About the Author

Joining the London Fire Brigade as a cadet at the tender age of sixteen, **DAVID PIKE** *was destined to become very much an operational firefighter. Awarded the Queen's Commendation for Brave Conduct as a young fireman, he rose steadily through the ranks during his thirty-plus years' service within the LFB. He commanded one of London's busiest and most challenging fire stations, Brixton. Heavily committed to raising monies for fire service charities, he rowed himself into* The Guinness Book of Records *whilst attracting many thousands of pounds through his, and his companions', endeavours. A regular contributor to the Brigade's in-house magazine, he now brings together many of its most notable stories and articles, combining them with a generous selection of the London Fire Brigade's most iconic images. He retired in senior rank from the Brigade in 1996. He is directing all the profits from this book to the fire service charity, Firemen Remembered. David now lives in Devon.*

By the same author

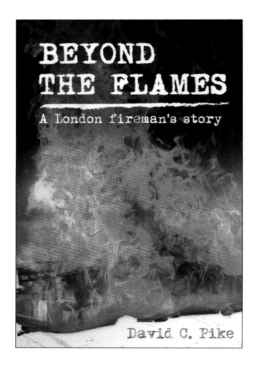

Beyond the Flames, David Pike's first book, charts his career and life in the London Fire Brigade. Published by Austin Macauley in 2013, it was shortlisted for the prestigious People's Book Prize in 2014 and was runner up in the non-fiction category. The book was also nominated for the Beryl Bainbridge Book Award and was a finalist in the Wishing Shelf Independent Book Awards 2014/15.

> *'A fascinating peek into the world of the London Fire Brigade. A FINALIST and highly recommended.'*
> The Wishing Shelf Book Awards, 2014/15

David C. Pike

LONDON'S FIREFIGHTERS

*Stories and articles from the
London Fire Brigade*

*With images of London's firemen, firewomen
and other firefighters too*

AUSTIN MACAULEY
PUBLISHERS LTD.

A CIP catalogue record for this title is available from the British Library.

ISBN 9781784555412 (paperback)

www.austinmacauley.com

First Published (2015)

Austin Macauley Publishers Ltd.
25 Canada Square
Canary Wharf
London
E14 5LQ

Printed and bound in the EU.

Dedication

To the men and women of the London Fire Brigade, past and present.

Contents

FOREWORD

By Gordon White, Editor of the London Fireman, 1970–82 and the London Firefighter, 1992–2002

The *London Fireman* magazine was spawned following the creation of the Greater London Council (GLC) in the mid-1960s. This was at a time when firemen's pay was very poor – the main reason why many members of the London Fire Brigade had to take second jobs purely to make ends meet. Morale was also low – a common complaint being that the Brigade rarely received any recognition by the news media or, even more galling, that the police were often reported as being responsible for work that firemen had carried out!

Under the GLC the Brigade opened a public relations department and the *London Fireman* came into being. It was published every quarter and every member of the Brigade had a copy delivered to their fire station. The magazine was generally well received and, fortunately, was more or less free of 'management-speak'. Apart from the editorial page (which was written by the Brigade's Public Relations Officer but was published under the name of the Chief Officer at the time), the *London Fireman* opened its pages to firemen, control room staff and civilian employees across the length and breadth of Greater London.

Apart from the front cover, which initially featured a large red circle placed carefully alongside a photograph, the magazine was entirely monochrome. Of great benefit to successive editors, the Brigade had a photographic section with a uniformed Sub Officer attached to each of the three watches, which later increased to four Sub Officers. The photographers, all previous operational firemen, attended major incidents, any fires involving fatalities, ceremonial occasions and, increasingly, sporting and social functions.

In 1970, after six years as a reporter with the *South London Press* and some freelancing for the London evening newspapers, I applied for a job as a Press Officer with the GLC, and rather to my surprise actually got it. I was told that after a one-month induction in the Press Office at County Hall I would be going to the London Fire Brigade for 'a year or two' as a Press Officer. That actually turned out to be 32 years! I was also told that I would be responsible for editing the *London Fireman.*

At the relatively tender age of 24 I had some trepidations about editing and overseeing the production of a prestigious house magazine – but I did not need to have any worries. Following the departure of the Brigade's previous Public Relations Officer, Geoff Bonell, work on the magazine had been left in the very capable hands of one Gordon Cruickshank. (I do believe he was the father of the television historian and architectural expert Dan Cruickshank, but I have never been able to find out if this is true.)

My arrival at Brigade HQ coincided – nothing to do with me! – in a revamped magazine: it was slightly larger than before and now, with the Brigade having access to colour photography, had more interesting front and back covers.

In any event, Gordon guided me through the various tasks involved in taking a magazine from start to finish and I shall forever be indebted to him for his kindly guidance. Interestingly, he later switched to County Hall to become a highly respected Press Officer. This, of course, was long before the computer era. All fire stations had typewriters but, more often than not, copy for the magazine arrived in various styles of hand writing and, I kid you not, we did actually received a small 'tit-bit' written on the back of a cigarette packet.

The magazine retained its overall format for most of its life, apart from changing its title to *London Firefighter* in the 1980s when the Brigade started recruiting female firefighters in 1982. The increasing use of colour photography, coupled with the fact that the profession of firefighting is often a highly visual subject, added much to the composition of the magazine.

The demise of the GLC meant we no longer had use of County Hall's expert print department, but fortunately a small design and layout department opened at Brigade HQ. They served us equally well. London's firefighters made good use of the magazine, not only with articles and reports but also with a 'small ads' page that we introduced. Eventually we started to sell advertising space in the magazine to well-vetted outside companies.

Towards the end of the 1990s and approaching the end of the London Fire and Civil Defence Authority, which had taken on responsibility for the Brigade from the GLC, I was given the task of seeking external sponsorship for the Brigade as a whole. This was time-consuming and I handed over the editorial reins to my very capable deputy Helen Atha. I remained as managing editor but, apart from writing 'The Chief Writes' column, my only role was to help Helen if there was a 'tricky' subject to deal with.

I departed in 2002; not long afterwards, the *London Firefighter* closed and was replaced by an intranet magazine. I was sad to learn of this as I have always been a great supporter of the printed word and published photographs. On reflection I think that *London Fireman* and *London Firefighter* served a very useful purpose, principally in helping to unite a very widespread workforce. I should like to thank all of those who contributed to or worked on these magazines over so many years.

INTRODUCTION

by David Pike

For very many years the **London Fireman**, later re-branded the **London Firefighter**, was the in-house magazine for the London Fire Brigade. Contained within its pages were a wealth of pictures and stories; tales of derring-do, of heroic deeds and acts of bravery. They were combined with an array of sometimes amusing and occasionally sad anecdotes, plus a fair sprinkling of fire service prose and poetry. In the twenty-first century financial cutbacks, and the growth of other forms of communication, sounded the death-knell of this acclaimed publication. This anthology seeks to resurrect many of those extraordinary stories and reflect upon the times and the people that made them: the protectors of London's population from fire and other emergency situations.

As London grew, expanded and became ever more complex, the London Fire Brigade had to rise to these challenges. Sometimes change in the LFB was not as some might have liked. Other changes, frequently driven by outside or financial forces, brought about alterations to previous working practices. In this collection of writings we cover various accounts of the history of the London Fire Brigade, its highs and lows, and the people that made it one of the premier fire brigades in the world.

With almost forty years of publications to choose from, the selected and edited material aims to deliver both a coherent history of London's fire brigade and a fascinating portrait of its people. It was, at times, a difficult and painful journey marked by the sacrifice of others. Yet it was also driven by the bravery, dedication and sense of humour of those most of whom you will never have heard of, but whose combined writing and photographic talents provide a unique insight into what made ordinary people who they were: London's firefighters.

ACKNOWLEDGMENTS

I am indebted to the copyright owners for their kind permissions to reproduce the images and tales that pay tribute to a once-excellent periodical, the London Fire Brigade's in-house magazine. In particular a special mention to those without whose active help this book would not have been possible.

Gordon White.

Terry Jones, London Fire Brigade.

Tom Gilmore, The Mary Evans Picture Library.

The London Fire Brigade.

Past London Fire Brigade photographers and contributors to the *London Fireman/London Firefighter* magazine.

Tim Jones.

Paul Wood.

Alan Dearing.

Walter Stephenson, Austin Macauley Publishers.

ALCOHOLISM

Alcoholism is a broad term for problems with alcohol. It is generally used to mean a compulsive and uncontrolled consumption of alcoholic beverages, usually to the detriment of the drinker's health, personal relationships, and social standing. It is medically considered a disease, an addictive illness; several other terms are used, such as alcohol abuse or dependence. In the 19th and early 20th centuries, alcohol dependence in general was called dipsomania. People suffering from alcoholism are often called 'alcoholics'. Alcohol misuse has the potential to damage almost every organ in the body, including the brain. The cumulative toxic effects of chronic alcohol abuse can cause both medical and psychiatric problems.

LIAM HACKETT *joined the London Fire Brigade in 1969 at the tender age of nineteen. His background was little different from so many of his generation, older teenagers who discovered the joys of having a drink with their mates, the occasional over-indulgence maybe and the odd happening of getting totally drunk. In those days Liam called himself 'Alf'. His was not a unique story: many in the London Fire Brigade were known to have a 'drink problem'. Some cleverly managed to disguise their drinking habits and their secretive dependency. What was special about Liam's tale is that he went public. He published his personal account for dealing with his alcoholism in the* **London Fireman** *magazine. This is his story as he told it.*

A triumph over one individual's demons

Imagine you are seated in groups of four listening to an after dinner speech at a medical convention. The speaker announces with some solemnity than one in four people in the community will suffer from cancer. He then goes on to describe the symptoms of the disease and, as each symptom is described a natural self-diagnosis will occur. With some nervousness the diagnosis may prove negative. Satisfied that you are not a sufferer your gaze will now be projected at your table companions and a feeling of sympathy will naturally ensue towards them, for you know one in four will be, or is a cancer victim – all perfectly natural, all rather sad, a situation which brings out fear and sympathy .

The speaker then goes on to say that one in four of the drinking community will become alcoholics and then continues to describe the symptoms. The same logical expectation of feelings? Not on your life! An evocation of fear or sympathy? No. More than likely, waggish remarks that, 'I'm not an alcoholic but my companion is,' amid gales of laughter. It wouldn't happen, you might say – but this is not a figment of my imagination. The above did happen not so long ago in America.

Unfortunately alcoholism is now the second biggest killer in this country after heart disease. According to NHS figures 13,500 sufferers pass through specialised units, of which there are only 23 [in the 1970s] in the UK, per annum. Of these only 30 per cent will achieve recovery.

You may wonder why on earth I am writing this. Alcoholism is not confined to any particular social class. Indeed I once thought that alcoholics were winos – derelicts of society, contemptibles not fit to live! Drink is consumed at all levels of society. Ethyl alcohol is a drug; addiction will follow with familiarity and abuse. It's as terrible as that. Indeed, one finds that people in the professions – journalists, lawyers, doctors, the military, even firemen, develop a dependence syndrome, simply because of the nature of the job and the socialising that goes with it.

I had to learn the hard way. *My name is Alf and I'm an alcoholic.*

My drinking started innocently enough. My father was a publican and once or twice a week I'd have a drink with my friends, nothing alarming, one or two pints, that's all. Life went on for me very normally, so I got drunk once in a while. Don't we all? I got married when I was 19, and needless to say, I had quite a stag night, but that's normal isn't it? I joined the Fire Brigade in 1969. This was the only job l ever wanted and I was determined to succeed.

A drink and a nag

Training School was enjoyable but hard work. The most natural thing in the world, maybe once a week, was for all the lads to meet next door, after work, in the pub and have a drink and a nag. I did well at Southwark and was posted to Chiswick fire station. Two days, two nights, two days off. Sometimes after days it would be down to the 'Hole in the Wall' for a jar or two, just to unwind and let the traffic die down. At no time did I, my wife or friends consider me to have a drink problem in those early days and, of course, I hadn't. I was one of the ordinary millions of social drinkers. One or two pints, occasionally, was all I needed.

Chiswick fire station, however, was not for me so I moved to Paddington fire station. I was in my heyday, I think, with plenty of jobs, plenty of excitement, a feeling of euphoria at work and a social centre on the station. I had plenty of good times at 'Padders' but it was about this time that I started to pursue my ambition, a simple enough one, to become Chief Officer of the London Fire Brigade. In those heady, youthful days I quite believed it. I started studying. It was all absorbing and my family life began to suffer. However, I thought I just had a nagging wife. Well, I was promoted to Leading Fireman and stayed at Paddington. The next stage was Sub Officer which came two years later. My total, consuming passion for study was beginning to take its toll. I found that I would drink more and more often. I would even take my books down to the local in order to establish a pattern for my study. If my wife objected I would storm out of the house using that as an excuse to drink.

My drinking was forming a habit and my waistline was getting bigger. Now this was causing me some little concern so like many others I decided to go on a diet but, alas, not to cut down on my booze. In 1976 I decided to go to Training School as an instructor. On reflection, and in absolute honesty, I went there for all the wrong reasons. I told them at the interview I wanted to give something back to the Brigade after all they had given me. They fell for it. What I didn't tell them was that I was on a gross ego trip of self-interest, not the Brigade interest. I wanted to be a Station Officer, even a temporary one, like, immediately.

I went to Southwark and found to my horror that I was bored stiff within a week. My inflated ego, however, prevented me from being honest and admitting it. Instead I went into the business of being an instructor with a resentment. This quickly developed into depression which as we all know has a panacea. My universal remedy for the ridiculous situation I had placed myself in was, you've guessed, drink.

I began to develop a taste for lunchtime drinking, something I had only done on Sunday before. However, drink is a depressant. After the initial lift from alcohol the return to melancholy is greater. I found myself going to the pub after work. Almost every night I would arrive home drunk. The rows got worse at home but I didn't care, because by now I was obese. I switched from pints of lager to Pils lager, which is sugar free. I lost a few pounds but I was drinking more than before. I was now well and truly on the road to insanity.

I was promoted to substantive Station Officer and posted to Silvertown fire station, in East London. I didn't go home in between nights but would start the day in all good faith exploring the ground. Come midday something would trigger in my brain and I'd end up in the pub. My habit was well established.

Alarming symptoms

Next I was posted to Southall fire station, near where I live, one week before the national firemen's strike. I remember little of the strike as the public, in their generosity, reduced me to a stage of semi-coma most of the time. I was developing alarming symptoms, retching in the morning without being sick, occasional trembling, a loss of memory following drinking bouts, but worst of all was a complete Jekyll and Hyde personality. More and more the monster came out in me. I would be violent, especially with my family, and always, always so remorseful the following day. I used to promise to stop but never went more than one day without booze.

I became the Fire Brigades Union rep, and then the divisional officers' rep. I used to preach the union gospel according to the word of Pils lager. More and more the Mr Hyde was in charge and finally took over. I was by now a thoroughly arrogant little runt, disliked by most senior officers who had the misfortune to come into contact with me. I could be told nothing but ruled like an idiotic despot. My wife was now fending for herself. No longer did she know me. She filed for divorce and I used this as another excuse to turn to my old friend drink. Still I did not see the harm it was doing.

One evening I decided to burn some rubbish in my garden. The fire smouldered and died. I wanted to go to the pub so I poured petrol on to it in order to speed up the process. It did. I became a fireball and suffered first, second and third degree burns to my back. If ever there was an example of lunacy from a professional fireman I was it. In hospital I was told to drink plenty of fluids. I did. Not quite what the doctor ordered, but the mixing of morphine and Pils lager was disastrous. When they found out and confiscated my 'fluids' I literally panicked. I used to crave for a drink in there and always managed to get one. Still I did not consider myself an alcoholic. My wife, who was still with me because of our financial hardships, told me over and over to stop drinking. I thought she was nagging.

One evening after a union meeting the first of many little miracles happened. My friend 'Bunny' called me to one side and asked if I had a drink problem. I immediately felt indignant, denied it and asked if he wanted to join me for a drink. He refused and I drove home. On the way I started thinking that there was a conspiracy so, just to keep everyone happy, but more to the point to convince myself that I didn't have a drink problem, I would go to my GP the following morning. When I arrived at the surgery my doctor asked what was wrong. I said I thought I had a drink problem. He lowered his spectacles, looked at me and asked me why. Confused, I said I didn't know. Now I was really uneasy, but to my relief he asked me a few questions and suggested I see a specialist. Not once did he mention the word 'alcoholic' so I felt rather pleased with myself. I left the surgery and headed straight for the supermarket to buy a can of beer. I went home smelling of beer with the good news. My wife was not impressed.

About two weeks and many drinks later I arrived at Ealing Hospital to see the specialist. He asked me the same questions as my GP and of course I had the answers. He finished his notes, looked up and said, 'Yes Mr Hackett, you are an alcoholic.'

I was horrified, astounded, hurt and…alcoholic. He suggested I enter hospital for a month. I argued that the Brigade wouldn't possibly tolerate that and refused. He said that if I carried on I wouldn't have a Brigade to worry about. This frightened me. He then said I wouldn't have a family, home or life to worry about either. He convinced me that it was the only thing to do.

So bewildered

On 14th September 1979 I was admitted to St Bernard's Hospital, Southall, as a patient in the alcoholic unit. I still could not believe I was a wino! I felt humiliated. I began a week of detoxification surrounded by alcoholics. Why was I here? I was so bewildered. The month dragged by. I kept it a secret only known to my wife, 'Dusty' my Sub Officer and my Divisional Commander. Every time the fire alarm rang, which was at least once a day, I would hide in shame lest I was seen. In about the third week I started to absorb some of the things the nurses and other patients were saying. Slowly, for the first time in my adult life, I was being honest with myself. I began to admit to myself that I was an alcoholic. I was just like everyone else in there.

The treatment was in fact to last for three months, mostly group therapy and introductions to Alcoholics Anonymous. I left the hospital on 14th December far from cured but, for the first time in a long while, sober. My wife had halted the divorce for the time being. On 16th December I returned to work. My watch at Southall had been marvellous and after the first month in hospital they got to hear about me and visited me frequently. They gave me a real lift when my world was disintegrating. I'll never forget that.

I now had to get on with the business of living. It wasn't easy at first. I went to AA meetings regularly and began to meet some wonderful people who taught me a simple philosophy, 'Just for today'. That statement is all I need to live. Yesterday is gone and finished, I can do absolutely nothing about that. Tomorrow doesn't exist for any of us. Today is all I can be sure about. Today I haven't had a drink, today I have had the choice to do what I want and not what the booze wants. If I can't solve a problem today then forget about it, don't worry, let go. 'Just for today' was to stand me in good stead for the months that were to come, some of the most traumatic dramas of my career to date and far worse than any fire I had been to.

On 20th March 1980 I was reduced in rank to Sub Officer following a disciplinary hearing, but that's life. I swallowed hard, prayed a little, thought a lot and let go. I didn't drink. That wouldn't solve anything. I'd proved that over and over. Once again, promoted back to Station Officer, I carried on with my duties as best as I could, and that was 100 per cent better than before. I was moved to Clerkenwell in April.

I continued with my AA meetings and found myself helping other alcoholics. My family life improved and I found I could listen to people, something I couldn't do before. My AA meetings have brought me into contact with all levels of society, from TV stars to once derelicts, all of them happy individuals with their simple programme for living. Only recently I have started voluntary work with the Probation Service and have talked at Borstals to youngsters with drink-related offences. I go back to St Bernard's regularly to liaise with staff and help in-patients.

Life is no longer self-centred.

I have written this article in order to give a message to anyone out there who, at this moment, may feel lonely and miserable and confused. You are not alone, you can recover. You don't necessarily need the extreme treatment I had. You can contact me anytime, I would feel privileged to hear from you. A small prayer I've learned, and I'm not overtly religious, says it all…

'God grant me the serenity to accept the things
I cannot change,
Courage to change the things I can,
And the wisdom to know the difference.'

Footnote

Alf (Liam) went on to have a successful fire service career in the London Fire Brigade, rising to senior rank. In 1989 he undertook a daring and dramatic rescue of a power-line worker from the upper levels of a high voltage electrical pylon in East London. His brave deeds were recognised by the presentation of the Brigade's highest gallantry award: a Chief Officer's Commendation. He was subsequently awarded the St John Bronze Life Saving Medal, a rare honour and one which is only bestowed on an individual who has performed a conspicuous act of bravery. Sadly, this act of bravery also brought his fire service career to a premature end. The harrowing rescue had serious consequences for Alf and he was diagnosed as suffering with Post Traumatic Stress Disorder, and he was medically retired from the Brigade. In retirement he returned to his native Scotland. Now known as Liam Hackett, he dedicated his life to helping others, working with international charities including the Order of Saint Lazarus. In 2013 he was invested as a Chevalier de l'ordre militaire et hospitalier de Saint-Lazare de Jérusalem.

Assistant Divisional Officer Liam 'Alf' Hackett prior to his medical retirement. (Permission of Liam Hackett.)

AT A BASEMENT FIRE

By Charles Clisby MBE, QFSM

London firemen in breathing apparatus (BA), circa 1930s. (Mary Evans 10535253.)

Reporter asked me, 'What's it like?'
I shrugged him off, 'I couldn't say:
You see I'm not a one for that.
Not one for bragging anyway.'

He pressed me hard and so I tried,
I hoped my tale he understood.
Could it be that telling him,
Might do the job a bit of good?

'If you put on six overcoats
And though you suffered hell from corns,
You cramped your feet in Army boots,
Wore on your head a crown of thorns.

Lay in a bath, first hot then cold,
Got out and ran a mile or so.
Into an oven squeezed yourself
And turned to nine the Regulo.

Climbed rapidly a mountain peak
And as night fell were all alone.
If to descend you had to try
Whilst praying hard each foot found stone.

Then with a bandage round your eyes
And wooden peg clipped on your nose,
You crawled around in concrete maze,
Could do the whole at once, suppose.

That's what it's like, hope that conveys.'
Reporter laughed, 'Can this be true?'
I looked him squarely in the eyes,
'FIVE overcoats I think would do!'

**London firemen
at a basement fire:
Covent Garden, London.
(Mary Evans 10731976.)**

AUXILIARY FIRE SERVICE

T he likelihood of a Second World War was already planned for in early 1930s Britain. Although not widely publicised the then National Government, under the premiership of Ramsey MacDonald, were considering what arrangements would be necessary to cope with enemy aerial attacks on its strategic population centres. This was just one of many problems for the Government, not the least of which was the vast economic trouble the whole country faced in the wake of the Wall Street Crash of 1929 and the subsequent widespread depression it caused.

However, despite this background, the Home Office (then responsible for the Fire Service) held a series of seminars and secret planning meetings to deliver a strategy in the event of war and subsequent fire attacks on the British mainland from the air. London was considered a particularly vulnerable target from enemy action, not least because it was the nation's seat of government and the City of London was crucial to the country's financial and business interests. The London of the 1930s took on a vastly different look to the London of today. The River Thames provided easy access for shipping to the vast network of extensive docks and associated warehouses. The dockland warehouses, from Southwark and Blackfriars on the south bank and Tower Hill on the north bank, ran eastward to the Essex and Kent borders.

Two London Auxiliary Fire Service fireman sharing a laugh. (Mary Evans 10793519.)

Advertisements on London fire engines were used to recruit men and women into the AFS. (Mary Evans 10535312.)

It was recognised at an early stage that it would require a massive expansion of the existing fire brigade(s) to deal with fires involving London's central maze of narrow streets, warehouses filled with combustible products such as oils and grains and dockyards with acres of stacked imported timber. Failure to respond to such a challenge could leave London little more than a smoking ruin.

The steady rise of Nazi Germany, and its expansion into surrounding countries, would bring about the inevitable conflict that saw Great Britain declare war on Germany in 1939. However, before that day arrived the Auxiliary Fire Service (AFS) was formed and from March 1938 their numbers grew. Attracting the 28,000 proposed volunteers who would supplement the regular London Fire Brigade was a major logistical exercise. A massive recruitment drive was launched. Whilst sixty fire brigade vehicles toured London's streets, a poster campaign was mounted and planes flew the over capital trailing recruitment banners. Even the Thames was used to advertise this new fire force and the Brigade's high speed fireboat flew similar banners seeking recruits to supplement the London Fire Brigade's river service.

The area we now know as Greater London had, prior to the outbreak of war, at least 66 fire brigades. This included the London Fire Brigade, the largest, which covered the whole of the former London County Council administrative area. Some of these other brigades were one fire engine outfits that only protected a small borough area while others had four or five stations such as West Ham and Croydon.

Buildings and vehicles were seconded into service to house and equip this basically trained corps of AFS firemen and women that had now greatly expanded London's fire service. Meanwhile garages, *filling stations and schools, empty since the mass evacuation of children, were taken over and adapted as fire stations. Some 2,000 London taxis were brought into service and used to tow trailer pumps. The taxis were large enough to carry a crew and the hose was stored in the luggage compartment. However, the accommodation was frequently poor at best and the new volunteer firefighters spent many hours making good their bases and building their own wooden beds. In addition to this they erected brick walls over windows and sandbagged entrances to protect themselves from blast damage.*

New AFS recruits undergoing basic hose drill under the watchful eye of a London Fire Brigade Sub Officer instructor. (Mary Evans 10536065.)

The basic training was provided by firemen from the London Fire Brigade. Detached from normal firefighting duties, they put the new recruits through 60 hours of practical and theoretical lessons. Whilst some women chose to undertake dispatch rider (motorcycle) duties and others opted for motor driving, most were trained in 'watchroom' duties and necessary procedures for mobilising fire engines and pumping units. Everyone underwent basic firefighter training. They were, of course, civilians. They had volunteered from every trade and profession, from every walk of life. Office workers, labourers, lawyers, tailors, cooks and cleaners had taken up the call to join the Auxiliary Fire Service.

AFS recruits were divided into different categories. This was based on their physical capabilities, their age, gender and skills. Men considered Class B performed general firefighting duties. B1s worked only on ground level, either pump operating or driving. Others recruited from trades on the Thames were classed for River Service work and whilst women would be in the thick of it none performed frontline firefighting duties. Those youngsters under 18 years of age became messengers equipped with either motorcycles or pedal cycles.

Those auxiliaries who became full-time firefighters on the outbreak of war received a weekly wage. Firemen earned £3 per week, women got £2. Those aged 17–18 received £1-5 shillings and the 16–17 year olds got £1 a week.

LESLIE BROUGHTON *was an operational firemen for twenty-four years before medical retirement brought his career to an early end. However, he became a Control Officer in the LFB, working from the 'E' Divisional headquarters at Lewisham. He recalled his early days in the AFS in the pages of the in-house magazine. This is his story.*

••

I became a full time operational fireman when all AFS personnel were mobilised on 1st September 1939 in readiness for the impending war.

As I was only 25 years old, the minimum age for operational firefighting at that time, there were no firemen younger than myself so I think I shall probably be the last of those thousands of London operational Auxiliary Firemen who served right through the war.

A London taxi converted to a wartime auxiliary fire engine in Lambeth High Street. (Mary Evans 10534504.)

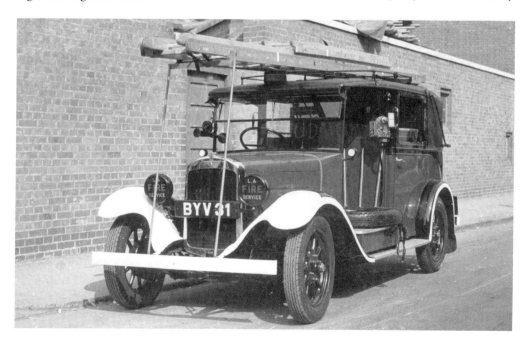

On that fateful in September 1939 we were notified on the radio to report for duty at our respective stations which in my case was '56 Eltham,' now Eltham fire station.

Groups of five men were formed into crews and were each allocated a commandeered London taxi, a couple of lengths of hose and a branch and were posted to man every street fire alarm in London, which at that time numbered thousands. We had no accommodation, no food, nothing and there we remained out in the streets for about a couple of weeks dependent on the good nature of the public to feed and water us.

Slowly, things became more organised, crews were taken off the streets and put into empty schools which became proper sub-stations, each with a manned watchroom and anything from ten to 20 trailer pumps manned by crews on a three-watch system, 48 hours on, 24 hours off, all for £2.18s.5d per week.

Taxis were gradually replaced by auxiliary towing cars. These were high-powered private cars, Ford V8s, Chryslers, Studebakers, Oldsmobiles etc, which had their saloon bodies converted into covered trucks. These vehicles with their trailer

The Surrey Commercial Docks and its warehouses ablaze on the first night of the London Blitz, 7 September 1940. (Mary Evans 10534574.)

pumps (mostly Dennis) bore the brunt of the firefighting during the following London blitz fires.

I was stationed at Pope Street School, New Eltham, and the usual procedure during the blitz was to order crews like us from the outskirts into inner London in anticipation of the inevitable air raids. We would often be out on a job for 24 hours or even longer, frequently bombed, occasionally machine-gunned, inevitably hungry, our one and only uniform soaking wet, and we would return to our stations so exhausted we would flop down on our straw mattresses just as we were.

Our casualties at this time were high. The flames we were fighting were the target for the approaching enemy bombers which had just dropped a stick of bombs, each bomb scream-ing on the way down and getting closer and closer. Whilst we were praying silently to oneself that the next one would fall anywhere 'so long as it's not on me'.

On 10th May 1941 London had its biggest air raid and 40,000 fires were reported. The fire service was stretched to its limit and only half of these fires were attended. For example, we were passing the Elephant and Castle on our way to a job when 'Jerry' dropped a load of incendiary bombs. When we returned the following day almost the whole area was burned out. The job we had been sent to was at Essex Street, off the Strand and close to St Clement Dane's Church, which was well alight. The whole of Essex Street was burning from end to end. The total attendance to our 'little job' was us; one pump and its crew!

To add to our difficulties during these raids the water mains were often destroyed and pumps had to be supplied from open water which all too frequently was a long way from the fires. This necessitated water relays being set up involving many pumps. Operating a pump in the middle of a water relay during a bombing raid is, believe me, the loneliest job in the world.

On the first large bombing raid on London we were ordered into the Woolwich Arsenal. There were fires everywhere and eventually I found myself operating a pump in the middle of a relay. I did not know where the water was coming from or where it was going to. I was on my own and bombers were coming over with monotonous regularity and dropping their cargoes. This was my baptism of fire and I was lonely and terrified. Every time a stick of bombs fell I threw myself down on a grassy embankment alongside my pump and as the long night went on I grew to love this embankment which gave me a modicum of protection. Suddenly, hundreds of incendiary bombs were falling everywhere and my grassy embankment was alight. At this point an 'Arsenal fireman,' the first person I

AFS crews take a welcome break and a morning 'cuppa' from a LCC canteen van after a night of fighting fires. (Permission of the London Fire Brigade.)

had seen for hours, came panting up to me. 'For Christ's sake get these flames out,' he gasped, 'this is a powder magazine.' You can imagine my feelings! The time it took me to beat out those flames with my fire tunic should be in the *Guinness Book of Records*.

The bombing pattern then changed to hit-and-run raids and, consequently, parts of the Brigade were re-organised. Mobile columns were formed in various Districts, each column consisting of 20 appliances plus motorcycle dispatch riders. We were geared to move in convoy to any part of the country that required our services.

Then there were the frightening occasions, like working on the roof of a burning building. We were seen like those serving in the armed forces, and our standing with the general public's eyes was terrific. The Press dubbed us as 'Heroes with dirty faces'.

If I had the talent I could write a book of the countless incidents that occurred; the amusing, such as the dear old lady who emerged from a badly damaged house after a nasty raid with a steaming pot of tea for the boys, saying, 'Excuse the pot, it's quite clean. I didn't have a jug that was big enough.' The pot in question was a chamber pot!

Then there was the foolish incident when we were ordered out into the playing fields of New Eltham, in the blackout, to search for a German magnetic mine dropped by parachute seen falling in the area. We were ordered to take off our axes and leave any metal objects behind as these would operate the detonator. It was not until a few minutes later that we remembered that our fire tunics were covered with metal buttons. Fortunately for us we failed to locate the mine which had drifted past our patch.

The mobile columns were used extensively during the V1 flying bomb raids. These would devastate an area as big as a football pitch and the loss of life and property became enormous. Worse was yet to come in the shape of V2s, the forefathers of the modern space rockets. With these there was no warning, just a terrific explosion and an even bigger area of destruction and a greater loss of life.

We were employed as general dogs-bodies at these incidents. Usually we were the first on the scene. We rescued people from their shattered homes, rendered first aid to the numerous

Directional sign to the Lambeth Road sub-fire station. (Mary Evans 10794289.)

AFS posters. (Courtesy of the London Fire Brigade Museum.)

injured, salvaged their furniture and belongings, patched up their doors, windows and roofs and did anything else that would make these unfortunate people a little more comfortable.

It was during this period, prior to the invasion of France, that the Allies decided to build the Mulberry Harbours. To those who may not know what this was, it consisted of dozens of huge concrete barges, built secretly on the Belvedere Marshes and other places close to the Thames river banks. These were eventually towed across the channel to form a harbour to facilitate unloading supplies for our invading troops.

The 'Mulberry Harbours' in position off the French coast after the D Day invasion landings. (Permission of the London Fire Brigade.)

These barges were constructed in great pits that were dug out a few feet from the bank of the river. As each one was completed, the bank that separated it from the river was dug away, and it became our job to cut a channel through the foreshore mud at low tide to enable the barge to be floated out to midstream and towed away to a secret rendezvous. We did this by using high pressure jets from radial branches, very large firemen's nozzles, and deluge sets. This activity had to take place in great secrecy to avoid being spotted by enemy planes and consequently we had to do our job in the dark, usually an hour or so before dawn. This job became known as 'mud larking' but believe me it was no lark. Thames mud has to be experienced to be believed. Chestnut paling fencing was laid out over the mud for us to stand on with our branches. This very quickly became covered with thick mud and disappeared from sight and we had to inch our way out, feeling for the fencing with our feet. Woe betide anyone whose foot missed the fencing. He would instantly begin to sink into the mud unable to assist himself.

We would have to throw him a line and try and haul him out. Sometimes we would be unable to do this, so tenacious was the mud, and we would have to enlist the aid of one of the tractors on the shore. As you can see, our job throughout the war was varied to say the least.

Needless to say it was not all work. Social activities were numerous and bearing in mind that we had people from all walks of life in the service, the talents that were available were numerous; painters, musicians, entertainers, engineers, carpenters and builders etc. I was fortunate to be included in a 'minstrel' show that was produced by one of the firemen and which reached quite professional standards and included a member of the Magic Circle. Also included was a mandolin band of eight firemen, who were all taught to play their instruments from scratch by another fireman and accompanied by yours truly on the guitar. We gave several shows at various large fire stations and were even invited to perform on the BBC radio series 'Under Your Tin Hat.' Unfortunately, the fire brigade would not give us the time off to appear!

Looking back over those war years I realise that it was an enriching experience being a wartime London fireman. They were a great bunch of blokes and I am proud that I was one of them.

London NFS firemen and firewomen entertain at Forest Hill School, south London, a large fire sub-station, during London's war years. (Mary Evans 10534714.)

AFS firewomen undertaking catering classes: they would become cooks, feeding London's front line firemen. (Mary Evans 10534798.)

The recruitment of women for fire brigade purposes was an unprecedented step and contrary to long established tradition. Women were recruited to the Auxiliary Fire Service for a wide range of duties as telephonists, clerks, cooks, dispatch riders and drivers, and most other work except actual firefighting. They provided magnificent assistance which released men for firefighting duties.

To provide auxiliary fire stations with accommodation for training, for meals and dormitory purposes, and for the storage of uniforms and equipment, including vast quantities of hose, premises as near as possible to existing fire stations were taken over. Disused factories, vacant schools, garages and even private houses were brought into use, especially if they had adjacent open space or a yard where drills and practice could be carried out. Training, given mostly during evenings and weekends by regular London brigade members who themselves had to be trained as instructors, consisted of sixty hours of drills or lectures followed by a passing-out examination.

Women were recruited into the fire service from 1938 onwards. In March 1943 there were some 32,200 women serving full-time, and 54,600 part-time, with the National Fire Service. While women still did not tackle major fires, they provided important back-up to their male colleagues. Some were trained to staff the communication centres in addition to the other varied roles they performed. During bombing raids both men and women dispatch riders were often the only means of communication between fire crews and their control rooms.

As a young woman, **PEGGY JACOBS** was amongst the first women to sign up to join the newly created AFS, thereby starting *a life-long association with the London Fire Brigade. She rose to senior officer rank and was awarded the British Empire Medal for her distinguished service by Lord Alexander of Tunis in 1965. Here Senior Woman Officer Mrs Peggy Jacobs recalls some personal memories of the AFS.*

I first joined the AFS nearly 30 years ago. It was the time of the Munich Crisis. I enrolled at my local fire station, West Hampstead, and in September 1939 I became a full-time AFS driver with the princely salary of £2 a week!

The first year of the war was the period which was later to be called 'The phoney war', as we watched and waited for the emergency which didn't come. At that time we were on duty for 48 hours followed by a break of 24 hours. The time was filled by sand-bagging, drills, turn-outs and training. We also found time for sports, concert parties and dances.

One particular personal memory of this period concerns a brush with authority, represented by the women officers at my station. I had returned from training school, well versed in all things squad drill, only to find that the women officers expected us to salute on the command 'Fall Out'. Going 'by the book' I refused, and to the consternation of the women's section I stood my ground for a whole week. Eventually, I was paraded before the regular station officer, who, to my delight confirmed that I was following correct procedure. From then on we saluted only on the command 'Dismiss,' and my enthusiasm for squad drill grew.

Although AFS firewomen did not fight fires they were all provided with basic firefighting skills, as here at Lambeth, the London Fire Brigade headquarters. (Mary Evans 10534526.)

Right: Senior AFS firewomen at the London Fire Brigade headquarters, Lambeth. (Mary Evans 10794304.)

Opposite: AFS firewomen in their roughly made sleeping accommodation in the basement of Southwark fire station in south London. (Mary Evans 10534661.)

A year later the Blitz brought the 'phoney war' to an end and life began in earnest as I was driving senior officers to the Surrey Docks fires. My own 'Blitz story' is of the night in December 1940 when the City was in flames. I drove a Superintendent to the fire at the Honourable Artillery Company building in City Road. In the early hours of the morning he came out of the fire holding his hand to one eye and told me to drive him to Moorfields Eye Hospital. Within five minutes of entering the hospital, he stormed out, his face redder than any fire could make it, to tell me, 'They take all sorts of things out there, but not from my eye!' I had taken him to a maternity hospital.

After the war and in 1949, at the time of the Berlin Airlift, the call for volunteers went out again. Although I was heavily involved in youth work I felt bound to return to the fire service which had come to mean so much to me during the dark days of the war.

I decided that I would give just one evening a week to AFS training, but this soon became two and then three. Promoted to an Assistant Group Officer in 1951, I subsequently became officer in charge of training, one of my most rewarding tasks. My particular memories of the 1950s are of squad drills and the concert party.

The concert party included both members of the AFS and the Brigade's uniformed and administrative staffs, and for a week in 1955 we played to packed and enthusiastic audiences. Since then people have asked, 'Why don't we have another concert party?' Could it be because we blotted our copy book by setting fire to the brigade lecture hall curtains during a dress rehearsal?

In 1964 I became the Senior Woman Auxiliary Officer of the London AFS and a year later for the newly created Greater London Council area. My last three years have been packed with activity, achievement and friends. 'Exercise Tercentenary' (which marked the three hundred year anniversary since the Great Fire of London) stands out as one of the landmarks of 1966. AFS women manned controls, acted as drivers and radio operators and coped with the enormous job of feeding the 5,000 auxiliaries who took part.

The Centenary Review by Her Majesty the Queen of the London Fire Brigade was of course the climax to that memorable year, when the AFS were proud to be reviewed along with their comrades of the London Fire Brigade.

Now, sadly, the AFS is finished. My years with the fire service were a rewarding experience, working with a team of women officers who accepted responsibility for the organisation and administration of the AFS women's section. None of this would have been possible without the encouragement and assistance of the officers of the Brigade, to whom we owe a great debt of gratitude. In the AFS we found a spirit of service which, I hope, will flourish elsewhere for the benefit of the community. Shall we meet again? I don't know, but in the meantime my happy memories remain and, of course, my pride in being associated with the London Fire Brigade.

AFS firewomen undertook important duties, one such duty was as dispatch riders. Here they are undergoing their basic training, which included motorbike maintenance. (Mary Evans 10534785.)

By the spring of 1941, after the winter of the German raids, it had become apparent to those most closely concerned with the organisation of firefighting that in the emergency conditions created by modern warfare fire services had to be brought under a national authority. One able to mobilise manpower and appliances quickly on a large scale.

In May 1941, the government decided to nationalise the fire services, merging all local regular brigades and the Auxiliary Fire Service into the National Fire Service. Thus, three years after its formation, the AFS was no more, but the auxiliaries carried on as 'regulars' throughout the war, many of them finding a new career which they continued in peacetime.

The wartime emergency over, the National Fire Service was returned to the local authorities on 1 April 1948. Only a year later international relations had so deteriorated that world peace seemed in danger once more, so much so that the government revived general Civil Defence precautions including the Auxiliary Fire Service. From then on, the auxiliaries trained to be available should they be needed in a national emergency. Several times a year they carried out large-scale exercises, and male auxiliaries rode to fires with the regular brigades to gain experience. In 1966, AFS men and women from far and wide played a splendid part in the massive exercise staged in the Port of London to mark the Tercentenary of the Great Fire of London Now, in 1968, the Auxiliary firemen and women were to 'ride' no more.

On 31 March, 1968, the Auxiliary Fire Service, after nearly 20 years of peacetime activity, was commanded to 'stand-down' as part of national economy measures. In London, as throughout Britain, more than 700 men and nearly 200 women reluctantly gave up a voluntary spare-time interest to which many were dedicated. Originally recruited to help save the nation, the AFS was forced to disband to help save the nation's finances...

....

The end of an era...

I n this issue of *London Fireman* we mark the end of an era in British fire service history, with the enforced stand-down of the Auxiliary Fire Service.

As an 'interested party' it would be wrong for us to enter into the argument over the wisdom of the decision to axe the AFS as an economy measure, but it would be equally wrong to let the AFS die without a word of appreciation for a body whose outlook has always been epitomised by the last word of its title – 'Service'.

The Londoner owes a special debt of gratitude to the AFS. Without the efforts of the auxiliary firemen and women the effects of the wartime raids on London would have been far more terrible, and the Service's long roll of honour tells its own story. Anyone who saw them in action during the dark days of 1940 and 1941 will always remember the way in which they stood alongside their regular comrades as the final defence against the fire raids of the Blitz, and the Churchillian phrase 'Their Finest Hour' takes on a special significance when used to describe the AFS of this period.

Many of today's [1968] regulars entered the fire service through the wartime AFS and a high proportion have since risen to senior commands, giving the Brigade a breadth of outlook and thinking which proved of great value in the planning and administration of London's fire services in recent years.

Editor of the **London Fireman** *Magazine.*

The Auxiliary Fire Service cap badge. (Mary Evans 10534759.)

BLITZ UPON LONDON

By David C. Pike

B

t was a Saturday. Saturday the 7th September 1940, at 4.33pm to be precise, that the air raid warnings sirens sounded in earnest over London. There had been plenty of false alarms but this would be different. The Blitz upon London had begun. German planes would deliver their deadly cargo on the nation's capital for the next 57 consecutive nights. They had but one aim. To bomb, blast and burn Great Britain out of the war and hopefully into submission. When that failed they continued with random bombing into the May of 1941.

When the bombs fell Londoners took, wherever possible, to the shelters. London firefighters stood their ground and prepared to fight. Both regular and auxiliary firefighters joined forces against the destruction that rained down from the skies. Many of the auxiliaries had day time jobs before starting the night shift at their designated sub-station, manning the taxi-trailer pumps or climbing on board the Home Office heavy units. In that first week of bombing no fewer than four regular LFB fire stations and seven sub-stations were destroyed by enemy action. Any raid might bring any range of high explosive ordinance. Oil bombs, land mines, parachute bombs all made up the enemy's arsenal of death and destruction. During that September and the following October London's firefighters attended more than 1,000 separate fires.

The aftermath of another night's bombing, and the resultant fires, in the City of London and close to St Paul's Cathedral. (Permission of the London Fire Brigade.)

The Honour Guard for the London Firemen killed following a direct hit on the Wandsworth fire station in south west London. (Permission of the London Fire Brigade.)

Opposite: A 100 foot turntable ladder at work as dawn breaks after another night fighting the flames. The smoke might be turning to steam, but that night the firefighters of London would be doing it all over again. (Mary Evans 10794770.)

An official wartime publication, *Front Line, 1940–1941* (left) records what happened: 'The auxiliaries, four-fifths of them with no prior experience of actual fire-fighting, faced the greatest incendiary attack ever launched. Shortly after midnight on the first night there were nine fires in London rating over 100 pumps. In the Surrey docks were two, of 300 and 130 pumps; at Woolwich Arsenal, 200 pumps; at Bishopsgate Goods Yard and at five points on the docks, 100-pump fires. All these were technically "out of hand".'

In Quebec Yard, Surrey Docks, was the night's biggest fire, immense in the area it covered, moving with disconcerting speed, generating terrific heat. It set alight the wooden blocks in the roadways, a thing without precedent. Fireboats trying to slip past under the lee of the opposite bank 300 yards away had their paint blistered.

Bombs fell incessantly all night, rekindling areas that had been laboriously conquered. As the Dockland warehouses blazed, pepper, rum, 'barrels exploding like bombs themselves', paint, rubber, sugar, tea and wheat all went up in flames, choking, asphyxiating, blinding and bewildering the fire-fighters. Two hundred and fifty acres of timber importing docks, stacked 20 feet high with mostly pine and resinous woods from the Baltic, were a sea of roaring flames.

Normal relief from duty in this monstrous situation was not possible: 'Many firemen were at work for forty hours, some officers for longer.' In the end the fire was mastered, and, as the official report put it, '**London's novices who helped to fight it had had, with their regular comrades, a concentrated experience without parallel in years of peace-time fire-fighting.**'

Right: London firemen salvaging their bedding and other belongings after their sub-station was bombed in Mansfield Road, NW3, during November 1940. (Mary Evans 10534626.)

By the end of that September in 1940 fifty London fire-fighters had died and over five hundred had been injured and invalided out.

Overnight almost, the attitude of the public to the AFS was entirely changed. From being somewhat suspect they became popular heroes. Weary pump crews returning wet and dirty from fires were cheered by Londoners trying to get on with life, despite the enemy bombing of their city and its suburbs.

Awards to LFB and AFS personnel

There were so many outstanding actions of courage: outstanding devotion to duty in the most harrowing of circumstances. Gallant acts performed by both men and women serving in either the London Fire Brigade or in the AFS, but importantly serving together against a common foe. Some acts inevitably got caught up, literally, in the heat of war and, sadly, went unrecognised. Others were commended for their meritorious actions. Here are but a very few (text courtesy of the London Fire Brigade Museum):

Awarded the GEORGE MEDAL. Divisional Officer Geoffrey Vaughan BLACKSTONE and Acting Sub-Officer Sydney Herbert BOULTER. A high explosive bomb demolished a building leaving one wall in a tottering condition. Five members of the Fire Service were on beds on the ground floor of the building and were entombed under the debris which was supported by iron girders inclined against the damaged wall. Bombs were falling in the district at the time and the blast made the wall sway dangerously. DO Blackstone, fully realizing the extreme danger of the wall falling, began to burrow into the debris. He worked continuously with his bare hands for about four hours in darkness and foul atmosphere and released three of the victims. In order to extricate them, he had to take the weight of a girder on his shoulders while passing debris back between his legs. DO Blackstone displayed conspicuous courage and suffered considerably from the effects of the gas and bad atmosphere in which he had been working. The tottering wall fell soon after the rescues had been effected. Sub-Officer Boulter, although wet through and exhausted, after seven hours strenuous firefighting, also assisted in the rescue of two of those trapped who were on the side of the ground floor away from the dangerous wall. He tunnelled downwards and, held by his feet, wriggled down vertically through the debris to a man who was pinned under a steel girder and covered in masonry. After three hours hard work in darkness and a gas-fouled atmosphere he released the man and brought him out alive. After this rescue Boulter assisted the other party until the last victim was recovered. Sub Officer Boulter displayed endurance and great courage in the face of extreme danger.

Divisional Officer Geoffrey Blackstone. (London Fire Brigade.)

Divisional Officer **GEOFFREY BLACKSTONE** *was also in command of firefighting operations in the Elephant and Castle District of South London on 10–11 May 1941. He was having to contend with broken water mains, burnt hose lines and firefighter casualties, including a direct hit on a pump that killed its entire crew. His recollections were included in an article in* **London Fireman***:*

'The stuff was beginning to drop. Quite a lot of it. I soon began to realize that this was a bit heavier than anything we had before. For a time we had the awful exasperation of lots of firemen, lots of pumps, lots of fires – but no water. Then a water unit arrived, which carried up to two or three miles of folded hose. It dropped a canvas dam and made its way to the Thames near Westminster Bridge. Four lines of hose were laid out waiting for water. Here was a most disappointing sight. Fires were showering embers onto the hose which was lying flat without water, burning it and charring it so that when the water arrived it would be wasted.

'As usual the decision had been made to let certain buildings burn out and concentrate on what seemed worth saving. For some reason the Elephant and Castle pub seemed to have some symbolic value. This magnificent piece of old London stood on a sort of island site in the middle of the six-road junction. I had a sort of urge to save it and perhaps wasted precious water and manpower on it.

'The fireman at the control point in the middle of the circus said, 'Cor, sir, what a wind – just our luck!' It was a perfectly still night, but the hot air rising from all the fires around was sucking cool air into the circus so that sheets of newspaper, sparks and burning rags were flying through the air around us.'

More than 1,400 Londoners perished on the night of May 10th–11th 1941. Among the dead, 22 firefighters on Blackstone's fire ground alone; a total of 36 across the city.

Viewing the tarpaulin covering the bodies, the Divisional fire officer counted eight pairs of leather boots, which were issued to London's regular firefighters, and 14 pairs of rubber boots, which were issued to the city's auxiliary firefighters.

'You are all equal now, mates,' Blackstone said to himself.

Opposite: Regular London firemen and AFS fought side by side, night after night. A blazing building casts its silhouette on a London fire crew standing by their wheeled escape ladder. (Mary Evans 50793646.)

• •

The Memorial Hall at the London Fire Brigade Headquarters building on the Albert Embankment, SE1. It was installed by the London County Council and it records the names of those members of the London Fire Brigade, the Auxiliary Fire Service and the National Fire Service (London Region) who lost their lives in the line of duty serving London and its population during the Second World War. (Mary Evans 10795531.)

Awarded the British Empire Medal for Gallantry. Firewoman (Aux) Bridget Gibson HARRIS. During an air raid a H.E. (high explosive) bomb fell within twenty yards of Auxiliary Harris and demolished a house in which fires broke out. In spite of the shaking she had received, Harris immediately began to clear away debris in an effort to reach people trapped in the basement. By the time further help arrived she had made substantial progress and she continued the work for over an hour, during which time more bombs were dropped nearby

33

and there was constant danger from falling masonry. During that night, Auxiliary Harris helped to layout many lengths of hose and on one occasion manned a branch. She displayed a high standard of courage and devotion to duty, and worked with tireless energy throughout the night, carrying out duties to which she was not normally assigned.

Firewoman (Aux) Joan Winifred HOBSON. During an air raid, a fire was reported but no appliances were available. Auxiliary Hobson, on her own initiative, took lengths of hose, a short ladder and equipment, and, commandeering a car, attended the fire with two auxiliary firemen. She fought the flames from the roof opposite for three and a half hours and succeeded in checking the outbreak, thereby saving the lower rooms and the surrounding buildings. During the time that Auxiliary Hobson was at work, bombs fell nearby. She showed remarkable initiative and courage throughout the incident.

Driver, London Fire Force; Miss Patricia DEWING. During an air raid Driver Dewing was driving a staff car when a high explosive bomb exploded about fifteen yards away, shattering the glass and severely damaging the vehicle. The roof of the car caught fire and Driver Dewing put this out with an extinguisher. Although bruised and suffering from shock, she procured another car and re-joined her Officer. The enemy attack was concentrated and lasted for some hours. High explosive and incendiary bombs were falling in the district most of the time. In addition to conveying vital messages during the height of the attack, Miss Dewing saved one building from fire by promptly removing two incendiary bombs from an upper floor. On another occasion, when firemen were injured, she volunteered, regardless of the danger from falling bombs, to go into the street to give first aid. Afterwards, on her own initiative she fought a fire in a fire station and prevented the flames from spreading. Driver Dewing has displayed great courage and devotion to duty.

Company Officer Sheila Rosemary BENTLEY. Company Officer Bentley has been on duty during nearly all the air-attacks on London and has at all times displayed great efficiency and devotion to duty. On one occasion when a fire station was almost entirely demolished by a bomb, she was on duty in the control room in the basement. The normal exit was blocked with debris but an emergency exit proved to be clear. After the Company Officer had assured herself that none of the women auxiliaries was injured she led them, notwithstanding heavy enemy activity, a distance of about one quarter of a mile to the secondary control station and in a very short time the service was being fully operated.

Section Officer Nellie MASON. Section Officer Mason has been present at her post, even reporting for duty when on leave, on practically every occasion when enemy attack has necessitated action at her station. On three occasions when H.E. bombs exploded within a few yards of the Watchroom, Section Officer Mason set an example of cool courage to the women auxiliaries under her, and as a result, the control room continued to function with all possible efficiency.

··

The Blitz ended on 10 May 1941. London was bombed for 57 consecutive nights by the Luftwaffe, destroying more than one million houses and killing more than 40,000 civilians.

Hundreds of members of the Fire Service died during the war, some many months after their injuries were sustained. Thousands more were injured, many disabled for life. In some cases their bravery was recognised by official honours but most remained unsung heroes.

Blitz statue at St Paul's Cathedral. (Courtesy of Paul Wood.)

BRIGADE BAND

By G. C. Bonell
(Past Editor, London Fireman)

Fifty years ago [1920] the strains of 'On the Quarter Deck' at London's Royal Exchange heralded the first performance of the London Fire Brigade Band. The original band was sponsored by members of Lloyd's who subscribed £1,500 to equip it as a token of their 'great appreciation for the efforts and bravery shown by the Brigade, particularly during the First World War London air raids.'

In those early days, before the advent of radio signalled the beginning of the end for musical 'entertainments' at home, there was no lack of available talent within the London Fire Brigade and there was usually a waiting list of firemen instrumentalists anxious to join. The band soon became part of the London scene, giving regular public performances in the London parks and playing at many Brigade and public events under its first bandmaster, Peter Anderson. Mr Anderson was succeeded in 1932 by Frank Burnell, a former bandmaster of

The London Fire Brigade Band playing in Victoria Park, East London, on the occasion of the Brigade's Annual Review, 1930s. (Mary Evans 10536076.)

the Devon Regiment, and in 1937 the baton passed to T. Kingston Jarvis of the King's Own Scottish Borderers.

The present bandmaster, Station Officer J. C. Wood, ARCM, has been musical director for the past 16 years. A former military musician, he came to the Brigade on retirement from the Army where he had been bandmaster of the 8th Queen's Royal Irish Hussars.

The purpose-built bandstand for the London Fire Brigade's band at the new London Fire Brigade Headquarters in Lambeth. The Headquarters was opened by King George VI in 1937. (Mary Evans 10536583.)

The London Fire Brigade band trumpeters preparing to provide a Royal Fanfare at Lambeth Headquarters with bandmaster Station Officer Woods. (Mary Evans 10795101.)

During the war years the band, then known as the Central Band of the London Fire Forces, was in constant demand. Many professional musicians had joined the AFS and there was a pool of top class talent to draw from. During this period the band became widely known outside London by its frequent radio broadcasts.

In the post-war period the band found itself in difficulties which have continued to a lesser extent to the present time. The 'professionals' returned to civilian life, and there was only a small core of the pre-war bandsmen still in the Brigade. It was only occasionally that a recruit entering the Brigade could 'play' an instrument, and the ruling that bandsmen must measure up to the physical standards required for operational purposes made replacements difficult to find.

The Greater London Council did provide limited financial assistance to the band, but it is largely self-supporting by means of the many public performances it gives in the course of a year. In addition to numerous official and private engagements it gives about 30 public concerts in the London parks each year. One of the band's most appreciative audiences are the men of the Star and Garter Home, Richmond, whom the band entertains every year with a programme specially selected to please the veterans of two world wars. Milestones in the band's progress were the Victory March in 1946, the South Bank Exhibition, and of course the many special events of the Brigade's Centenary in 1966.

Next month the band will celebrate its jubilee with a special concert at the Queen Elizabeth Hall on October 2nd. If you haven't got your tickets yet you had better hurry as it looks like being a 'sell-out'.

BRIGADE'S COLDEST FIRE

By G. C. Bonell
(Past Editor, London Fireman)

Moderate or fresh North East winds; bright intervals; snow showers; very cold.' This was London's gloomy forecast for Saturday 7th March, 1931. In Chelsea, athletes due to represent Oxford or Cambridge Universities that afternoon at Stamford Bridge, read the forecast, looked at the sky, and prophesied slower times and shorter jumps. In Southwark, at the headquarters of the London Fire Brigade, firemen read the same forecast, looked at the same sky, and wondered why they chose a career that made them get up on such a morning.

London firemen at the scene of the Butler's Wharf fire in March 1931. (Permission of the London Fire Brigade.)

The riverside view of Butler's Wharf, 1931. (Permission of the London Fire Brigade.)

In a warehouse on Butler's Wharf near London Bridge a fire was in its infancy. Shortly after 10 o'clock the Brigade was called for; the bells went down and firemen, their breath condensing beneath their brass helmets, scrambled aboard their machines and sped to the scene. A pall of black smoke hung over Shad Thames and as they drew nearer the acrid fumes of burning rubber stung their nostrils.

The fireboats Alpha and Beta ploughed their way towards the wharf and crowds gathered to watch the spectacle. On arrival the firemen immediately got to work and attacked the blaze from the street and from adjoining premises, they even used the cargo ship 'Teal' as a standing platform. In charge of these operations was the Chief Officer, Mr Arthur Reginald Dyer, and also on hand were the men of the London Salvage Corps under the command of Captain Miles.

The Brigade managed to confine the blaze to the single building but it was a long time before the last flame was quenched. All day it burned and when darkness fell searchlights were brought into action. Compared with other conflagrations this fire was not very large, but it was the unbelievably cold conditions that made the firemen's job so difficult. Water froze as it ran down the walls, sheets of ice spreading across the road made even the most limited of movements hazardous and everywhere hung monstrous icicles like the serpents of Medusa after her decapitation by Perseus.

We will leave the last words on the subject to another, more qualified to speak, a fireman from Southwark. 'The temperature was so low that all branches had to be wrapped in sacking, or it would have been impossible to hold them.'

BRIXTON RIOTS:1981

BRIAN WILLIAM BUTLER, *known affectionately as 'Bill', was born in Brixton in the mid-nineteen thirties in the shadow of Brixton Prison. Whilst parts of Brixton reflected the relative affluence of a part of London that spoke of the grandeur of its former Victorian London heyday, with its tall spacious terraced houses, wide streets and open spaces, he was raised in a compact terraced house. His childhood open spaces were those created by Adolf Hitler and his V1 and V2 rockets*

Well-grounded after attending the nearby Clapham Secondary Central School, in his late teens he completed his compulsory National Service having been selected to serve in the Grenadier Guards, first performing pubic duties and then seeing active service in Egypt. At the age of twenty he joined the London Fire Brigade and was trained at Lambeth, the Brigade Headquarters, which was then the Brigade's Training School.

Brian William Butler MBE, QFSM. (Permission of the London Fire Brigade.)

His first posting was to Lambeth fire station itself, serving on the Red Watch. Gifted with an intelligent mind he listened to, and learnt from, the advice offered by the more experienced firemen who had served throughout the Blitz on London. He honed his operational skills and rapidly gained promotion. At the relatively young age of 28 and after only eight years' service (a meteoric rise in the early 1960s) he was promoted to Station Officer in charge of his own watch. After a brief spell in East London he returned to the newly opened Clapham fire station, frequently attending calls in the Brixton area. Brixton was to play its part in his evolving career as he returned there twice as Station Officer. His local knowledge, combined with a proven talent as a competent fire officer, proved invaluable in those formative years and it would do so again.

Brixton fire station and its two fire engines. They were two of London's busiest fire engines in the early 1980s. (Author's picture.)

With over ten years served in Station Officer rank, and as an outstanding operational officer, promotion to senior officer rank was inevitable. It was, however, a steady progression through the senior ranks, and one that saw him gain valuable experience within Fire Prevention – rebranded later as Fire Safety – and operational training in London's A Division, which covered the West End. In 1980 he returned to Clapham, only this time as the Divisional Commander responsible for its eleven fire stations and the Fire Prevention department. As a Deputy Assistant Chief Officer he also had a wider operational role that required taking charge of major fires and other emergency incidents. However, the Brixton Riots, in 1981, were totally unprecedented. There had been skirmishes with stone-throwing youths attacking fire engines before, normally on Bonfire Night, but nothing on the scale that was to unfold. There were no published Fire Service rules of engagement or procedures when confronting a riot. Brian Butler was about to change that. This is his story...

Saturday 11th April 1981 and late on that fateful Saturday afternoon, the Brixton riots started. Their impact would have lasting implications felt across the capital, and beyond. This subsequently brought about both social change and much heated political debate. It certainly changed the public's perception of the Metropolitan Police and its pervading culture of racism that had, sadly, been demonstrated so forcibly by the officers involved in dealing with black people in the build up to the riot.

Railton Road on Sunday morning following a night of rioting. (Permission of the London Fire Brigade.)

During that Saturday morning Brixton fire station's pump had been driving through the very streets that would, all too soon, be illuminated by the many fires that had been deliberately started. These would burn out of control, destroying pubs, local shops, houses and numerous overturned cars. To those riding Brixton's fire engines that morning something was definitely in the air. It was palpable. Lines of police 'tactical support vehicles' (transit vans) were parked in the side roads around Railton, Mayall and Effra Roads. There was a strong presence of uniformed policemen everywhere. Many were just standing on street corners, looking tense, and waiting for something to happen.

A fierce exchange had already taken place the previous evening, involving the police and the young black men who frequented the private clubs and back street bars of Railton Road. This exchange had resulted in a number of arrests. Whilst the Station Officer from Brixton fire station had tried repeatedly to speak to the duty officer at Brixton Police Station on Saturday morning to gain an assessment of a clearly tense situation, no information was forthcoming. It had seemed obvious to those local firemen as they had driven around, looking out from the safety of their fire engine, that all it needed was another spark to ignite the blue touch paper. To them the police appeared more than happy to supply the matches.

Having passed on his concerns to the duty senior officer at B Divisional headquarters, the Station Officer suggested that local stations be advised of the potential for trouble around the Railton Road and Mayall Road area. The message came back at 1.30pm saying the police were of the opinion that no flare-ups were likely to occur before nightfall. Clearly someone had spoken to the wrong policemen since those in the locality were planning to get the action going long before then. With Brixton's Station Officer required to leave the fire station for a meeting in the early afternoon it fell to his deputy, a Sub Officer, to take charge of the station. Unbeknown to the firemen at Brixton fire station rioting had already broken out in the area of Railton Road and Atlantic Road in central Brixton, where police and black youths had clashed on Friday night. That disturbance was soon stamped out but the trouble that Saturday evening, which began after the arrest of a young black man, quickly spiralled out of control. When other police officers arrived and tried to make more arrests the ever-increasing crowd started throwing bottles and bricks. Despite the strong police presence in the locality reinforcements from other police areas were called in. However in the 30 minutes it took for them to arrive the violence had escalated sharply. A charge by about 200 officers with riot shields and batons down Atlantic Road misfired when they were forced to retreat under a hail of missiles.

One of 61 private vehicles destroyed by fire during Saturday night's rioting. Firemen in the background continue to damp down building remains in Mayall Road. (Author's picture.)

It was at 5.30pm that Brixton's fire crews got their very first taste of a civil disturbance. So much for nothing until nightfall! Ordered to a house fire in Railton Road they never reached the incident. They were prevented from doing so by brick throwing mobs involved in street to street fighting with the shield wielding police officers. The mob was filling Coldharbour Lane, Atlantic Road and Railton Road. Brixton's attempt to get a police escort to take their fire engine towards the pall of smoke, clearly visible in the distance, failed. The senior police officer present on the ground was not committing his officers and told Brixton's Sub Officer to forget it because of the volatile crowds and the danger they posed.

During the early stages of the riot West Norwood's pump escape had been sent to a blazing car in Railton Road. As they approached the incident from Brockwell Park a policemen waved the appliance through their cordon. However their route became increasingly congested by people spilling onto the roadway. The Station Officer, Alan Lowles, had to order the driver of that appliance to slow down. The crowd, that had until then been attacking the police with bricks and stones turned their hostility onto the approaching fire engine. First the windscreen and side windows were quickly smashed and missiles hit the firemen inside the cab. The driver, fireman Michael Harding, was concentrating on his driving and was unable to protect himself. He was hit several times by brick-bats. One particular missile, a large lump of concrete, hit him in the chest, it breaking two of his ribs and rupturing his spleen. Despite his severe pain Harding continued to drive in accordance with the Station Officer's instructions. Reaching the Atlantic Avenue end of Railton Road, and in the protection of the police again, the Station Officer summoned an ambulance for Fireman Harding whilst his crew dealt with the severe vehicle fire.

Brixton's pump crew had by now been joined by the crew of West Norwood's pump escape who had just made it down Railton Road. What was happening to London Fire Brigade crews was a new and the unprecedented experience for them all. Unable to attend the very calls that some were ordered to they did not know if lives were in danger or not. The situation in, and around, Railton Road was deteriorating rapidly. Both firefighters and police officers alike were in considerable danger from the constant hail of bricks, bottles and sharpened lengths of wood being hurled at them by the hordes now gathering in numbers and charging at the police lines. Unable to return to the local fire station, lest it be attacked, Brixton and West Norwood crews were ordered to a temporary holding point, a nearby coach station, just outside the immediate danger area. Widespread damage and looting had by now spread as far as central Brixton. Brixton's crews were ordered by radio to attend further calls, including Burtons, the tailors, where the looters had fired the shop as they left with their arms filled with their spoils. By now other fire station crews were being ordered to the numerous 999 calls that the mobilising control at Croydon was receiving continuously. Fire appliances, in the minds of the rioters, had become a legitimate target for their ferocious attacks.

The disturbance very quickly escalated into major proportions. News of the events in Brixton had spread via a cultural grapevine and others joined in the street violence having travelled in from surrounding areas. Several hundred members of the local community and the wider society added their weight and acted in an extremely riotous manner. Their number was to swell into the thousands. It was something that police, at this stage, were totally unable to contain. In fact these were the first serious riots of the 20th century, and the first entailing substantial destruction of property since the formation of the Metropolitan Police.

Due to the very pressure that the police were put under the level of protection which could be afforded Brigade personnel and their equipment, whilst trying to fight the fires started in this area of Brixton, was minimal. Crews from various parts of

London were called into the area and they encountered previously unseen hostility that caused the most severe and difficult circumstances in addition to the normal hazards of fighting fire. Fire engines were bombarded with missiles, crews targeted for attack from bricks, masonry and bottles. Brigade equipment was sabotaged and even stolen whilst in operational use!

As the evening moved into night the day shift crews were slowly relieved and night shift crews took over. They too would face a night of increasing violence, running street battles and having to deal with several major fires that were seriously under-resourced. This was the capital's most serious public disturbance in modern times and radicals and extremists from various parts of London were willing and eager to join in the violent assault on public order, coming out of the ground like rats from Brixton and Stockwell tube stations.

It was into this scene of chaos that Brian Butler, the local fire brigade Divisional Commander, found himself projected. He already knew that the mobilising control-room at Croydon was working under the most extreme pressure because of the riots. He had been monitoring the radio traffic on his 'listening post' located in the Commander's office at Clapham. Booking 'mobile' to Brixton he sped through Clapham's busy streets towards Brixton. He knew that in addition to the many fire crews already on the ground he also had at his disposal his team of duty senior officers, and he had access to more of each if required. But he soon realised that if 'normal' mobilising was maintained then fire engine crews would be sent unwittingly into hostile areas and exposed to an extremely dangerous and volatile environment. On his arrival he immediately took overall command of the fire brigade actions and its mobilisation within the area of the civil disorder. This was uncharted territory in Fire Service operational tactics. Because of the number of fire engines in the vicinity the Divisional control unit, based at Clapham the Divisional headquarters, had already been sent into the area and was now located at the Effra Road 'Orange' coach station, which itself was now in imminent danger of attack.

Despite the smaller riot in the Saint Paul's district of Bristol, in the same month in 1980, and the attacks on Avon fire engines and their crews, no national fire service advice or guidance had been published in respect of dealing with such disturbances.

Brixton Prison is located on Brixton Hill. Whilst close to Brixton town centre it was not in any immediate danger of attack from the rioters. Access into the prison is via Jebb Avenue, a no through road. Brian Butler choose this location as his forward command post and set about establishing a safe marshalling area for his appliances and crews. His were new operational tactics and they were being developed on the hoof. It was the first time that the deployment of a forward control point had been used in the British fire service. His vast operational experience as a command officer and his intuitive and decisive decision making, together with an intimate knowledge of the affected area, served to provide a comprehensive and effective plan of attack that the fluid and rapidly changing situation demanded. He made sorties into the area to make a personal assessment of the situation and ensured the best use was made of his personnel and the resources available.

With the Divisional control unit relocated and designated a 'forward mobilising control' a number of appliances were held in readiness under the command of a nominated senior officer who dispatched the appliances into the riot zone. The control at Croydon had been instructed not to mobilise fire engines into the Brixton area but to refer all calls to the forward mobilising control. Fire engine crews were fully briefed of the prevailing situation and strict observance of the necessary changes to normal firefighting techniques because of the very real threat posed to personnel by the rioters.

Painting a picture in words to anyone not directly involved in this situation, over those prolonged fraught hours, is difficult, if not impossible. This would be deemed a major 'civil disorder'. It was a breaking news story that would go global. But not in today's terms of instant 24 hour news coverage. The wider public would only awake to graphic images of the street violence, and the aftermath of the destruction, that had erupted on South London streets on the front of their Sunday morning newspapers and that which was contained in BBC and ITV news bulletins.

A burnt out builder's merchant in Railton Road. One of 127 buildings seriously damaged by fire started during the riot. (Author's picture.)

The remains of the Railton Road post office and adjoining motor accessory shop being damped down. Two of the 28 premises destroyed by fire. (Author's picture.)

Brian Butler was not the only one to face severe challenges that night. The acting Station Officer of Brixton's Green Watch had to fight a most serious fire involving a three-storey public house with only two fire engines and eight firemen. Something which in the normal course of events would have demanded eight fire engines plus special supporting crews. Needless to say the pub, which was well alight when the crews arrived, was a burnt out shell by the early hours of the Sunday morning. However the crews fought hard and successfully prevented the fire spreading to other property.

Saturday night turned to Sunday morning. A massive police presence was mobilised and reinforcements, from all over London, arrived in Brixton. Despite their weight in numbers the police tactics remained one of containment. Something that those rioting on the streets took scant regard of as their ferocious attacks, withdrawals then attacking again kept the police engaged and the fire brigade crews working in the area under the ever present threat of serious harm from this violence. However the plans put into action by Brian Butler were working and to good effect. The fact that injury to fire brigade personnel was restricted to a relatively small number was due to his presence of mind and his leadership qualities, together with those fire officers taking their crews repeatedly into such a hostile environment.

By the early hours of Sunday morning it was possible for Brian Butler to escort the Chief Fire Officer, who had arrived to see for himself the plans Brian Butler had put into action, and to view the work of his firefighters on the ground. Both Brian Butler and the Chief were impressed, but not surprised, by the highest possible commitment from members of the Brigade who had demonstrated, in so many ways, the finest qualities required of a firemen.

By sunrise there was an uneasy calm. The forward command post was closed down and it was not necessary to reinstate it again over the following two days. The Metropolitan police flooded the area, but those with what riot equipment the police had available then maintained a discreet presence, sitting in police vans parked in side streets. It was the traditionally clothed policeman that stood on the street corners and, together with the Brixton locals, surveyed the scene of considerable devastation that surrounded them.

Sunday evening, and with high risk of more riots, Brian Butler ordered the evacuation of Brixton fire station. It was not something the crews at Brixton were happy about. But it was obvious that this was not an issue for debate as far the Divisional Commander was concerned. Ten minutes later the station was secured and empty! Brixton's pump and driver headed off to West Norwood fire station whilst the pump-ladder was driving towards Clapham fire station. Brixton's fire engines would cover its ground from these two adjoining fire stations.

It was clear that fire engines remained a legitimate target as far as the rioters were concerned and for those that had started their hostility and aggression for a second consecutive night, but thankfully without the same mass destruction that had taken place only twenty-four hours earlier. That night the tension and running street battles were confined to the rioters and the police who now presented a massive presence in the affected area. None of the numerous arson attacks that had materialised Saturday night were repeated.

Monday. Brixton's night duty watch reported for duty at 6pm. They expected the same evacuation drill as nightfall came. None came and they remained at Brixton. Just before supper their first shout of the night was received. It was to a house alight in Mayall Road and new tactics were now in place to ensure better crew safety in case of a hostile attack. Driving as close to the incident as possible the drivers were told to reverse the fire engines down the cul de sac to ensure a quick exit if necessary. Working directly from the street hydrant the derelict house, which was blazing merrily, was soon extinguished.

At 9.30pm both Brixton's fire engines were ordered to a car alight in Railton Road and they rapidly applied the tactics that Brian Butler had insisted upon. The car was blazing fiercely as they approached. Stopping and turning the appliances around, they reversed the last one hundred and fifty yards towards the incident. The street was illuminated by the light of the burning car and the air was heavy with the acrid smoke of burning rubber and the car's interior. With water again used directly from the street hydrant the street filled with clouds of steam as the jet made contact with the white hot metal of the car. It was so hot that the car lay flat on the road surface with all its tyres completely burnt away. There was still no police escort despite their now strong presence. But these were not local Brixton policemen and they had little or no knowledge of the area. Small groups of stone-throwing black and white youths were playing cat and mouse with the police and causing a great deal of confusion as they attacked, waited for the inevitable chase and then disappeared amongst the narrow alleys and pathways leaving the police increasingly frustrated and angry.

That was the last fire attributed directly to the Brixton Riots. However fourteen Brigade personnel sustained injuries from bricks and other missiles and eight fire engines and one staff car were damaged. 299 police were injured, and at least 65 civilians required hospital treatment. The triangular area most affected by the arson attacks at the height of the rioting looked like a war zone. Damage to buildings and property was on an unprecedented scale for peacetime in London. Some fires, that crews were prevented from attending, spread and involved other surrounding premises. In one particular case five buildings were destroyed after the initial blaze spread out of control. Some 61 private vehicles and 56 police vehicles were damaged or destroyed, mostly by fire. 28 premises were burned down and another 117 damaged and looted. 82 arrests were made. Molotov cocktails were thrown for the first time on mainland Britain. There had been no such event in England in living memory.

The shell of The George public house, gutted by fire following an arson attack whilst a news reporter gets his story in the aftermath of Saturday night's riot. (Author's picture.)

Notes

1) In 1981, Brixton's Afro-Caribbean community comprised roughly 25% of its population. It was an area of high unemployment, particularly for black men, where rates were as high as 50%. Brixton was also an area of high crime, and in that April the Metropolitan Police initiated 'Operation Swamp'. Within just six days, a massive police presence on Brixton streets (including plain clothes officers) had led to almost 1,000 people, mostly young black men, being stopped and searched. Police operated then under the 'sus' law. In order to stop someone, a police officer need only 'sus', or suspect that they might be intending to commit a crime. The police were exempt from the Race Relations Act, and seemed to some to be operating the 'sus' laws on the basis of racial prejudice.

Many found that the prevailing attitude of so many police officers swamping the surrounding streets of central Brixton made them feel increasingly uncomfortable. Police officers' attitude towards the black population was adversely impacting on the very public order task that they were meant to be performing. It would later come to light that very many were racist. They seemed to be itching for a fight with anyone of a skin colour different from their own, which was universally white. This was not just a local problem as they came from all over London, bussed into Brixton to police the area while it slowly reverted to normal.

Black people, especially youths, were more likely to be targeted and challenged in ways that would not be applied to white people. In the days and weeks following the riots much was reported nationally of the causes and implications of this civil unrest and the disturbances in Brixton. But it would take future public inquiries to recognise the 'pernicious and institutional racism' that prevailed throughout the Metropolitan Police Force. The Stephen Lawrence inquiry conducted by Sir William MacPherson and published in 1990 highlighted these very attitudes and the 'institutional' racism that had been witnessed in 1981.

Following the Brixton Riots Brian Butler received many invitations to talk and comment on the lessons learned that had tested not only him but those under his command. He spoke far and wide and his actions set a new benchmark in the Fire Service response to civil disturbances. The events of that April were not only unprecedented in the history of the London Fire Brigade but the British Fire Service. It was something that would not be repeated on such a scale for thirty years and the widespread riots that erupted in 2011.

2) At the time of the Brixton Riots Fireman Harding had been a Brigade heavy goods driver for only two weeks. Fireman Michael Harding and Station Officer Alan Lowles (West Norwood) were awarded a Chief Officer's Commendation and a Chief Officer's Letter of Congratulation respectively. Fireman Michael Harding was subsequently awarded the Queen's Commendation for Brave Conduct.

Deputy Assistant Chief Officer Brian 'Bill' Butler was awarded Membership of the Most Excellent Order of the British Empire (MBE) for his actions, leadership and officership during the Brixton Riots in April 1981.

CALAMITY IN LONDON

A poem by Sir William Topaz McGonagall

'Twas in the year of 1897, and on the night of Christmas day,
That ten persons' lives were taken away,
By a destructive fire in London, at N° 9 Dixie Street,
Alas! so great was the fire, the victims couldn't retreat.

In Dixie Street, N° 9, it was occupied by two families,
Who were all quite happy, and sitting at their ease;
One of these was a labourer, David Barber and his wife,
And a dear little child, he loved as his life.

Barber's mother and three sisters were living on the ground
    floor,
And in the upper two rooms lived a family who were very
    poor,
And all had retired to rest, on the night of Christmas day,
Never dreaming that by fire their lives would be taken away.

Barber got up on Sunday morning to prepare breakfast for his
    family,
And a most appalling sight he then did see;
For he found the room was full of smoke,
So dense, indeed, that it nearly did him choke.

Drawing of the Metropolitan Fire Brigade in action with a horse drawn steam fire engine at work. (Mary Evans 10794408.)

Then fearlessly to the room door he did creep,
And tried to arouse the inmates, who were asleep;
And succeeded in getting his own family out into the street,
And to him the thought thereof was surely very sweet.

And by this time the heroic Barber's strength was failing,
And his efforts to warn the family upstairs were unavailing;
And, before the alarm was given, the house was in flames,
Which prevented anything being done, after all his pains.

Oh! it was a horrible and heart-rending sight
To see the house in a blaze of lurid light,
And the roof fallen in, and the windows burnt out,
Alas! 'tis pitiful to relate, without any doubt.

Oh, Heaven! 'tis a dreadful calamity to narrate,
Because the victims have met with a cruel fate;
Little did they think they were going to lose their lives by fire,
On that night when to their beds they did retire.

It was sometime before the gutted house could be entered in,
Then to search for the bodies the officers in charge did begin;
And a horrifying spectacle met their gaze,
Which made them stand aghast in a fit of amaze.

Sometime before the firemen arrived,
Ten persons of their lives had been deprived,
By the choking smoke, and merciless flame,
Which will long in the memory of their relatives remain.

Oh, Heaven! if was a frightful and pitiful sight to see
Seven bodies charred of the Jarvis' family;
And Mrs Jarvis was found with her child, and both carbonised,
And as the searchers gazed thereon they were surprised.

And these were lying beside the fragments of the bed,
And in a chair the tenth victim was sitting dead;
Oh, Horrible! Oh, Horrible! What a sight to behold,
The charred and burnt bodies of young and old.

Good people of high and low degree,
Oh! Think of this sad catastrophe,
And pray to God to protect ye from fire,
Every night before to your beds ye retire.

DUNKIRK

When the London fireboat Massey Shaw first left her river moorings for Dunkirk, she had only ever been to sea once before. That was on her maiden journey from the Isle of Wight to the Thames in 1935 after being constructed at the John Samuel White's boatyard at a cost of £18,000. Following her final fitting out at Greenwich she was placed into operational service with the London Fire Brigade that summer. The Massey Shaw was never intended to be a sea-going vessel but had, until the time of Dunkirk, been stationed at the Blackfriars river station, adjacent to Blackfriars Bridge in London. Her two massive 8-cylinder, 160 hp diesel engines had more than enough power to propel her up and down the Thames at 12 knots. However, they were principally intended to operate her 3,000 gallon-per-minute centrifugal pumps to put out fires along London's river front.

She had been named after Captain Eyre Massey Shaw (1828–1908) who, at the age of thirty, was the first Chief Officer of the Metropolitan Fire Brigade (see page 175). Her first major operational test was, literally, an ordeal by fire. An eight-storey riverside warehouse, Colonial Wharf, containing rubber products and located in Wapping High Street, burned for four days from 27 September 1935 and had also required 60 fire engines to contain the blaze. This was the first major incident, and test, for the new fireboat and one where she greatly assisted land crews, who were hampered by inaccessibility. The Massey Shaw's single monitor threw vast quantities of water high

The crew of the Massey Shaw starting her exploits in the evacuation of the Dunkirk beaches in May–June 1940, taken as the fire-float heads down to the English Channel. (Permission of the London Fire Brigade.)

into the inferno, thus allowing the land crews to regroup and prevent the fire from spreading to adjoining warehouses.

However, that was not to be her most noticeable service achievement. Shortly after the start of World War II, the London Fire Brigade volunteer fireboat crew of the Massey Shaw would perform heroically as they joined the fleet of 'Little Ships' that evacuated British soldiers from the beaches of Dunkirk in Northern France. Navy sailors, volunteers with their small craft and London firemen all worked side by side to rescue members of the British Expeditionary Force trapped by the German Army on the French beaches.

On 29 and 30 May 1940 the Massey Shaw's crew had seen tugs coming down the river towing strings of small boats, yachts, lifeboats and even dinghies. Then they heard that their destination was Dunkirk, and Massey Shaw was to follow them from her mooring at Blackfriars. Her volunteer crew of 13 was chosen and with a formal send-off they departed from the Brigade Headquarters river station by the Albert Embankment in Lambeth.

Thirteen was more than her normal crew complement because they had expected to spend several days fighting fires off the French coast without relief. A river pilot took them to Greenwich and another onto Ramsgate. Her sparkling brass-work and fittings were covered with grey paint on the way. A young Royal Naval Sub-Lieutenant came aboard to take command of the Massey Shaw. He carried nothing more than his steel helmet and a chart to show him how to navigate through the minefields across the channel from North Goodwin Lightship to Bray Dunes, the beach where they were to pick up Allied troops.

The Massey Shaw did not even possess a ship's compass, but the firemen had bought one hastily from a chandler's in Blackfriars. There was no time to swing and correct it, which made it rather unreliable since the large steel hull of the fireboat caused a massive deviation. As a result, despite the excellent landmark of smoke from Dunkirk's burning oil tanks, they were well outside the swept channel when they got to the French coast. But the boat's shallow draught enabled them to cross the hazardous sandbanks without grounding.

The fires ashore were what the Massey Shaw's firemen crew were used to, but the bursts of high-explosive shells, bombs and anti-aircraft fire were a new experience. As they steamed parallel to the beach, they saw columns of men wading out in the shallows, waiting to be picked up by a host of small boats. Late that afternoon, they anchored off Bray Dunes.

They used a light skiff, picked up at Ramsgate Harbour, to go ashore and collect the first of the men. Most of the soldiers were non-swimmers and at first, too many of them tried to get aboard so they swamped and sank the skiff. There were many other small boats operating from the beach, but each of them already had its own ship to fill. After many attempts to find a suitable way of ferrying soldiers to the Massey Shaw, a line was made fast to a derelict lorry and a small boat was used to ferry altogether 40 of a company of Royal Engineers aboard the Massey Shaw.

The young naval officer, having spent most of the day in the water between the fireboat and the beach, then safely navigated her back to Ramsgate where they arrived next morning. They escaped major damage, despite an attack by a German bomber which had spotted the Massey Shaw's phosphorescent wake, but whose bombs missed by a boat length. The crew of the Massey Shaw re-fuelled hastily, got some food and left for another trip. Some of the exhausted firemen were replaced by naval ratings and they brought a Lewis gun on board as a defence against air attack, but this was never used. Another Royal Naval Volunteer Reserve Lieutenant came aboard to command the ship and they brought two stokers to take care of the engines and a beach party commanded by a second young naval officer to handle the embarkation on the other side. They also took a 30 foot ship's lifeboat in tow as a tender.

At 2300 they arrived and anchored off Bray Dunes in 10 feet of water with their prow facing the shore. The fires of Dunkirk gave them enough light to work by and the thick blanket of smoke provided some cover from air attack. But the shelling from German guns was relentless. The two naval officers set a splendid example of calm and the beach party rowed ashore, fixing a line to maintain contact with the fireboat. After four or five journeys, the Massey Shaw was full once more with troops pressed together in the cabin and standing shoulder-to-shoulder on deck. Her load of nearly 100 men was transferred to a troopship at anchor in the channel and she returned to be re-loaded.

This was only possible after some engine trouble that the naval stokers, who were unused to the Massey Shaw's machinery, eventually managed to overcome. Stretcher cases now began to arrive and these were hard to handle and transfer to the troopship. They made about five journeys from the beach to a paddle steamer and it was estimated that they embarked 500 men in this way. As dawn broke, the troopship was full and left for England. The Massey Shaw returned to the beach and started loading again. At this point, on a falling tide, they began to bump on the sands and were in danger of damaging their propellers but, with their engines throbbing at full power, they just managed to get back into deep water. At 0330 they were the last boat to leave that part of the beach. Halfway across the channel, the naval skipper began to have doubts about the compass, but then, to his relief, came across a drifter towing two small boats packed with troops. They followed them into Ramsgate where they arrived at 0800 on Sunday 2 June, landing 30 or 40 more soldiers.

Fireman Dick Helyer, a crew member on the Massey Shaw Dunkirk crossings. He was later promoted to Station Officer and in 1951 awarded the British Empire Medal. (Permission of the London Fire Brigade.)

The Massey Shaw returned to Dunkirk again the next evening with a London Fire Brigade crew. This time they went to the jetty of Dunkirk harbour. It was difficult for soldiers to board her from the towering jetty and she came away empty. After returning to Ramsgate, she was ordered back to London. Off Margate, the Emile de Champs, a French ship which had sailed to England from Dunkirk laden with troops the previous night, was passing her at a distance of 200 yards when it struck a mine and sank almost immediately. The Massey Shaw picked up 40 men, all severely injured and took them back to Ramsgate. Early on Wednesday 5 June, she finally returned to London and as she came up the River Thames she was cheered as she passed each fire station. Finally the wives and families of all those on board were waiting at the Lambeth Headquarters when the boat docked at the Lambeth river station to great jubilation. The crew were given a splendid reception at the Headquarters station.

Sub-Officer A. J. May was subsequently awarded the Navy's Distinguished Service Medal, a rare honour for a civilian. Two of her firemen, Henry Ray and Edmond Wright, were also mentioned in Dispatches (Kings Commendation).

*A member of that crew was fireman **DICK HELYER**. Later he would be promoted to Station Officer rank but here he recalls what it was like to be part of that armada of 'little ships'.*

∙∙

W e knew that things were not good in France. Sub Officer May had called a group of us together and said, 'We're in trouble. The British Army is stranded on the beach not far from Dunkirk. Will you volunteer to go over there?'

We agreed readily and scampered around getting the things we needed. There was a bit of a delay while we got a certified river pilot because they wouldn't let the Massey Shaw out of the Thames without one, but we eventually got one and shoved off about four o'clock.

Our crew came from the LFB and the AFS and most of us on the Massey were stationed at Blackfriars. At Ramsgate we tried to get some metal sheeting for the engine covers and some Lewis guns, but as I recall we weren't successful. From this point we had a naval officer in charge of us and flew the white ensign. Our crew comprised Jack Gillman, Beaumont Hinge, 'Speaky' Lowe, Mr Youngman and Sub Officer May, who was a really courageous bloke.

There were dozens of boats of all shapes and sizes moving out to cross the Channel. Spitfires and some twin-engined Blenheims cruised around overhead. Left to my thoughts in the engine room I wondered what I had let myself in for. Many of the crew had been in the First World War, but I was the youngest member of the crew at twenty-two.

We had a look out of the hatch occasionally and when Dunkirk appeared on the horizon there was a thick pall of smoke going from across the seafront. We steamed in towards Dunkirk and then turned along the coast towards De Panne. There were bombers overhead, but I was down below and could only hear things rather than see them which was as much as I wanted at the time. When I did poke my head out of the hatch I could see a French destroyer, completely burnt out.

The Massey Shaw.
(Permission of the
London Fire Brigade.)

It was a dead calm sea and there were wrecks everywhere. You could see masts sticking up out of the water from boats that had received direct hits from enemy bombers. In our engine room you could feel the shock waves from the explosions. We were unable to get right into the beach because of our propellers, but smaller boats were picking up soldiers. There was a lot of machine-gunning and bombing going on. Eventually we got soldiers on board from one of the other boats and after a while we could hardly move down there.

Coming up on deck for fresh air I could see the troops still on the beaches. The sky was thick with aircraft while out to sea there were four or five destroyers lobbing some stuff inland. At one stage we wanted to get a line to a launch with our rocket line system but it fell short. I put on a lifejacket, pulled on the rocket line and swam ashore with it. The bombs and shells were coming down all the time and it really was very frightening. Anyway, I swam to this RAF launch which was crowded with soldiers. They said they were stuck until the tide came in, but somebody gave me a hand and we tied a bowline from the Massey to the towing bollard on the launch. A naval officer said we'd never pull them off with all the soldiers on board; he was right, it was useless. Someone on the launch unhooked the line and threw it off. I had to swim back to the Massey.

We had nearly seventy soldiers on board and nearly all of them were drying off in the engine room. A few sat on the upper deck where they could find room. We were on the go all the time. Putting the engines into ahead, stop, astern, stop, ahead, you get the picture.

Eventually we got away at about three o'clock in the morning – one of the last to go. There was a red glow all over Dunkirk and the fuel oil tanks at the entrance to the harbour were well alight. We got back to Ramsgate without being machine-gunned. We had a cuppa tea and digestive biscuit but I remember we were still very hungry and absolutely exhausted. After we had gone off the Massey they put a Navy crew on board and after they came back from Dunkirk they sent another crew down from London for a third trip.

A welcome return home from family and friends as the volunteer crews of the Massey Shaw land at the Lambeth HQ fire-float moorings. (Mary Evans 10535414.)

When we moved out again we were warned about mines which was particularly worrying for us as we had no protection against magnetic mines. We were nearly opposite Margate and I was in the engine room when I heard a tremendous crash. I nipped up the hatch to look and saw a plume of smoke not very far away. It was the Emile de Champs, a French auxiliary vessel. She had struck a mine. She sank within two minutes. She had something like 350 people on board and nearly all were lost. We picked up 39 survivors, all of them badly injured. The first survivor we picked saw the monitor of the Massey, thought we were the enemy and tried to swim away rather than be rescued.

It was a real mess and we felt so sorry for those poor devils. One man was split like a kipper, from his hip to his heel. We put them everywhere, all of them seriously injured, and covered in blood and with broken arms and legs. To make matters worse, just as we were about to move off we got a line round one of our screws and had to put one of the engines off the run.

We signalled to HMS Albury, a minesweeper loaded with French troops, to ask if they could take the injured, but she replied that she had no doctor on board. We were about to head back to Ramsgate when the Albury signalled again to say they'd found some French doctors on board so we went alongside and transferred the injured before making our way back to Ramsgate.

As we came off the Massey Shaw we were told that somebody was needed to make a broadcast to Canada, There were no volunteers so, being the youngest, I was chosen. I came home by car and recorded the broadcast about Dunkirk at Broadcasting House. Whether or not it was ever broadcast I don't know because, believe me, I was so tired that all I wanted to do was to sleep.

• •

As a footnote to Dick Heyler's story, it was not the last time the magazine would describe his exploits at Dunkirk. Fifty years after the evacuation he would be reunited with one of the very soldiers that he had helped save. It was an emotional reunion that took place in April 1990 when **JOHN OVERY***, a former Sergeant with 2nd Royal Horse Artillery, knelt on the now restored decks of the Massey Shaw and, Pope-like, kissed the deck. His friends were laughing.*

'This boat saved my life,' he told them. He saw the Massey Shaw again in Dunkirk for the 50th anniversary celebrations. The occasion brought his memories flooding back.

John Overy's regiment had been in France since the outbreak of war in September 1939. Pushed back by the German onslaught they found themselves, together with hundreds of thousands of other British, French and Belgian troops, on the Dunkirk beaches. Operation Dynamo was the name given to the evacuation plan. John's first rescue attempt had ended in failure when the Dutch boat he was on took a bomb down its funnel and sank. 'I was lucky,' he recalls. 'I went over the side and swam back to the beach. There were so many dead lying around.' John waited a further two days before his eventual rescue by the Massey Shaw.

....

The Massey Shaw fireboat returns to Dunkirk for the 25th anniversary of the beaches evacuations in 1965. (Permission of the London Fire Brigade.)

Enemy bombers constantly flew low over the beaches every ten or twenty minutes. With the onset of darkness, at about 6pm, a man (Dick Heyler) had swam to shore from the Massey Shaw bringing a line with him as a guide back to the boat for those waiting rescue. By this stage two smaller craft had already been overwhelmed and sunk in their attempts to ferry troops to larger waiting boats.

John had grabbed the line Dick Heyler had secured to the shore line and hauled himself to the safety of the Massey Shaw's deck. He found himself in the crowded company of other servicemen, many injured, and all of them drenched.

It took two or three hours to reach the relative safety of Ramsgate and with no first aid equipment the injured were looked after with torn shirts used as bandages.

At first we didn't realise we were on a fire tender. When we realised that these were not seamen but firemen, we all said a silent prayer to them. We were all so glad we had been saved.

On resuming her normal duties, Massey Shaw was the first fire appliance to be fitted with radio communication. She played a major role during the Blitz, pumping water ashore for the land appliances hampered by huge demands on the water supply, or when bombing had destroyed the water mains. In 1947 her original open canvas dodger and screen were replaced with a purpose-built enclosed timber wheelhouse. Another claim to fame came in this year when a secret meeting in the Thames Estuary between Herbert Morrison (Member of Parliament and Chairman of the London County Council) and Aneurin Bevan MP eventually resulted in the formation of the National Health Service.

No other London fire brigade appliance, or sole piece of equipment, has been responsible for the rescue, or bringing to safety, of so many individuals. Some 710 soldiers were either ferried to troop ships or landed safely on English soil. The Massey Shaw resumed her operational (war-time) duties in London and was one of some twenty other fireboats and floats swept up in the creation of the National Fire Services (London Region), making up part of the River Thames Formation.

E

ELDON STREET – A SIXTY PUMP FIRE

An account by Charles Keevil, Historian of the London Ambulance Service

Some time ago I was walking around the area near to the old London borough of Finsbury and the City of London when I thought some of the buildings seemed vaguely familiar. Then I saw the street nameplate: Eldon Street. This caused my memory to flash back over 50 years.

The scene of devastation at Eldon Street after the collapse of the upper wall onto firemen and their equipment. (Permission of the London Fire Brigade.)

Whilst on one side it was very much the same, the other was entirely different. Back in December 1951, Eldon Street contained two wrecked London Fire Brigade turntable ladders, several broken 50 foot wheeled escapes and debris in the road covering hoses and other fire-fighting equipment. Unfortunately in those days I did not have a camera so I missed some prize photographic opportunities.

The building in question was the former British Railway's Eldon Street warehouse, also known as the Broad Street Goods Station. It was a five storey open-plan building with brick load-bearing walls containing both a basement and sub-basement. It was bounded by Finsbury Avenue and Eldon Street. In size it was 112 by 256 feet with a capacity of some 2,500,000 square feet. There were no internal walls, and the upper floors were carried on steel joists.

The first floor was brick arches supporting steel girders on which rested a wooden floor. The roof was on timber trusses with close boarded timbers covered with waterproof felt. Items stored in the warehouse included carpets, hosiery, rubber flooring, cotton, wool, textiles, paper, glass and stationary. On the second floor an area had been partitioned and used to hold

The fatal building collapse at Eldon Street and the subsequent fire brigade funerals. (Permission of the London Fire Brigade.)

records on timber racks. There was also a canteen and kitchen. The ground floor was used as a loading and unloading area while the basement was sub-divided and stocked with wool; this was undamaged by the subsequent disastrous fire.

To add to the London Fire Brigade's problems, Eldon Street was 40 feet wide, whilst Finsbury Avenue was only 22 feet wide. It would be discovered that a 'late call' was made for this fire! The last known person left the building between 5 p.m. and 5.30 p.m. when there was no indication of the inferno which was to follow. The two cleaners who were working on the second floor left about two hours later.

Timetable of events

At 7.15 and 7.20 p.m. the 'dolls' eyes' (indicator panels) actuated on the private telephone exchange alarm system. The switchboard operator took no action. Two railwaymen in the canteen heard a thud that might have been caused by falling furniture at 7.25 p.m. but also decided to take no action. At 7.33 p.m. off-duty City of London police officer (PC Armfield from Bishopsgate Police Station) and two colleagues were walking in Finsbury Square when he saw smoke issuing from a second floor window. He ran to the gatekeeper's cubicle in Eldon Street and was told by the occupant, 'We know all about it', or words to that effect. At 7.34 p.m. the PC saw smoke still coming from the window and returned to the gatekeeper. Only to be told: 'Everything is all right, my people have been told.' The gatekeeper later denied all knowledge of these events. The switchboard operator said he received an internal call at 7.34 p.m. asking for the Fire Brigade to be called. This time was later challenged, as a worker who 'clocked off' at 7.41 p.m. saw the glow of a fire on the second floor. He reported this to a member of the railway's own fire brigade. Then they both went to investigate and discovered a well-established fire. The railway fireman, with others in the brigade, tried to get a jet hose to work but the water supply had been turned off! The first person then went to the gatekeeper and told him to call the 'LFB.' This call was received at 7.49 p.m. Someone also went to a public telephone booth which was in use.

The initial attendance was pump escape and pump from the then (B32) Bishopsgate fire station, and pump from (B33) Redcross Street, whilst the turntable ladder came from (B35) Cannon Street. In addition a pump from (B27) Shoreditch station, with a fire station officer, was mobilised. Bishopsgate's appliances arrived 7.45 p.m. The leading fireman in charge of

Bishopsgate appliances made 'pumps four' three minutes later. The Sub-Officer from Redcross Street made a swift survey and made 'pumps eight' at 7.50 p.m. At this stage Assistant Divisional Officer Varndell arrived and made 'pumps 20' and turntable ladders '3' at 7.53 p.m. The ambulance service also attended and stood stand by in Broad Street junction with Eldon Street. At 8.01 p.m the Chief Fire Officer arrived, having been preceded some three minutes earlier by his deputy.

Meanwhile jets from the three turntable ladders and 15 other jets had been got to work from the tops of escapes or from the ground.

At 8.46 p.m. pumps were made 40. Two minutes later the first major wall collapse occurred.

Deputy Chief Officer McDuell, pictured here as a London Divisional (District) Officer in the 1930s. (Permission of the London Fire Brigade.)

The construction of the building had large unprotected steel joints across the building and as they expanded they forced the walls to bulge dangerously and structural collapses occurred. The major collapse in Eldon Street happened at 8.49 p.m. as an evacuation from the street was 'in progress'. The deputy chief officer (Mr McDuell) lay pinned down by masonry and suffered serious injuries to his right leg – later to be amputated in hospital. Two firemen (Edward Harwood and Leslie Skitt) were killed with a third (Thomas Joy) succumbing to his injuries in hospital. Seven other firemen were injured and detained in hospital, with a further three being treated in hospital but released after treatment. At 8.59 p.m. the duty ambulance station officer called for an additional three ambulances. At the same time St Bartholomew's, The London and St Leonard's hospitals were all put on standby. The ambulance chief superintendent was informed and attended.

Thirty firemen were taken to hospital, with others being treated at the scene for minor injuries. The attendance by the LFB included 62 pump escapes and pumps, including an Auxiliary Fire Service (AFS) pump from Euston, eight turntable ladders, both the Brigade's emergency tenders and a hose layer. Soon after midnight the initial crews were relieved by 20 relief pumps, including five pumps each from Kent, Essex and Surrey Fire Brigades. During the night and following days 37 relief crews attended with the last crew being withdrawn on December 27th, six days after the initial call.

This was the largest attendance at any peace-time fire in the County of London. I do not have the attendance of the Smithfield Meat Market fire when more appliances were involved, but spread over a much longer time. I understand the maximum attendance was 40 pumps plus specialists. It is interesting to note that ambulances were conveying three stretcher patients at a time. One on each bed and one on a Furley stretcher in the gangway of the rear of the vehicle. At this period of time the LAS did not have radios in their vehicles, therefore the duty station officer had to find a telephone, either in a public telephone booth or one in private property. The LFB did not have spare radio capacity, and some years were to elapse before ambulance vehicles were fitted with radios. It is also interesting that at Smithfield Meat market, where the fire started in the basement lined with cork insulation, that radiated heat was felt in the basements of buildings more than 60 feet away, whilst at Eldon Street, goods in the basement were left undamaged. The turntable ladders that sustained damage came from Kingsland and Cannon Street Fire Stations.

Press cutting of the Guard of Honour for the firemen killed at the Eldon Street blaze.

PASSING THROUGH LINES OF FIREMEN AFTER LEAVING WHITEFRIARS FIRE STATION : THE FUNERAL PROCESSION FOR THE THREE FIREMEN KILLED AT THE ELDON STREET FIRE. Elsewhere in this issue we publish photographs of the disastrous fire at the Broad Street Station warehouse, Eldon Street, on December 21, in which three firemen lost their lives. The funeral of these men took place on December 29 at the South London Crematorium, Streatham.

ENTRAPPED PROCEDURE

By Anon

There was a deathly silence save for the plip-plop of the mica valves in the breathing tubes of Pete's breathing apparatus set. He could see absolutely nothing through the thick smoke, not even the heavy timber joist which made it impossible for him to move under the pile of rubble that trapped the lower half of his body. Making himself as comfortable as possible he tried to relax and reflect on how he had got into this predicament.

Only a couple of hours ago he was sitting snugly in a warm comfortable fire station listening to the earthy humour of his fellow firefighters. Tonight was old George's last night. After spending nearly thirty years in the one station it was time to hang up his axe, tunic and helmet forever.

Now Pete was buried up to his waist in rubble, unable to move, all on his own and the small cylinder of oxygen he carried in the small of his back, nearly empty.

Like all firemen Pete loved to ride to fires. True, he would cuss when the bells went down in the middle of the night, but to compensate there was that strange mixture of excitement tinged with fear when the appliance left the station. No other job he could think of was quite the same. However, when the 'bells went down' on this occasion all the crew were a bit peeved.

'Always happens when there is a "Do" on. Don't move a wheel for days and then crash, just when you're enjoying yourself.'

The staccato sound of the two tone horn disturbed the peace of the deserted streets in this part of London. Then, as the speeding fire engine turned a corner, there was a glow so bright it could have been mistaken for the rising sun. A disused dockside warehouse was ablaze from end to end, the heat of the fire already starting to blister the paintwork and scorch the brickwork of houses and the factory on the opposite side of the street.

The next few minutes sped by, 'Make pumps 20'. 'Find the hydrant.' 'Get your BA sets on you lot.' Coarse commands filled the night air and competed to be heard over the sound of the raging fire.

There was feverish activity and the blaring of horns as more and more machines sped to the fire. Slowly the huge red glow of the fire started to dim. Lengths of hose, intertwined, snaked their way into the building. While overhead turntable ladders poured on tons of water from the outside.

Pete was standing near one of the appliances, taking in some fresh air, when a screaming woman ran up to him. He was already exhausted and in no mood to face panicking members of the public. 'If there is anything you want Missus find one of the men wearing a white helmet,' he said. 'I'm only an ordinary fireman.' But the woman was not going to leave him and clutched at Pete's arm. 'I think that my two boys could be in there. I've just come out of the pub and they are not at home. The woman next door says she saw them playing about in there earlier.'

Pete turned and grabbed the first fireman he could see. As luck would have it, it was George. Fancy making him ride on his very last night, thought Pete, whilst quietly delighted to have George at his side. 'This woman here says her kids might be in there George,' shouted Pete. 'Keep her quiet,' said George, 'I'll find the Guvnor and we'll organise a search party.'

But the woman had no intention of staying quiet. 'Please fireman,' she sobbed. 'My neighbour's certain they're in there.' The thought of the woman's children lying in some smoke filled storeroom spurred Pete into action. George could be ages, he thought. Firemen everywhere, but when you want someone you can't find them.

In the rear cab of the appliance he was standing near to he saw two unused Proto breathing apparatus sets hanging on their racks. Pete had only just done his own Proto course and knew he couldn't get into the building without one. He grabbed one of the sets and, without bothering with the head harness, slung the set over his shoulders, turned on the main valve, clamped his teeth over the mouthpiece and charged into the warehouse, leaving the woman to tell George where he had gone when he returned.

Never go alone

Inside he couldn't see a thing, even with his 'Ceag' lamp turned on. He shuffled forward, keeping his weight on his rear leg and probing with his foot and the back of his hand as he'd recently been taught in Training School. He could imagine his instructor's voice speaking to him. 'Never go into a building alone. Work as a crew. Always remove your tally and hand it to a BA control officer. Always test your set before you use it. Follow the correct starting procedure.'

'It's okay for him to be so clever,' thought Pete. 'Not much chance of him ever wearing a set again. This is the real thing, not a smoke chamber, and there's real life at stake.' The crashing of falling masonry made him realise this was no time for an imaginary argument.

The noise stopped and Pete strained his ears. He could hear nothing and was aware only of the thick black smoke swirling around him. He raised his goggles to peer at his pressure gauge. 'That's funny, only 60 atmospheres,' he thought. 'The low pressure warning whistle will start soon. Surely I haven't used up that much oxygen already?' But instead of making his way back to fresh air he kept going forward. 'I must find those kids. I'll have plenty of time to get out when the whistle sounds.' He continued to shuffle forward, unaware of the faint hissing sound coming from the connection of his warning whistle to his pressure gauge tube.

Groping his way forward he felt the outline of a door frame with the back of his hand. There was no door, so probing carefully feet first and keeping his weight on his heels he commenced his search. He worked his way round the walls, then diagonally from corner to corner. Then, before he realised what had happened, his legs shot through some rotten floorboards and with a sickening crash he went through, ending up buried to the waist in debris.

His first instinct was to tear out his mouthpiece and yell for help, but he knew that would do him no good. He still had the use of his hands and tried to claw his way out, but his legs were pinned by a heavy wooden joist. 'Don't panic!' The times he had heard those words. Easy to say round the mess table or in a BA drill, but this was no drill and that smoke was no harmless chemical that could do nothing more than make your eyes smart. By now all thoughts of the children he had come to rescue were forgotten. His only concern was how to get out in one piece.

'My God,' he thought. 'I don't suppose anyone knows I'm here.' Without realising it, Pete started to pray and suddenly, as if in answer, he heard his BA instructor's voice. 'Entrapped procedure – a fully-charged oxygen cylinder can be made to last up to six hours.' Pete felt euphoric. There was nothing to worry about. By the time six hours were up he would either be found or the smoke would have cleared.

So many things to learn

Then, like a bombshell, it hit him. He wasn't quite sure what to do. He vaguely remembered demonstrating it to the Assistant Divisional Officer when he qualified in Proto, but there were so many other things to learn and he'd never liked classroom work much anyway.

He racked his brain and slowly it came back to him. Sound your distress signal unit. Make yourself comfortable and relax. Finger on the pressure relief valve, gently inflate the breathing bag using the by-pass. Close the main valve and keep your hand on the cylinder wheel. Try not to fall asleep. Re-inflate bag when nearly empty. He did all this and tried to relax but had a horrible feeling he'd forgotten something. But what? He went through it all again and nothing seemed amiss.

He kept glancing at his pressure gauge. Only 40 atmospheres now; why was he using so much oxygen? He could hear a slight hissing sound coming from somewhere near his pressure gauge. 'Must be a loose connection or a washer missing,' he thought. He tried to tighten the gauge by hand, but the hissing sound persisted. 'I just can't understand it. There can't be anything wrong with the set. After all, it's worn and used for at least 30 minutes every month, then it's stripped down and tested. It's given a general check every time someone takes it over.'

A horrible thought suddenly occurred to him. Did he always test his BA set properly? Especially a Proto set that's hardly ever used. He almost screamed aloud. 'I'd like to put my hands round the neck of the bloke who last tested this set. Calm down! No use getting upset. You'll only use up the oxygen more quickly. Maybe old George has found the guvnor. They might be searching for me now…!'

In fact this was exactly what was happening. George, and the guvnor had seen the BA set missing and realised what had happened. They had started a full scale search, but with no guide line to follow the task for the BA emergency rescue teams was difficult.

Pete looked at his gauge and filled his bag with oxygen for the last time. It registered zero, but there was always a little left. Even so, a few minutes at most, and then…

Now he was back in Training School. He was on the end of a right rollicking from his instructor. 'How many times do you have to be told? Knucklehead, when you close the main valve and your gauge reaches zero you close the pressure gauge valve.' *Close the pressure gauge valve!*

Sitting there in the smoke and darkness it suddenly became crystal clear. That's why he had to keep inflating the breathing bag so often. There was a high pressure leak in his set. Now he could see why his set had run down so quickly. Why hadn't he thought of it before? He'd been told enough times. 'The pressure gauge valve is a built-in safety device. In the event of a leak or damage to the pressure gauge or tube and when in entrapped procedure you turn it off.'

Pete turned it off. Now there was nothing to worry about. His oxygen supply would last a bit longer. He would soon be found and strong, willing hands would free him. He might even get a commendation. How proud his wife would be.

Next day, at the bottom of page four in a national daily newspaper, there was a headline: 'Blaze in derelict warehouse.' The story read: 'A fireman was killed, overcome by smoke and fumes, in a fire that swept through a derelict warehouse in Wapping last night. Fire chiefs are puzzled as to why a small safety device which could have saved his life wasn't used. Two children presumed missing were later found playing safely in a nearby park.'

FIREBOATS I: FIRE FLOATS

A host of the innovations introduced during the London Fire Brigade's long and distinguished history can be laid at the door of James Braidwood (see page 170). He was its first Superintendent (Chief fire officer equivalent), although he never actually served in the LFB. His was the era of the London Fire Engine Establishment (LFEE). But it was thanks to Braidwood that the first 'fire' steam floats were introduced into the metropolis of London. They provided fire cover on one of the then busiest waterways and dock systems in the world, the River Thames and the rapidly growing Port of London.

Riverside wharfs and warehouses had an extensive history of providing London's fire brigades with many of its fiercest peacetime fires and also its greatest challenges. One such fire would cost Braidwood his life. James Braidwood was born a Scot. He was considered, by many, to be the founding father of London's fire brigade having established new firefighting standards in the recently created London Fire Engine Establishment in 1833.

Braidwood also took account of the fire risks associated with the increasing volumes of river traffic and the large swathes of riverside buildings with their combustible contents. His initial solution to the problem was the use of 'large floating engines' (called fire floats). They

A drawing of the London Fire Engine Establishment in action with their horse drawn manual pump worked by 'volunteers'.
(Mary Evans 10535436.)

THE FIRE-BRIGADE.

were, in effect, very large rowing boats fitted with manual fire pumps. Propelled only by oars they were crewed by as many as eighty men (called pumpers) whose job was to work the manual pumps fitted to the craft at a fire. Offers to fit the craft with a steam fire pump were originally rejected by Braidwood who, at the time, was wedded to the concept of only employing manual fire pumps in the LFEE. However, the use of these fire floats proved both expensive and problematic. Expensive because the eighty odd men called 'pumpers' were paid in beer for working the pumps and problematic because the pumpers could only work for so long without a rest and then additional pumpers had to be ferried to the fire float from the shore. It all came to head at one particularly large riverside fire when the pumpers stopped working several times, demanding more beer! This experience lead to a reappraisal of the cost of this method of firefighting from the river. It was discovered that the savings in men, wages and beer money more than covered the cost of a specially built fire float with a steam engine that provided both propulsion for the craft and power to the pump.

A pen and ink sketch of Braidwood at Tooley Street at the moment of his untimely demise.

Braidwood's own demise came about at a riverside blaze, a massive blaze at that. In his book Stories of the Fire Brigade (1894) the author **FRANK MUNDELL** gives an insight into the man and his untimely death.

• •

Braidwood was not only a skilful organiser, but he also possessed great presence of mind and an unusual amount of personal courage. He was in every respect a successful leader of men, and he inspired those under his command with the same courageous feelings for which he was so conspicuous.

He preferred sailors as firemen to any other class of worker. Their experience on board ships had made them hardy, active and obedient. They were also able to bear great fatigue, accustomed to keeping cool in moments of danger, and to act with great presence of mind.

In a short time Braidwood's Brigade became as famous as the body of men he had previously trained in Edinburgh. The Brigade, too, was most popular with the public, and could always count upon any necessary assistance in their labours. The system of rewards given to whoever was the first to bring a call of fire, the liberal gratuity to the policeman who first reached the burning premises thus preventing undue confusion and, by keeping the street door closed, shutting off a strong draught of air from the flames, and the handsome pay to the ready throng of strong armed men who worked the engines, secured every co-operation from the public, beyond that naturally springing from a general admiration of a brave and well-trained body of men.

Various improvements in the engines, scaling ladders, and fire escapes were made from time to time. Braidwood placed floating fire engines at certain points on the Thames, ready for use when fires broke out in any of the great warehouses on the banks of the river. The most important improvement was the introduction of a steam fire engine.

In June 1861, one of the greatest fires of modern times and the most destructive that had taken place in the City since the Great Fire of London in 1666, broke out in a jute warehouse in Tooley Street. In a few hours the conflagration spread at such an alarming rate that, for a time, the Brigade could do little or nothing to arrest its progress.

The whole force at Braidwood's command, and the fire engines on land and water, were soon engaged in an attempt to cope with the devouring element. The combustible nature of the contents of the warehouses – hemp, sugar, saltpetre, rice, cotton, tallow and spices – made the work almost hopeless.

Braidwood was everywhere, directing and encouraging his men and devising plans to prevent the fire from extending over the adjoining property. Towards evening he visited a body of firemen who were almost worn out with fatigue; he was just giving them some refreshments, when, suddenly a terrible explosion took place. The next moment the whole front of a warehouse, many storeys high, was seen to totter and fall outwards. The cry 'Run for your lives' was heard. The men ran, and down came the huge building with a mighty crash. All escaped, but two, and one of them was James Braidwood, the brave chief of the Fire Brigade. He was killed instantly, and buried beneath a mass of ruins.

The men were much affected by the loss of their chief, but they continued to battle the flames, which spread from house to house and from warehouse to warehouse. It seemed as if half the City would be laid in ashes. At length its further progress was arrested, but it continued to burn for several weeks. The cost of that terrible fire was said to be £2,000,000.

Braidwood's death was regarded as a national calamity, and the great fireman was honoured with a public funeral. His pall bearers were six of the men with whom he had been most associated in his great work, and a procession a mile and half in length followed him to the grave.

With the exception of the great bell of St Paul's, which only tolls on the occasion of the death of a member of the Royal family or of a Lord Mayor in office, the bells of all the churches in the city were booming slowly throughout the day, and so evident was the general sorrow, that it could be truly said that the heart of the nation mourned.

Drawing of a Metropolitan Fire Brigade fire-tug and raft, with its steam-driven fire pump, heading to a Thames side blaze. (Mary Evans 10535424.)

···

The collapse had buried Braidwood under tons of hot brickwork. It was not possible to recover his body until three days later. This was a huge conflagration and had cost the insurance companies dearly. Even the wages and beer money ran to £1,000, which amounted to four years of Braidwood's previous annual salary.

Braidwood's successor was Captain Eyre Massey Shaw (see page 175). He was appointed by the City insurance companies who still controlled the LFEE brigade. He had come from Belfast where he had been both the Chief Fire Officer and its Chief Constable. But the Tooley Street fire had lasting consequences. Insurance companies started to increase their fire premiums to such an extent that City merchants protested to the Lord Mayor. The outcome of this was the creation of the Metropolitan Fire Brigade by an Act of Parliament passed in 1865. The Metropolitan Brigade came into force on 1 January 1866 with Shaw as its first Chief Officer and answerable

77

to the newly created Metropolitan Board of Works. It was not a good first day! A serious fire occurred, once again in riverside property, only this time in St Katherine's Dock. Despite the greater use of steam fire engines, the cost of this blaze was £200,000 – many millions of pounds in present day values.

Captain Shaw built on Braidwood's original ideas. He combined his steam fire engines, which were sat on rafts (river-barges), and had them towed along the river by steam tugs. This was something that would continue for almost fifty years.

However, a massive expansion programme was put into place by Captain Shaw in those early years: more stations, more men, more engines and an improved River Service with new river stations provided at Southwark and Rotherhithe. Shaw was a very hands-on Chief. A strong disciplinarian, he was considered to be fair but with his own sense of justice by his firemen.

The following is an extract from the 1931 book Fifty Years of Firefighting in London *by **JOHN HENRY (JACK) WHILE**, a journalist who reported on the work of the London Fire Brigade for over fifty years. It provides a glimpse of Shaw's management style and the shenanigans of some of those early firemen.*

When Captain Shaw knew an officer or man thoroughly he trusted him implicitly, but if he suspected him of neglect of duty he would watch him like a cat watching a mouse, and never cease his vigilance until he had caught him red-handed. And he had his own peculiar ways of doing his detective work too, as I will show.

The Beaver tug and the Metropolitan Fire Brigade barge with its steam fire engine on board. (Permission of the London Fire Brigade.)

There were from the start [1866] river-floats for dealing with waterside fires. One of these was at moorings at Southwark Bridge, and another lower down the river, near Rotherhithe.

It came to the ears of 'The Skipper' (Shaw) that the crew on the Cherry Garden Pier, Rotherhithe, float were not keeping watch properly, in fact the officer-in-charge and his men were all in the habit of leaving the vessel altogether and having an occasional pleasant 'sing-song' at an adjacent riverside hostelry. This was good enough for Captain Shaw, who, as his men said, was 'like the blooming fleas – he only got lively at night.'

One night he ordered his van (carriage), drove to Southwark Bridge, had the whistle blown for the boat, and was taken on board the float. I should mention that he always knew the state of the tide, almost to the minute. He instructed the pilot to proceed alongside the Rotherhithe float and hail her. There was no response.

'Oh,' said Captain Shaw, 'there must be something wrong here. You had better take the float in tow.' So two lines were fixed, and the float was towed down the river to a point where she could be left high and dry on the mud and carefully fastened so that she could not break away. Then the Chief dashed back to Southwark, hastened to headquarters, and telegraphed to the Superintendent of the district, asking him where his float was?

The Superintendent had to turn out in the middle of the night, and proceed to the spot on the shore close to where the float was usually moored. By this time the frightened crew, with their officer, had assembled there too, having left the local pub and the cheery concert to find they had lost the vessel which was supposed to be in their charge.

It can be imagined that there was a pretty hullabaloo. Let me know where she is, had been Captain Shaw's last message to the Superintendent, and that much-worried officer proceeded to institute a search which was by no means as easy as it sounds. Shipmates of the pilot eventually came to the rescue with information, and the float was manned and returned to her moorings.

The rest of the story is obvious. There was a formal court of inquiry; there was no disputing the evidence; the neglect of duty had been going on for some time; the officer in charge had lost all sense of power or discipline. He also lost his job and the other offenders were dealt with suitably. It was drastic treatment, but it served its purpose, and made possible offenders think twice before they allowed themselves any slackness of duty.

FIREBOATS 2: ALPHA, BETA, DELTA AND GAMMA

T*he Thames of the late nineteenth and early twentieth century was a vastly different Thames than the one you see today. It was like rush hour on the M25, a very congested major waterway. Cargo ships were berthed right up to London Bridge and were moored at riverside warehouses, wharfs and filled an expansive docks system. On the Thames wharf-sides there were rows of ships and boats, two, sometimes three, abreast. There was a whole lexicon of names for people working on or by the river: stevedores, lightermen, porters, bargees and watermen, who lifted, carried and transported goods to and from the many ships. Much of the Thames waterfront was an array of wharves and ware-houses, some as much as eight or ten storeys high. Moving between the various ships, docks, warehouses and wharves were barges, some under sail, some steam driven and newer motor driven craft. Each plying their trade and handling, moving or storing goods and*

The London County Council London Fire Brigade fireboat Alpha on the River Thames. (Mary Evans 10536184.)

commodities that were coming in and out of the Port of London and its associated dock areas.

The efficiency of the river fire service improved greatly during Shaw's time although the muddy banks of the river still remained the principal difficulty when dealing with riverside fires. This problem

Fireboat Alpha in action at a major warehouse blaze on the banks of the River Thames. Early 1900s. (Mary Evans 10534845.)

plagued the Brigade for many years until the river began to be artificially banked.

Captain Shaw resigned as Chief in 1891 after a falling out with the fledgling London County Council that had replaced the Metropolitan Board of Works. Upon his retirement he was knighted by Queen Victoria; her son the Prince of Wales had been both a friend of Shaw's and an occasional, 'part-time' fireman, riding from the Chandos Street fire station where he kept his Royal fire gear. Shaw's successor was a man named James Sexton Simonds who left under a cloud in 1896 after questions were asked about his book-keeping! It fell to Captain Lionel de Latour Wells, a former Royal Naval officer, to be given command of the Metropolitan Fire Brigade. He drastically cut the Brigade's river service, not least because of the vastly improved water supplies on land. However, he also saw the introduction of the first self-propelled steam-driven fireboats that were based on the then Royal Navy's gunboats. These boats were specifically designed for river work and their shallow draught, of only two feet, meant that they could get close to the banks of the Thames.

The first of these craft, Alpha, was put into service in 1900. Captain Wells caused some concern with the LCC's Fire Brigade Committee since the cost of Alpha was £6,300 but his arguments for dedicated fireboats won the day. The Alpha was moored at Blackfriars. By 1913 it had been joined by three other similar craft: Beta, Gamma and Delta. It is perhaps no coincidence that in the intervening years the Brigade was commanded by two further former Royal Naval officers, one a Rear-Admiral, the other a Lieutenant-Commander. Beta joined

London Fire Brigade fire-float Beta III off the Southwark river bank of the Thames in 1926, the year it came into service. (Permission of the London Fire Brigade.)

Alpha at Blackfriars, whilst Gamma was stationed at Battersea river station and Delta moored at Rotherhithe, Cherry Garden river fire station. These four boats formed the backbone of the river service for the next twenty years.

Fireboat Delta off the Victoria Embankment. (Permission of the London Fire Brigade.)

By the mid 1930s a new fireboat was being built on the Isle of Wight for the Brigade, the Massey Shaw. This boat, with an improved all steel hull, could navigate in shallow waters and pass under all of London's bridges irrespective of the state of the tide. With the imminent outbreak of war another fireboat was brought into service, a small faster fireboat named the James Braidwood. It had a top speed of 20 knots and was capable of discharging 750 gallons (3,375 litres) per minute from its monitor. Other craft would be pressed into river service and many temporary stations were set up during the early war years. The river service became a separate command in August 1941 with nationalisation of the British fire service.

The fireboat Massey Shaw was commissioned in 1935; this sixty-pump fire was her 'ordeal by fire' as it was the first major blaze she help tackle on the Thames. (Permission of the London Fire Brigade.)

83

The National Fire
Service crest of
the River Thames
Formation, 1941–1948.
(Mary Evans 10534923.)

Fireboat Gamma
alongside the newly
opened London Fire
Brigade Headquarters
in Lambeth, 1938.
(Permission of the
London Fire Brigade.)

Now under the guise of the National Fire Service (NFS) the River Thames Formation progressed to employing larger vessels, equipped with pumps to cover the lower reaches of the Thames. However, that was to come; in the meantime London's Massey Shaw and the James Braidwood were joined by upgraded fireboats, the Beta III and Gamma III.

FIREBOATS 3: FIREBRACE AND RIVER TRAINING

Fireboat *Firebrace was built in Anglesey in 1961. This sturdy craft had made her way around the Welsh and English coastline entirely under her own steam and had no problems coping with the varied sea conditions. She cut an impressive figure as she travelled up the River Thames and was London's first new fireboat since the end of the Second World War. With Massey Shaw covering the downstream reaches of the Thames the Firebrace was moored at the Lambeth pontoon, directly opposite the Brigade Headquarters building on the Albert Embankment. She had been named after Commander Aylmer Firebrace, another former Royal Naval Officer, who had been London's Chief Officer for only twelve months prior to the outbreak of the Second World War. Gifted with a brilliant mind and exceptional organisational skills he was seconded to the Home Office and was the principal architect of the Fire Service's wartime organisation. Later he oversaw the establishment of the National Fire Service from 1941 to 1948. Never returning to London as Chief he was knighted for his services and became the Chief Inspector of Fire Services prior to his retirement in 1948. (He died in June 1972.)*

Firebrace was a purpose-built craft. An all-steel vessel, it was sixty-five feet long, had a beam of thirteen feet and a draught of three feet eight inches. The two powerful diesel engines provided the boat with a maximum speed of nearly twelve knots. All the engine room controls were operated from the forward wheelhouse which had a connecting door leading to the crew's accommodation and a small galley. Access to this area was also possible from the stern of the boat. The Firebrace had two sets of pumps, each capable of pumping 2,000 gallons of water per minute. Mounted on the deck, immediately behind the wheelhouse, was the boat's sole monitor, its three inch nozzle capable of throwing a solid stream of water hundreds of feet into the air. More importantly, it could reach the tops of any riverside wharf or warehouse standing on the banks of the Thames, delivering tons of water per minute in the process. With its distinctive livery of red and black bodywork and white painted pump outlets and fittings, it made an imposing sight as it patrolled the upper reaches of the Thames, from Wapping to Teddington weir. (Although if one fireboat was unavailable the other would cover the whole length of London's River Thames.) The normal crew for Firebrace was seven but they could ride four as a minimum plus a river service trained (RST) fireman, making five. If the crew fell below the minimum, anyone in the Brigade who was fireboat qualified could be ordered to stand-by on the boat.

*I, **DAVID PIKE**, had been posted to Lambeth fire station in 1967 after leaving Southwark Training School. A former junior fireman, Lambeth was my first station, a station that had both a land station and a separate river station. As a mere teenager I still loved riding the fire engines and had little interest in the fireboat on the other side of the Albert Embankment. Serving at Lambeth fire station meant doing out-duties to the fireboat if they were short of personnel, but before you could do that you had to undergo a basic river service training course. I did everything in my power to avoid this and put off that damn river course, then one day I ran out of options and was detailed to get over to the float. This is my own tale.*

**Fireboat Firebrace.
(Permission of the
London Fire Brigade.)**

One aspect of station life I hated, besides doing watchroom duties, riding the canteen van, driving the divisional lorry, in fact, anything that stopped me riding either the PE or pump, was the possibility of standing by on Lambeth's bloody fireboat. So far my stand-by's had only been to other land fire stations, but now I was eligible to attend a River Service Training Course, which in essence was a familiarisation course that guaranteed I would stand by on that darn boat.

Eric, the next junior buck on the watch, had already done his RST training and I knew my turn was coming. Finally, caught like a rat in a trap, I went like a petulant child over to the pontoon to undertake my familiarisation. The training would last two weeks but I could not be considered to be a crew member during that time.

I soon had to eat humble pie for it was far more interesting than I had thought possible. Being taken out training on the river every day duty was an eye-opening experience. I learnt about the drills and manoeuvres required of the Firebrace and its crew. The boat required a qualified coxswain and an engineer at all times, plus, if he was not the coxswain, an officer in charge. Station Officer 'Dodger' Long was the Red Watch's fireboat governor; he loved the river and was a fount of knowledge regarding all things riparian. His knowledge was encyclopedic. He was also a good trainer and made the course interesting and varied. Days were filled by 'man overboard' drills, rowing the skiff pulling hose ashore, pumping vast quantities of water out of the river and putting it back in again. If only the fireboat got some working jobs it would be much more interesting; as this happened only rarely you can see why I did not want this qualification. Fortunately it fell off my list of qualifications some time later, when I typed out new watch personnel cards.

On the last night duty of my training course I was to see just how hard the fireboat's crew would have to work when called upon to do so. Although a couple of shouts came in for the fireboat during those two weeks we never once arrived, being returned to base, unwanted and unloved. In the late evening on my last night duty the station bells rang and the white light came up: a shout for the boat. Leaving the land station and running across Albert Embankment we all trotted down the gangway on to the pontoon. Whilst the experienced hands cast off the mooring lines I went to the bridge and waited for an opportunity to ask where we were heading. I knew we were going downstream on an ebbing tide, so not all the two weeks' training had been wasted on me. The Station Officer told the crew that we were ordered to Battle Bridge Lane, Tooley Street, adjacent to Tower Bridge on the south side of the river. The shout was on Dockhead's ground and the call was to a fire in a warehouse. Even with the tide behind us the fireboat was not renowned for its rapid arrival at an incident. We were just approaching the Charing Cross railway bridge when Bravo two-four-two (Dockhead's pump) sent a priority message over the radio, making pumps a straight ten. Calmly, Station Officer Long announced, 'We've got a job lads', which I thought amusing; given that the youngest fulltime crew member was at least twenty years older than me.

There were still four bridges to pass under, Waterloo, Blackfriars, Southwark and London, before we saw Tower Bridge and the blazing warehouse on its southern approach. The tide had run its course and the Thames was at its low water mark by the time we reached Southwark Bridge. One of the old 'floaties' who was busy making a brew in the galley below called out, 'It means bloody hose ashore by skiff.' It was the first and only time I've had a cup of tea going to a shout.

Clearing the next bridge another priority message came over the radio, this time from Bravo one zero (B Division BA control van) making pumps fifteen and requesting the ETA of the fireboat. It would eventually become a thirty pump fire. 'Blimey we're wanted,' mused the coxswain whilst trying to get the maximum revs out of the engines. Even from the wheelhouse we could see the glow illuminating the night sky on the far side of London Bridge. Charts were pulled from the wheelhouse drawers as the Station Officer and the coxswain looked for anchorages and low water lines. A message was dispatched to Brigade Control giving our ETA as five minutes and requesting instructions from the fireground as to what was required of us.

We were now passing Hays Wharf head offices, its white clean stonework making it a distinctive feature of the riverside façade alongside the old and dirty buildings that surrounded it. Three large sculptured reliefs, symbolising Capital, Labour and Commerce, fill the centre of the building's river frontage. It was this company's warehouses that totally dominated the vast warehouse and wharfages that run between London and Tower Bridges: these included Chamberlains, Cotton, and Wilson's wharves. Many were now lying idle or empty, their former days of hectic trading and unloading goods from all over the globe now consigned to the history books from when London had been the 'Port of the Empire'. Gaps in the riverscape told the story of those already lost to the ravages of fire; others would follow before developers would once again bring life and wealth back into the area, not least with the creation of London Bridge City and the conversion of warehouses to prestigious inner city apartments and flats.

The fireboat was detailed to lay offshore and supply water to the quayside, to feed the pumps that would redirect the water to crews fighting the fire. The large, ugly, brick warehouse was well alight by the time the fireboat stood by at its station laying about fifty yards from the exposed shoreline. The quayside stood thirty feet above the shoreline; here the river frontage, that included Mark Brown's wharf, had enormous baulks of timber sunk into the river bed. This timber had been used to

Opposite: The Firebrace in action at Tower Bridge in July 1968 when the summer heat wave caused the roadway to expand, and the bridge was unable to be opened. Both land and river crews cooled the bridge's roadway for three hours before the bridge could finally be raised again. (Mary Evans 10793369.)

construct a wooden jetty where once famous ships, like the Baltic Trader, would have moored to discharge their valuable cargos of goods and commodities. Now it was just rotting and derelict, yet another obstacle to getting the hose and much needed water ashore.

The fireboat crew had been busy getting long lengths of flaked three and a half inch hose ready, coiling lengths of grass line that would be used to pull the heavy lengths of hose ashore. The Station Officer had already decided it was too dangerous to use the rocket line from the boat but his crew could use it from the shore to fire over the boat. It would trail a line that would be connected ultimately to a grass line that would haul the hose through the water onto the shore. I was seeing at first hand the methodical workings of the boat's crew. On land firemen were frequently like sprinters, going for the quick all-out physical assault required for a snatch rescue, or the speedy attack on a blaze. But here they were like marathon runners, maintaining a steady powerful rhythm, preparing for the long haul.

The skiff, which had been towed, was now pulled to the side of the fireboat, two hundred feet of flaked hose line was placed aft, the rocket line box placed forward, and wearing lifejackets for the first time four of the crew prepared to row ashore. With the end of the hose line connected to the pump outlet they rowed and trailed the hose line out behind them. Crews who were waiting on top of the jetty had lines thrown down to pull up the hose to deliver the desperately needed water. I was watching all this activity, detailed to remain on the fireboat. As the skiff crew reached the shore the first man jumped clear, immediately sinking into slimy ooze that came up to his knees. It took the combined efforts of all four men to haul the single line of hose though the mud to the jetty wall where it was hauled aloft and connected to the first pump. Giving the water-on signal the hose was charged with water. Taking on the image of a giant python, the hose was slowly engorged with water as it snaked a path through the mud-filled foreshore, then slithered up the jetty wall.

The skiff's crew moved on to their next task. Still wading through mud, two found a vertical iron ladder and climbed to the quayside with the rocket line in its special carrying box. Positioning themselves opposite the fireboat they opened the box and removed the hand held rocket launcher which looked like a large flare gun. In the box, made up on a special 'former' was the thin nylon line that would be fixed to the rocket. Taking the former out and turning it upside down, the line fell out in a crisscrossed free running pile on the ground. With one end tied to a fixing on the rocket and the other secured to the ground, the crew member took careful aim and fired the rocket over the wheelhouse of the fireboat. With a whoosh the rocket passed overhead and fell into the river, its line now lying across the fireboat. Pulling the free end in, it was secured to a long line that was pulled back to the shore by the two crew members still waiting by the skiff. Tied to that long line were two two-inch grass lines. Grass lines were special ropes that floated on the water; these were used to pull the next lengths of hose ashore. Finally, to each grass line was secured a length of three and a half inch hose. With all four crew members now back on the foreshore and, joined by other land crews, the process of trudging the hose lines through the mud, up the jetty and connecting to another pump was repeated and completed. It had taken nearly an hour to connect the final hose to its pump but now an endless supply of water was available to the fire ground. The crew rowing back from the shore were almost unrecognisable; even their helmets were caked in black slime and mud and they stank to high heaven. Smiling, the Station Officer shouted, 'Don't even think of going below until that lot's washed off,' before he returned to the warmth of the wheelhouse to monitor the pump controls.

We pumped water all night. There was little hope in saving the warehouse; its empty floors rapidly collapsed, leaving high walls dangerously exposed and unsupported. Crews were withdrawn and reluctantly the fire was fought from the outside, not the London way. With the roof finally gone the building was just a shell when the first rays of light brought a new day.

Crews had protected the surrounding property but had just unfortunately provided National Car Parks with a new site once the building was demolished and the land cleared. But, for now, crews would be here for two or three days, putting out the last remnants of flame and making the site safe for the demolition crews to move in. With the White Watch crew delivered by a brigade personnel carrier we were finally relieved at about ten that morning and made our weary way back to Lambeth. The fireboat would remain on station for the whole of that shift but now moored on the jetty until the tide changed again. My two weeks had ended in style. I now had a greater appreciation of the role of the fireboat and even greater admiration for the crews, who were, in the main, long-serving land-based fireman who had transferred their skills to the fireboat. They might not have to use them very often, but when called upon, they won my respect and admiration every time.

FIREBOATS 4: FIRE HAWK, FIRE SWIFT AND PHOENIX

By the early 1970s the nature of the River Thames and London's northern and southern Thames shoreline had undergone radical change. Gone were the last of the London docks and the shipping that fed them. Old crafts of the Thames were vanishing and had in many cases vanished completely. People were becoming the main commodity in these Thames side warehouses, which had been converted to residential use, and in many instances, very expensive riverside accommodation. The water-filled highway that flowed through the capital had taken on a new character, one that focused more on recreational activities than the previous trades it had supported.

The Greater London Council, then London's fire authority, had required the Brigade to review its river service provision in 1969/70 as part of a wider fire cover review. Central Government was also putting pressure on fire authorities to find ways of reducing or revising cover to minimum levels. The Massey Shaw was considered to have reached the end of her useful service and was sold off in 1971. The Firebrace would follow suit in 1975. The Massey Shaw spent her latter years stationed at Woolwich river station and her last major 'shouts' were a serious fire at the Tate and Lyle's sugar factory at Silvertown, close to the site of the present London City Airport, and the major cargo ship fire on-board the SS Paraguay Star moored in the Royal Victoria Dock, where she fought this blaze alongside her sister fireboat, Firebrace.

Sea trials of the Fire Hawk. (Permission of the London Fire Brigade.)

*The Massey Shaw almost suffered an ignominious end in 1990.
Following a period of near total neglect and having been purchased by
a restoration group, she sank, close to the London Fire Brigade headquarters at Lambeth. Years of restoration work were undone as she
lay submerged underwater for several tides. Thankfully, the boat was
salvaged and the restoration work started all over again. Today, the
boat has been lovingly restored and returned to her former glory, now
saved for the nation by the efforts of the Massey Shaw Preservation
Society.*

*Different approaches were tried by the Brigade to meet the chal-
lenges caused by the changing face of the River Thames. The then
Ministry of Technology ran a feasibility study with a Hovercraft to be
stationed at the new Dowgate fire station. Financial costs prevented
the adoption of this scheme. Sea-trucks that looked like small landing-
craft were very successful on their trials but again finance, or lack of
it, was cited as the reason for not changing to these highly manoeu-
vrable and versatile craft. However, the fact that it was run aground
by river firemen resulting in the sea-truck suffering considerable
damage (especially as it was only on loan!) did not bode well. It was
often said by those in authority within the Brigade that you could lock
a fireman in a sealed, empty room with two steel ball-bearings and
he would lose one and break the other! Sometimes we just seemed to
prove the saying right.*

*After much debate, two craft were eventually purchased as replace-
ment fireboats. These were the Fire Hawk and the Fire Swift, costing
£46,000 and £60,000 respectively. They were mono hull craft and
carried portable pumps to feed the small, front, mounted monitor.
They had more the look of a boat you would go sea fishing in rather
than a fireboat. Increased financial pressure by Government on the
fire brigade had brought about the closure of the downstream river
fire station at Woolwich, because supporting its continued operational
existence proved difficult to justify.*

*In the early 1980s the London Fire Brigade had sought approval
to commission a new, and impressive, fireboat at a cost of one million
pounds! At the same time the Greater London Council (GLC),
London's fire authority, was in its death throes. The GLC would not
go down without a fight though, especially under the leadership of Ken
Livingstone. It was abolished in 1986 by the policies of a Thatcherite
Conservative Government. However, before then the Chief Officer
submitted a report seeking approval to purchase the craft. His report
extolled the virtues of the proposed replacement boat whilst omitting
to highlight its probable shortcomings. With less scrutiny than might
normally have been applied to such an expensive purchase, the Fire
Authority was given approval by a now belligerent GLC.*

The Rise of the Phoenix

The crew of the
Phoenix at drill on the
Thames. (Courtesy of
Paul Wood.)

PETER W. HUMPHREYS *now lives in Australia having emigrated after his retirement from the London Fire Brigade. As a young man Peter had lived in Surrey. During 1962 he had gone to visit a family friend who was a patient in Westminster Hospital. Sadly he was dying from cancer. His friend had wanted his son to join the fire brigade and follow in his own footsteps. He was a serving fireman at Richmond fire station, then in Surrey, though sadly he would never return to duty. His son had other ideas and was not interested in joining the fire brigade, so Peter said that he would give it a go. It was a decision he never regretted.*

Joining in July 1963, he was first posted to Barnes fire station which was soon amalgamated with Richmond fire station. On 1 April

1965 Peter found himself serving in the London Fire Brigade upon the creation of the Greater London Council, as Richmond was one of many fire stations incorporated into the enlarged LFB.

His next 22 years were spent mostly south of the River Thames. By 1972 he was promoted to Station Officer of a watch. After a short spell serving north of the river he found himself going south, again posted to Battersea, where he spent almost the next eleven years. It had a small fire ground but was one of the busiest in South West London.

In April 1984 he took his annual leave in Florida with his girl-friend, staying in Fort Lauderdale. It was there, amidst the multi-million dollar gin palaces that he saw a US fireboat. The craft looked impressive and the crew knew it. That looks an interesting job, thought Peter, giving the matter little heed until he was back behind his desk at Battersea fire station. He takes up the story below.

• •

I was looking through the accumulated paperwork that builds up whilst you are away. Something had caught my eye, an advert contained in an information bulletin asking for Station Officers to apply to lead the crews for the new fireboat the Brigade had just commissioned, the London Phoenix. I applied, and the image of cruising the Thames and looking out at the equally scantily clad young ladies flashed across my mind! However the selection procedure soon put such thoughts to the back of my mind as the candidates were whittled down by the rigorous process we were put through by Brigade principal and senior officers. Finally there were just six remaining and I was one of the six being dispatched off to Newcastle that September to start an intensive six week course. If successful we would have a certificate of competence to work on boats. If not it was back to a fire station.

The course was ran by the Northumberland Police's marine division and I found myself somewhere between Newcastle and Gateshead. We were based in police accommodation and trained on police boats, similar to those used on the Thames by the Metropolitan Police during the 1980s. But they also had a fast 45-foot Marine patrol boat that could do the best part of 40 knots. The course was looking good.

Prior to my departure from London I was sent to see Assistant Chief Officer Cliff Colenutt. He was responsible for all things Phoenix at the time. A handsome looking man in his fifties, he was third generation London Fire Brigade, the Brigade coursed through his veins. A keen sportsman still, he had a reputation as being both a good fireman and outstanding senior officer. Until his recent promotion he had commanded the A Division that included the whole of the West End. A confirmed bachelor, he seemed to many to be wedded to the Brigade, which was probably true, but he was also a man's man and considered to be a pleasure to work for. 'Look here old Humphreys,' he said as I entered his office, 'I need you to be the liaison officer and deal with matters that may crop up with the Northumberland police.' There was no debate, I was nominated.

Our first taste of the course got fed to us at the marine police station overlooking the Tyne. Boat handling, navigation, chart plotting, flag signals, marine radio procedure was all part of our assessable programme of intensive learning. It sounded all very professional, which was more than can be said for our mode of transport from classroom to boat yard as we sat uncomfortably in the back of a Ford Transit van that usually ferried police dogs around. With no windows and hard wooden slatted seats, by day three, the novelty of the uncomfortable 20 mile daily drive was wearing thin. Our evenings were spent in police accommodation that was full to overflowing with the reinforcements sent from all over the country because of the miners' strike that was in full swing.

In response to my complaint about getting shuttled about in a canine unit I was told to report to the Chief Inspector, who was in charge of the marine unit. It was a meeting that did not go well. Knocking on his door I got no reply. I waited then knocked again, still nothing. So having been summoned I entered the office. I was greeted by the sight of an enormous desk with a little chap sitting behind it, the Chief Inspector. Clearly used to ruling all he surveyed, as I walked in he looked up and shouted, 'What the hell do you think you are doing?' 'Please don't talk to me like that. I am not one of your constables, I'm a LFB fire officer and as such I expected to be shown some respect.' Respect was not high on his agenda of management skills as his irritation that had already turned his face purple with rage, was getting deeper as the seconds passed.

Quietly irritated myself now I took a chair and sat, without being invited, in front of his desk. I then reminded him of our complaints and that we required it to be addressed. This all appeared to be something of a culture shock for this little man, who in his best 'Geordie speak' said, 'Don't you know that there is a miners' strike going on?' – clearly now unable to hide the irritation in his voice. 'Of course I do, we are kept up half the night with all the policemen in the billet counting up their overtime. But we are not here for that are we?' This exchange went on for about ten minutes before he begrudgingly said he would see what he could do. We were given some cushions to sit on and I got reported back to Cliff Colenutt by the little chap behind the desk.

Dog van aside, the course was both demanding and rewarding. With the ending of course examinations completed, both practical and theory, we compared notes and I thought I let myself down with a question or two in navigation. However, I consoled myself by thinking that I had only got to turn left or right on leaving the river station at Lambeth. Regrouped at Brigade Headquarters the six of us were presented to the deputy Chief, Gerry Clarkson, who was to give us our course results that determined who went onto the Phoenix. He started with number one, by the time he came to number three and my name had not been called out I was getting worried. When I wasn't named the number four I lost the plot. Standing up to the deputy Chief I said, 'I'm pissed off with this.' Not a man to be intimidated Gerry said, 'If you're pissed off, then piss off.' So I did.

I spent the next six months at Brigade Headquarters, mostly bored, covering the other Station Officers on the Phoenix when they were on leave. Not my finest hour. However before then I had secured good passes on the Port of London grade II certificate and the necessary first aid sea certificate that allowed me to administer injections. Now we six were reunited and ready to go to sea.

The Phoenix was built as a catamaran. For some inexplicable reason she would affectionately be known as 'Nellie.' At 60 feet long and 23 feet wide it was thought she would provide a stable platform for a 70 foot Simon Snorkel (hydraulic platform). Her twin Perkins diesel engines provided 340 horse power and her two pumps were capable of pumping 2,000 gallons (9,000 litres) per minute through her monitors mounted fore and aft, and a foam monitor mounted ahead of the wheel house. Sadly the Snorkel never made it past the sea trials.

Whilst we were swanning around in Southampton Water an engineer from Simon's was in the elevated cage and he swung out at a 90 degree angle to the Phoenix at exactly the same time as the boat decided to rise over the wash of a Red Funnel Streamer that was making the crossing to the Isle of Wight. The Snorkel snapped at the end of the main extension and the poor engineer was in danger of becoming a sub-mariner until we pulled him from the sea. It was back to the drawing board for Simon's and their subsequent modifications just added a monitor to the shortened arm which now doubled as a crane. The remainder of her sea trials proved a lot less eventful and in April 1985 the Phoenix was placed in operational service, operating from Lambeth's pontoon. I was at last given my own watch on the boat and was conscious that many of my watch were far more experienced boatmen and sailors than myself. Some had worked on the river previously and had joined the fire brigade on the demise of the River Thames trades. One, Peter Mursell, was a former 'lightermen' and had intimate knowledge of the Thames. His ability to throw a mooring line directly over a cleat beggared belief. He was good for at least 25 feet whilst I could only manage 20 feet at best. Another outstanding hand was Norman Wooldridge, he was my leading fireman and came with an excellent pedigree, level headed and someone you would like at your side in a tight spot.

Going out on patrol on the River was always an education and there was always something new to learn or to experience. The movement of the Thames at certain times, the river's eddies and the various anchorage points was all useful knowledge gained on almost a daily basis. Interesting snippets gleaned such as the hangman's gibbet that still stands close to Wapping river police station, or the familiarisation visits to Tower Bridge

London Phoenix fireboat at her Lambeth pontoon on the Albert Embankment, SE1. (Mary Evans 10536014.)

or the Thames Barrier added spice to the numerous VIP visitor trips when the Chief or the Deputy (or both) brought the latest batch of personages over to the Phoenix took them on a trip on the Thames and showed off their latest acquisition. In the first couple of years the enthusiasm of all the boats crews was tremendous. In fact we did more VIP trips than we did fire calls.

There were emergency calls naturally, a lot of automatic fire alarms to riverside premises where we rarely got to work. I am sure we pulled more bodies from the Thames than we attended working fires. There was the odd occasion where the Phoenix came into her own, like the riverside warehouse fire, which was filled with newsprint paper, and Nellie pumped water through four lines of hose taken ashore for 16 hours without a blip. That is what the fireboat was designed for, a floating pump that would never run out of water.

However, there were downsides with Nellie and getting to all places up or down the river was more a matter of luck of the draw, or rather state of the tides. She could not navigate Hammersmith or Westminster bridges on the top of spring tides as there was insufficient head room (air draught). The opposite was true of Westminster Bridge on low spring tides as the Phoenix drew too much water. These things were a known quantity but sadly they did not go into the mix when the Phoenix was being designed. They certainly did not go in to the Committee Report, presented to the Greater London Council, seeking their approval to spend 1 million pounds on London's latest fireboat!

FIRE STATIONS

I n the late 1960s and 1970s a regular feature of the in-house magazine was 'Focus On', where one of London's fire stations would be profiled. In those days the London Fire Brigade was organised into three Command areas: Southern, Eastern and Northern. So in the interest of fairness one station has been selected from each of those Commands: Deptford from the Southern, Silvertown from the Eastern and Soho from the Northern Command. All the articles were penned by the Editor of the **London Fireman**, **GORDON WHITE**.

Deptford

The first Deptford fire station, opened in 1872 in Evelyn Street, SE8. The 50 foot wheeled escape ladder is parked on the station forecourt. (Mary Evans 10535840.)

Deptford, which nestles alongside a broad loop of the Thames where the river winds its way from the Pool of London down towards Greenwich, is steeped with maritime history.

In 1513 Henry VIII, from whom Britain's emergence as a major sea power stemmed, decreed that a naval storehouse be built at Deptford.

From that relatively small beginning Deptford grew to become a thriving and bustling district. Based on the riverside yards which reverberated to the sounds of shipbuilders' tackle as they strove to meet their monarch's demands for a fleet capable of gaining supremacy on the high seas. Sir Martin Frobisher and Sir Francis Drake were just two of a long line of illustrious seafarers who set sail from Deptford on conquests and missions that were to make this country's navy a feared force wherever it sailed.

Deptford expanded to become an integral part of London's dock land and paid a heavy price during the last war when the Luftwaffe flattened a square mile of the Surrey Commercial Docks. This area contained 250 acres of imported timber in stacks 20 feet high. The inferno engulfed ships and warehouses and could be seen for miles around.

The present Deptford fire station, opened in 1904 (the year the Metropolitan Fire Brigade changed its name to the London Fire Brigade), and typical of the period with the firemen's accommodation above the station. It is pictured here in the early 1980s. (Permission of the London Fire Brigade.)

The Surrey Commercial Docks are closed now and riverside activity is on a very small scale, but Deptford remains a heavily-populated area as it moves through a period of transition.

Deptford fire station is situated in Evelyn Street, named after the 17th century diarist John Evelyn who wrote extensively about the area and its people. Evelyn, incidentally, lived for a number of years at Wotton House near Dorking, the home of the Fire Service Staff College (until it was later closed down).

The foundation stone, outside the present station, was laid on 27 July 1903 by Edward Smith JP, chairman of the London County Council Fire Brigade Committee. The building work was carried out by the council's works department, partly on the site of the previous Deptford fire station, and was completed in 1904 at a total cost of £10,424.13s.2d.

The station complement was one station officer, eleven firemen, three coachmen and two pairs of horses to man one steam fire engine, one horsed escape, one manual escape and one hose cart.

In common with a few other London fire stations, Deptford is reputed to have had its very own ghost, and at one time nobody would sleep in the television room on the ground floor because, at night, footsteps could be heard approaching from the floor above. It was said the footsteps were those of a station officer attached to Deptford who was killed at a fire in the Surrey Commercial Docks. His fire gear was brought back to the station after his death and it was thought he had returned to look for it. In any event he must have found it, for the footsteps have not been heard for a few years now!

Silvertown

For members of the grouse-shooting fraternity the 12th August or the 'glorious twelfth' as it has become known, is one date on the calendar that stands above all others. It is then that the grouse season starts, and suitably tweeded, deerstalkered and armed, the followers of this upper-crust sport can head for the moors. But the date has just as much significance for Silvertown fire station in the heart of the East End's grimy dockland. It marks the anniversary of two of the area's more serious fires in recent years – both on ships belonging to the same company. Still fresh in the memory is the long battle that firemen had last year [1969] on the Paraguay Star, where bulkheads and deck plates blistered the skin and choking smoke filled the bowels of the stricken ship.

The burning ship
SS Paraguay Star
in London's Royal
Victoria Docks, 1969.
(Permission of the
London Fire Brigade.)

The Paraguay Star was saved from a grave in the Royal
Victoria dock, but has since been condemned to the breaker's
yard. A better fate, perhaps, than the Scottish Star, a sister ship
which caught fire in dry dock on 12th August a decade ago
and which again was saved only after a long, tiring struggle by
firemen. The ship survived to sail again, but now lies trapped
in the blocked Suez Canal, bereft of a crew and, seemingly, no
further use to anybody.

'Fortunately ship fires are much fewer now than they were
ten or 15 years ago,' says Station Officer Charlie Phillips, whose
long service at Silvertown, stretching back to West Ham Fire
Brigade days, has made him one of the best-known figures
in and around the docks, wharfs and riverside factories. 'The
ship owners are much more fire protection minded these days
and the majority of them have guards constantly patrolling the
vessels.'

Minefield

Station Officer Phillips and his colleagues are sitting in the
middle of a veritable minefield at Silvertown, an area solidly
in the A-fire risk category. From the top of the station's drill
tower, almost as far as the eye can see, it is one expanse of
cranes, ships' funnels and masts and giant factories and other
buildings.

The local 'customers' include the British Oil and Cake Mills,
Pinchin and Johnson paint manufacturers, two massive Tate
and Lyle sugar refineries, an edible oil factory, and petrol and
oil 'farms' owned by SP, Esso and Gulf Oil. Almost overshad-
owing the station are the vast Spiller's flour mills, where the

danger of a dust explosion is one which the firm, and of course the men at Silvertown, are naturally extremely conscious of.

Snowmen

The flour mills also present another problem, as Station Officer Phillips explains. 'When the wind is blowing from the direction of the mills everything here gets covered in a white dust. If you're out in the drill yard for ten minutes or more you end up looking like a snowman. It can make it difficult to keep things clean.'

In West Ham days Silvertown boasted a pump escape, pump, and turntable ladder and foam tender, but the last two machines were transferred to Plaistow and Stratford fire stations respectively prior to the changeover in 1965.

Two machines may not sound enough to cover a fireground that includes 635 acres of docks and 11 miles of quayside and is virtually an island, being completely surrounded by water and only linked with the 'mainland' by a swing-bridge in the east and a flyover in the west. But reinforcements are rapidly available from surrounding stations, and a call to one of the big local factories always brings a pump and turntable ladder hurrying along from Plaistow. 'In the old days this used to be called the punishment station,' said Station Officer Phillips, 'because it was an extremely difficult place to get to. Fortunately public transport around here is much better now.'

Disaster

There is little residential property in the area, although the sky-scraping system built blocks of flats which have become a familiar feature of East London spiral up from the ground in the not too far distance. One of them, the ill-fated Ronan Point serves as a grim reminder of the disaster two years ago when Silvertown firemen were called to the scene to help in rescue operations.

The first Silvertown fire station was opened in October 1914 – and badly damaged three years later by the blast from an explosion at an ammunitions factory across the road when many people were killed.

The station was repaired and served the area for another 50 years before it was replaced on the same site by a new station in August 1968. It was officially opened on August 13th last year by Mr Robert Mitchell, chairman of the Greater London Council's Fire Brigade Committee, while the fire on board the Paraguay Star was still being fought.

An oil painting completed on the evening of August 12th by a local police chief, dedicated to 'our brave colleagues in the fire brigade' and depicting the Paraguay Star fire, was presented to the station at the opening ceremony and now hangs proudly in the fire station mess room.

The collapsed corner of Ronan Point tower block in East London. (Mary Evans 10793577.

Soho

The 'temporary' replacement Soho fire station, which stood for over 35 years after the original was destroyed during the Blitz. (Permission of the London Fire Brigade.)

From plush apartments and ritzy hotels to dingy hovels and back street brothels, from theatres and cordon bleu restaurants to strip-clubs and seedy cafes, Soho fire station's ground certainly stretches from one extreme to another. From the outside the station in Shaftesbury Avenue looks, and is, a relic from the past: a patchwork of brick and iron sheeting. The station yard, if you can call it that, is small and cramped, while the mess room and sleeping accommodation would not seem ideal for boosting any fireman's morale.

Yet Soho is how one always imagines from boyhood a fire station should be. Rambling, yes. But a real fire station all the same where the crews have an intense and fierce pride in the job they do. The number of people who have asked to be transferred away from Soho is infinitesimal. The number who have expressed a desire to move there, enormous.

Why? Partly the station's past reputation, partly the station's ground, partly the high number of calls, partly many other things as well. 'This station's ground must surely be one of the most interesting in the world,' said Station Officer Alan Marshall, who leads his crews in a buccaneering yet conscientious style that courts both respect and admiration. 'You never know what sort of call you're going to get next. It could be a blaze in a club or restaurant where you have the problem of the buildings being so tightly packed, or it could be to a bad car smash where some late night reveller has had too much to drink and slammed his car into a lamp-post.'

In a world away from the standard two-bay station, Stn O Marshall sat in his office overlooking the choking late-night traffic and added: 'The lads here come from places miles out of London, but they would never dream of getting a transfer to a more local station. I think it would drive them mad, not having the calls to answer. The biggest problem here is the non-operational stuff – the London Building Acts visits, the hydrant tests, and the paper work. There just isn't enough hours in the day to get it all done. I think the time will have to come when this station will have to have a permanent fire prevention officer.'

Leading Fireman Martyn 'Turk' Manning echoed his guvnor's views: 'Once you've been here you can't really imagine serving anywhere else. As far as we are all concerned this is the best station in the Brigade and is going to remain the best.' Soho's normal complement is pump escape, pump, and turntable ladder. Although when I visited the station recently the escape was off the run following an argument with a Knightsbridge lamp post.

The turn-out into Shaftesbury Avenue, never easy because of the heavy traffic, is always done on the bell at night, for the benefit of patrons in the Palace Theatre opposite. 'They can never stage a play there because of this station, only musicals or revues,' said Stn O Marshall. 'The two-tone drowns anything being said or sung on stage, and although they can still hear the bells when we turn out it's not so bad. Once Norman Wisdom was appearing there. The audience was applauding him at the end of the show when Soho got a shout. He asked for quiet, beckoned towards the sound of the bells and said, "They're the ones who deserve applause."'

FIRST FATAL

The former Chief Officer of the West Ham Fire Brigade Cyril Demarne OBE in his role as Senior Instructor at Sydney Airport in Australia. (Permission of the Demarne family.)

CYRIL THOMAS DEMARNE OBE was born in Poplar, London on 7 February 1905. As a boy, he recalled seeing troops marching from Woolwich through the Blackwall Tunnel with horses pulling the guns. Most distinctly, he remembered the Zeppelin raids on London during 1915 and witnessing the downing of the German Schutte-Lanz SL11 class airship in 1916, for which Captain William Leefe Robinson was awarded the Victoria Cross.

For thousands of people, including Cyril, this was without doubt one of the most memorable events of the entire war that Londoners witnessed. It is difficult to imagine one lone pilot achieving anything more spectacular. With the blazing wreckage of the SL11 slowly falling to earth in a field in Cuffley, Hertfordshire, even before it reached the ground London was celebrating in boisterous fashion. Crowds of people, oblivious to the fact that other enemy airships were overhead, erupted in a frenzy of rejoicing. Those dramatic events were but a precursor of the relentless bombing of the capital some 25 years later.

In 1927 at the age of twenty-two Cyril joined the West Ham fire brigade. By the outbreak of war, in 1939, he was a Sub-Officer instructing firemen in the recently created Auxiliary Fire Service. He served in London throughout the Blitz. After the National fire service was returned to local Authority control he served with the London Fire Brigade as a senior officer, based at the Manchester Square fire station. In 1952 he was promoted to Chief Fire Officer of West Ham fire brigade. He was awarded an OBE prior to his retirement in 1955 and moved to Australia. In 1956 to 1964, at its inception, he became the Senior Instructor of the Fire Service Training School at Sydney Airport. In retirement, he wrote several books based on his wartime experiences.

It was Cyril who had the idea of raising a memorial to the firefighters of the Blitz. A sculpture by John W. Mills has become the National Firefighters Memorial, erected to the south of St Paul's Cathedral and unveiled by HRH Queen Elizabeth the Queen Mother in May 1991. It was later relocated and rededicated in 2003.

Cyril Demarne was married in 1930. His wife died in 1986. Cyril died on the 28th January 2007 at the age of almost 102. A frequent contributor to the **London Firemen** *magazine, one of his many tales is retold below.*

Cyril Demarne OBE at the re-dedication ceremony of the Blitz statue at St Paul's in 2003. (Permission of the Demarne family.)

After a few years of experience in a busy urban environment, the average fireman is apt to become a trifle blasé. The sight of a large factory or warehouse on fire does not excite him unduly; his thoughts are more likely to dwell on the certainty of a wet shirt and hours of slogging work in dangerous and unpleasant conditions, normal routine. But, utter the words 'persons reported' and the adrenalin immediately starts to pump, dangers and discomfort are forgotten.

The words of the training instructor return to mind. 'Lots of fire, lots of water, QUICK.' You can't walk into a blazing fire without getting burned, same as anyone else. And you've got to get in quick to have any chance of rescue. So, don't forget; 'persons reported' means plenty of water, quickly.

The words stick, but the reality behind them – the searing heat and the choking smoke, the thumping heart and the responsibility of locating and rescuing a fellow human being from great danger – must be experienced to become comprehensible. Some of us remember our first fire, others do not: the details of our 'first fatal' usually are imprinted so deeply in our minds that they remain long after retirement.

I attended my first fatal fire in November 1928, just before Guy Fawkes Day. It was about 6 p.m. on a raw afternoon when a man came running to report a fire in a newsagents shop in Martin Street, just across the road from Stratford fire station. Turning the corner into Martin Street, we saw a great plume of flame leaping from the open door and sweeping up the face of the building. I had been riding to fires for only twelve months but my limited experience was sufficient to tell that this was no ordinary shop fire; something of a highly flammable nature must be involved.

'Hydrant on the corner,' yelled the Sub Officer as the pump escape pulled up with a jerk and we leapt into action. I grabbed a branch and my mate yanked the hose from the locker. Out of the corner of my eye I saw our number five haring across the road carrying the hydrant tools and a standpipe. Behind him a policeman was struggling with a woman, but I had other things to do than watch what I took to be a street disturbance.

My mate joined me at the branch. 'Water on,' we shouted as we took up position beside the door. Then up ran a policeman shouting, 'There is a little girl in there.'

My first thought was one of dismay: no one could be alive in that inferno. Then came a confusion of thoughts racing through my mind. 'Maybe she is upstairs and we've got a chance? Perhaps she's not in there at all, we've had these scares before.'

There had been no lack of urgency before, but now we reacted with every ounce of energy we possessed. The jet spluttered and popped before getting a solid stream as we set about the fire. As we entered we were met by a wall of heat that seemed to take the skin off my face and hands. We put our heads down and ducked to get below the worst of it, swinging the branch around and striking at the fire in all corners. In those first seconds I was forced to close my eyes and mouth tight against the bite of the heat, only opening my eyes in a series of blinks to see where I was going. The steam cloud that followed penetrated my heavy tunic and I felt as if I was being passed through a steam-press machine. Painful as they were, the heat and difficulty in breathing seemed only part of the background, the dominant thought in my mind was of the child, somewhere in that mass of flames.

We were knocking the fire down faster than we had dared hope and moved towards the back room, also well alight, over loose debris littering the floor. Behind us came our second crew with hose reel and emergency lighting, peering around and searching every corner. Suddenly, someone called, 'Here she is.'

I looked back into the shop, now brightly lit by the box lamps, and saw two firemen bending down behind the counter. The space was strewn heavily with newspapers and there beneath the litter lay the body of a pretty little girl about five years of age. Remarkably, the fire had by-passed the paper behind the counter and the child, apparently, had burrowed beneath the heap in an effort to escape the fire, only to suffocate.

I found myself trembling with shock. But there was still much to do before the premises could be left and I realised for the first time that I must not let my mind dwell on the tragedy, I must 'work it off.'

My mate on the branch had suffered more than I. My face and hands were scorched and tingling painfully, but I had not blistered. As we came out for a breather I noticed that the skin on the tip of his nose had broken and was curling back around his nostrils. White blisters hung from the lobes of his ears like pearl earrings.

**'Ladders made of wood, firemen made of steel.'
(Mary Evans 10795541.)**

We heard later that the shop had been doing a brisk trade in fireworks. A substantial stock was displayed for sale in open trays when someone had thrown a lighted squib into the shop, turning it into an inferno in a matter of seconds. The woman struggling with the PC was the child's mother and was restrained from running back into the shop.

In the drill class we had been told about the strange places in which people sought refuge when trapped by fire. 'Look under the bed and in the wardrobe when searching a bedroom,' our instructor had told us. He recited the case of the servant girl trapped in a fire in Wimpole Street and who had immersed herself in a bath filled with water in an effort to escape flames roaring up the staircase. The fire did not reach her, but the smoke did. She too was suffocated.

But the stark reality of these events only came to me with this tragic episode. It sharpened my perception and I realised that drill class lectures were not just stories told to entertain, but were sound practical guides to young firemen embarking on the serious business of firefighting.

THE GEORGE CROSS

G

The GEORGE CROSS was instituted by King George VI in 1940 specifically to recognise acts of conspicuous gallantry in circumstances of extreme danger by civilians, or by members of the Armed Services when not in the immediate presence of the enemy. The award ranks with the Victoria Cross, which is awarded for valour in battle; it is worn before all other decorations except the VC. In the modern history of the London Fire Brigade only twice has it been awarded to its firefighters, one of which was granted posthumously. It would be most remiss not to mention them in this anthology.

••

The KING has been graciously pleased to award the GEORGE CROSS to Auxiliary Fireman Harry ERRINGTON. (Supplement to the London Gazette, *issue No 35239, 8th August 1941, pg. 4545.*)

High explosive and incendiary bombs demolished a building. Fireman Errington and two other Auxiliary Firemen were the only occupants of the basement of the building at the time of the explosion. The blast blew Fm Errington across the basement, but although dazed and injured he made his way to the other two Auxiliaries, whom he found to be pinned down, flat on their backs, by debris. A fierce fire broke out and the trapped men were in imminent danger of being burnt to death. The heat of the fire was so intense that Fm Errington had to protect himself with a blanket. After working with his bare hands for some minutes he managed to release the injured men and dragged them from under the wreckage and away from the fire. While he was so engaged, burning debris was falling into the basement and there was considerable danger of a further collapse of the building. He carried one of the men up a narrow stone staircase partially blocked by debris, into the courtyard, made his way through an adjoining building and thence into the street. Despite the appalling conditions and although burned and injured, Errington returned and brought out the second man. Both Fm Errington's comrades were severely burned but survived. He showed great bravery and endurance in effecting the rescues, at the risk of his own life. (Twenty people, including six firemen, died at this incident.)

Harry Errington GC. (Permission of the London Fire Brigade.)

113

Harry, a Savile Row tailor by day, continued to serve with the AFS throughout the war. He had a lifelong interest in basketball and managed the basketball competition in the 1948 London Olympics. He was always a welcome visitor to 'his' Soho fire station and on the occasion of his 90th birthday he attended a birthday party there given in his honour. He died on 15 December 2004, aged 94.

The KING has been graciously pleased to award the GEORGE CROSS to Frederick DAVIES (deceased). Fireman. No. 34 (London) National Fire Service. (Second Supplement to the London Gazette, *issue No 37455, 5th February 1946, pg. 805.)*

The premises, which consisted of a shop and house of five rooms, caught fire. The N.F.S. (London Region) were informed that two children were in the front room on the second floor. The escape was immediately slipped and pitched to the middle window of this floor. Before it was in position Davies ran up the escape. At this stage flames were pouring from the windows on the second floor and licking up the front of the building. Upon reaching the window Davies at once tried to enter but bursts of flame momentarily halted him. Undaunted, however, he climbed into the window with his back to the flames and entered the room. He was seen to endeavour to remove his tunic presumably to wrap it around and protect the children

Opposite: The rescue by Frederick Davies, from a reproduction of the original that hangs at Tottenham fire station. The original painting, by Reginald Mills, is displayed at the Fire Service College, Gloucestershire. (Photograph courtesy of Paul Wood.)

but his hands were too badly burned for him to do so. During this time Davies was moving around the blazing room in an endeavour to locate the children, and after a short period he returned with a child in his arms whom he handed out of the window. He then turned back into the room to find the other child. He was next seen to fling himself out of the window on to the escape, the whole of his clothing being alight. He was helped to the ground, the flames on his clothes were extinguished and he was conveyed to hospital suffering from severe burns. Later he died from his injuries. The gallantry and outstanding devotion to duty displayed by Fireman Davies was of the highest order. He knew the danger he was facing, but with complete disregard of his own safety he made a most heroic attempt to rescue the two children. In so doing he lost his life.

GHOST STORY:
THE SITTER

by L F Bee (Anon)

While clearing out some old papers in my flat recently, I came across a photograph given to me by a man called Mahoney, whom I knew very well. Mahoney was in the fire service, and just before he retired and moved away from London, he told me one of the most fantastic stories I have ever heard. It concerned something of a supernatural nature which happened to him on a night duty. He swore that every word of his tale was true. I have had good reason during my life not to disbelieve in the supernatural so I have always kept an open mind about Mahoney's story. Now I am convinced of its truth. However, it's you, the reader who must now judge for yourself.

Sub Officer Mahoney, a brigade photographer, was late coming on duty that evening. Fog which had been gathering over London during the afternoon had begun to settle, and his car became jammed in a stream of rush hour traffic which crawled along slower and slower as the fog grew thicker. By the time he had collected his fire-gear and stowed it on the photographic unit, visibility was practically nil. It was one of those dense London fogs which are now happily a thing of the past. A killer fog (smog), which would snuff out numberless lives already hanging on a thread of uncertainty before it dispersed.

As Mahoney started to cross the Lambeth drill yard to go to the rear Headquarters block, where the Brigade's photographic section was housed, he was totally engulfed in a dense, swirling, blackness which snatched at his throat and made his eyes sting, isolating him, and robbing him of all sense of direction. The familiar sounds of the appliance room he had just left were suddenly hushed and sounded far away. Soon there was no sound at all. Moving forward at a snail's pace and shuffling with his feet, as though moving through smoke, and often groping with his hands, Mahoney at last reached his goal. He breathed a sigh of relief as he entered the brightly lit office and felt the comforting warmth of the central heating.

Lighting a cigarette, Mahoney started to check on his night's work. A booking in the diary for Divisional Officer Massey to have his photograph taken that evening made him smile. 'The fog's put paid to that anyway,' he thought. DO Massey commanded one of the Brigade's outer Divisions. He certainly would not risk going 'mobile' in such dense fog for anything less than a fire or other serious incident. Mahoney knew that the DO was due to retire the following week. It was not unusual for retiring senior officers to have their pictures taken for publication in various fire journals, including the Brigade's own in-house magazine. Mahoney remembered having made this booking himself about three weeks previously. Then the DO had told him that he had to attend a meeting at Brigade headquarters on that particular night, and that he could kill two birds with one stone by having his photograph taken at the same time. The DO had been very precise about the time – 8 o'clock. Mahoney's smile broadened as he remembered this, for Massey was well known for his fussiness about keeping appointments on time. 'That's one appointment he won't keep; not in this lot!' thought Mahoney.

It was then that Mahoney became conscious of the, almost, eerie silence. It seemed to actually bear down on him, all of a sudden. He was quite alone on the first floor of the rear block, and experienced an unpleasant feeling of being cut off. There was a suggestion of menace in the dense blackness pressing in against the windows. It made him feel distinctly uneasy and he longed for someone to talk to. He dialled the General Office with the intention of asking whether the meeting Massey had mentioned had been cancelled. He knew it was a stupid question before he asked it, for there could be no doubt that it had. But it gave him the excuse he wanted. An expression of annoyance crossed his face as he listened to the continuing burring of the phone at the other end. But there was no reply and he replaced the receiver. He tried to comfort himself with the thought that DO Massey might turn up after all, knowing full well that such a possibility was extremely remote. But he arranged everything in readiness, placing both the camera and the photo floods in position, plus a chair for the DO to sit on, in front of a screen. Then he went into the darkroom to make a start on some prints which were required by the following morning.

It was dead on 8 o'clock when Mahoney came out of the darkroom. The first thing that he noticed was that the fog seemed to have penetrated into the office, as if a window had been opened; a cold draught against his cheek seemed to confirm this. He was about to check on the windows when he saw the tall, gaunt, figure of DO Massey emerge from the shadows of the drawing office, which adjoined the photographic office. It made him jump, for he hadn't heard anybody enter. The thought flashed through his mind that the DO must have arrived when he was in the darkroom and, for some unknown reason, had opened one of the drawing office windows. He was disconcerted too, by the way the DO was staring at him, and it was a moment before he could find his voice. 'Good evening, Sir. You gave me quite a start. I didn't really expect you because of the fog. But I've got everything ready; if you wouldn't mind sitting down here.' Mahoney indicated the chair which he had placed in readiness in front of the screen.

The DO inclined his head in acknowledgement, and without saying a word crossed the office and sat down, crossing his legs and folding his arms, his eyes staring fixedly at the camera lens. Mahoney was disturbed by the DO's abrupt manner. He knew that some men hated having their photograph taken, but he never had a sitter who so obviously wanted the job over as quickly as possible. He switched on the photo floods and then realised how dreadfully ill the DO looked. Mahoney prided himself on his ability to put sitters at their ease and make them look pleasant, but the DO's ashen face and staring eyes seemed to rob him of speech. A feeling of unreality came over him, almost as though he was dreaming. He heard himself speaking rather than being conscious of doing so; asking his sitter to look left, or right, and so on. It never occurred to him to ask the DO to smile.

Mahoney took three exposures, then the phone bell rang, stabbing his consciousness with its shrill sound and bringing him back to reality. Muttering an excuse, he crossed the office and picked up the receiver. It was the General Office, and Mahoney experienced a feeling of relief as he recognised the cheerful voice at the other end of the line. It seemed that the caller just wanted to chat and it was a few moments before Mahoney could get a word in. 'Look, I'll call you back later,' he managed to interrupt at last. 'I'm tied up just for a minute.' As he said this, Mahoney glanced over his shoulder and caught his breath. Divisional Officer Massey was no longer in his office. He still held the receiver to his ear, and speaking aloud to himself exclaimed, 'He's gone!'

'Who's gone?' he heard his colleague in the General Office ask. 'DO Massey,' answered Mahoney. 'He was in the office a moment ago. He must have left while you were talking.'

'DO Massey?' the voice sounded surprised. 'I thought he was sick. Yes, that's right. I heard today that he was in a pretty bad way, too.'

Mahoney gripped the receiver tightly and a slight shiver ran down his back. The DO's waxen and expressionless face flashed in his mind. There seemed to be a dreadful implication in what he had just heard.

Mahoney was possessed by an urgent desire to develop and print the negatives he had just taken. Immediately he put down the receiver, grabbed the slides and hurried into the dark room. He came out some minutes later with the wet prints in his hands. The pictures were about as bad as they could be. DO Massey looked ghastly, but at least they proved that he hadn't been dreaming. But he wondered why he still felt confused about what had happened when he took the exposures. For one thing, all the poses were exactly the same, and he couldn't account for that. He gazed at the prints and frowned. Quite clearly he would have to take them again.

Before going off duty the following morning, Mahoney took the batch of prints he had prepared over to the main Headquarters building, including the pictures of DO Massey. There were two officers talking together when he entered the General Office. It was impossible for Mahoney not to overhear their conversation. 'Yes I've heard about DO Massey,' one was saying. 'What damned bad luck, just about to retire too. Jones told me that you were there when it happened.' The other officer nodded. 'Yes, it was lucky that I was. I don't know what his wife would have done without help. When I got there poor old Arthur was staggering down the stairs. He was delirious and kept rambling about an appointment he had to keep at Headquarters. We had an awful job getting him back to bed. He was struggling a lot too. I suppose that is what really finished him off.'

The noise of the traffic rumbling past the building suddenly roared and thundered in Mahoney's ears and his legs seem to turn to jelly.

'What time did Mr Massey pass away?' he heard himself ask.

'Just about 8 o'clock,' the officer replied, and both of them looked at Mahoney curiously as they saw the Brigade photographer snatch a print from the bottom of the batch he was holding and staring at it intently. The print actually showed very little, just a chair placed in front of a screen.

I destroyed the photograph which Mahoney gave me. A photograph of a chair placed in front of a screen. You see, when I turned it out with some old papers in my flat recently, the chair was no longer unoccupied. There was something with a uniform on it. The details of the uniform were very clear, particularly the rank markings. But the thing on which the uniform was draped frightened me. I suppose it's a human impulse to destroy things of which we are afraid…

H THE HILLS HOTEL FATAL FIRE

Arthur Nicholls OBE, QFSM. (Permission of the London Fire Brigade.)

ARTHUR NICHOLLS was born in North London in 1921. Educated at Tottenham Grammar School he joined the army in his late teens and during World War two served with the Army in China, Burma and then Italy. After the war he became a police constable in Palestine before returning to the UK and in 1948 joined the newly created Middlesex Fire Brigade. Serving at Wood Green, Tottenham and Edmonton this intelligent young man rose to the senior rank of Assistant Divisional Officer in Middlesex before it was absorbed into the new Greater London Council's London Fire Brigade in 1965. His talents were quickly recognised and in 1967 he was promoted to Deputy Commander of London's 'A' Division, covering the West End of London, Chelsea, Kensington and Paddington. A year later he was promoted to be the Commander of that Division. He would eventually rise to principal rank, and in 1974 he became an Assistant Chief Fire Officer.

*An accomplished writer, he was a frequent contributor to the **London Fireman** magazine. His acclaimed account of the fire at the Hills Hotel (an annex of the New Langham Hotel), Kensington Gardens Square, W2, won him a prestigious writer's award from a panel of national journalists. His account of that challenging, and tragically fatal, blaze is recalled here.*

• •

A t varying times before six o'clock of the evening of 10th May 1971, according to the distances they had to travel, a number of men left their homes in and around London. With a nod, a cheerio, an affectionate kiss or just a friendly pat on the arm, they took their leave of their families and set off on their journeys to the fire stations at which they would be on duty for the coming night.

Arriving, they dressed in fire gear ready for the roll call. The usual exchange of banter, the voicing of complaints, 'Not my turn. I was on the pump last night as well.' 'Not my turn in the mess, what about Harry, he hasn't done it for weeks.' 'Me? Stand-by. Has he gone sick again? I ought to get some of his bloody pay!'

After the roll call and allotted to their various appliances, the men check the equipment, test the BA sets. Replenish petrol/ diesel, oil and water as necessary and stand ready for what the night has in store.

The work programmes are arranged; drills, lectures, equipment maintenance, hydrant tests, visits to risks, each station according to the pressing need of the time. But already at some stations the programme is disrupted before it is even under way.

The urgent ringing of the fire bells sends the men running to their appliances, which in turn roar out of the station in response to the urgent call for aid. On through the evening the calls mount. Time and time again at fire stations here and there all over Greater London appliance bay doors crash open and the big red fire engines sally forth carrying their black-helmeted crews. With warning horns, or engine bells sounding, they are cursed for their noise by all but those in trouble and anxious for their aid. The radio wave, carrying the message from the appliances reporting the situation they were meeting, were seldom stilled:

'Stop for Commercial Street. Flat of five rooms. Half damaged by fire. Two hosereels, BA.'

'Stop for Southwark Bridge Road. Unoccupied factory of four floors. 40 feet by 50 feet. 50% of third floor, 25% of top floor damaged by fire. 3 jets. BA.'

'At Under Croft, Westcombe Park Road. Smell of smoke on second floor, Crews investigating.'

'Stop for Chapel Farm Road. Sports pavilion of one floor. 20 by 60 feet. 25% damaged by fire. One jet.'

'Priority... From Station Officer Vaughan at 23 Croydon Road. Persons reported.'

'Stop Kingston by-pass. One car and one bus in collision. One person trapped, injured, released. Five persons injured. All removed to hospital by ambulance. Police in attendance.'

The variety was unending. A small fire here, petrol spilled on roadway there, a false alarm caused by burning rubbish, fire and explosion in a cable tunnel, etc. Then, soon after 10 p.m. in Commerce Road, Brentford, a fire in a paint manufacturers that was only to be quelled by the combined sweating and gut straining efforts of the crews of 25 pumps and two turntable ladders. While the fight to control this blaze is still at its height an urgent (priority) message comes for reinforcing pumps to help deal with a fire at Friern Barnet Hospital, in North West London.

The city quietens

Still the score of other incidents mounts, although the rate slows down as life in the capital city quietens and people turn to their beds to sleep. To sleep, they hope, in peace, until the morrow. For most, this is to be. For some, the night will hold its terror. For some, it will demand the ultimate – life itself.

But first, the men at Croydon are called to a warehouse in Selsdon Road. Again the fire is of such proportion that they ask for more assistance pumps and once more the men of the LFB sweat and toil in blinding heat and choking smoke to combat the scourge of mankind.

In London's West End it was an average night. The men at the stations had only snippets of news about what was going on elsewhere. Some of their appliances had been involved at the Brentford fire, indeed some were still so engaged. But generally the pace was normal. The clock passed midnight and ticked on.

At Paddington the fire station grew quiet, some men talked over a cup of tea, others reclined to rest. In a hotel annex, less than a mile from the station, staff and guests settled down for the night. Destiny would have it that these two separate groups of people would meet this night to play out a drama together. A real life drama of fire, death, destruction, pain, agony and courage, rarely to be met outside the realms of fiction. For those in the hotel, the drama began when fire flashed through the corridors and stairways of the hotel in minutes to mushroom through the upper floors. For the firemen it began at precisely 00:48 hours when the silence of the station was broken by the harsh sound and continuous ringing of the call bells. Automatic lights flashed on throughout the station and in the watchroom the teleprinter clacked out its cryptic message: 'Fire. Hills Hotel, Kensington Gardens Square.'

A red angry glow

Away they went, these men, some young, some not so young. Ordinary men who are 'dad' to their children, 'son' to their parents, 'uncle this' or 'uncle that' to nephews and nieces. Who are 'dear' to their wives or 'mate' to the man next door. Away they went to Kensington Gardens Square. Their journey was short. One hundred and twenty seconds in time as they sped along Bishops Bridge Road and on into Westbourne Grove.

Over the tops of the tall buildings that they passed en route there could be seen a red, angry glow reflected against the night sky. Inside and outside the hotel the drama was already being enacted. Some of the residents, frightened but unharmed, had made their way out safely. These were the lucky ones. Others, not so lucky, had crawled along a wide ledge at fourth floor level into the window of an adjoining house. They suffered burns and shock but were safe. One man, trapped at a ground floor window, and prevented from escape by a deep basement area surrounded by heavy iron railings, was helped by passing policemen, who bridged the gap by pushing a wooden plank to him. A woman, caught on the upper floors, made her way via a metal fire escape at the rear of the third floor, which led her via intervening buildings to an adjoining house. Badly burned in making her escape, she fell and sustained other injuries en route.

A young girl, clinging desperately to a window sill on the upper floors, driven by heat and smoke lost her grip and fell to be impaled on railings surrounding the property. At windows at the front of the hotel men and women stood crying desperately for help. A crowd, already gathered, called encouragingly. 'Don't jump, they are coming', for in the distance could be heard that most delightful of all sounds to those in peril from fire, the urgent sound of two-tone horns as fire appliances speed on their way.

Thus it was as the first appliances turned the corner. Flames spewed from the windows of the two upper floors at the front of the building, thick smoke spilled from the windows of the lower floors. A man and a woman called excitedly from the second floor, below them on the first floor another man and woman screamed their distress.

The pump escape pulled in first. Its doors opened and men leapt out before it slowed to a halt. The escape ladder was slipped, turned and extended as only a well drilled crew, working as a team and reacting automatically, can do. The appliance itself then moved on to clear the area of operations. Its driver, acting on instructions, radioed the priority message. 'Make pumps six-persons reported'. As background to his voice as he transmitted the message could be heard the cries of the crowd and of those in distress.

Now the other appliances from Paddington, the ET and TL, halted at the scene. One man raced to the escape and began mounting it as the top of the ladder crashed to rest at the second floor window. He was closely followed by a second fireman. As the first man reached the top, the trapped woman was already on the ladder. He moved aside to let her pass and went on into the room where the man still waited and then helped him on to the ladder. Both people were assisted down to the ground by other crew members. While waiting until the ladder was clear of people, the attention of the fireman, still in the room from which the man and woman had been assisted, was drawn to an adjacent window. There he saw an elderly lady standing in the thick smoke. Clambering along the top of a narrow balustrade, which fronted the windows, he made his way into the room to comfort the woman.

A crew from Kensington fire station, arriving with a pump, pitched its thirty foot extension ladder to them. Its head rested two feet short of the window of the room. With difficulty, and assisted by a fireman on the ladder, the lady was helped to it and down to safety; and none too soon for the heat and smoke was worsening rapidly, and fire was breaking through the door to the room. Meanwhile the escape ladder had been re-pitched to the first floor and the man and woman trapped there were brought to safety.

By now a clearer picture of the fire situation was available. The hotel, taking up a corner site, was comprised of two and five floors. It was alight on all five floors. Flames were roaring from a doorway at the side of the building and had engulfed the two storey section and was licking from the windows at the side of the hotel. At the back, the windows of one half of the building showed red with the fire inside. Already the roof had collapsed, flame licked skywards, and myriads of sparks shot high and the whole scene reflected the angry red glow.

The raging fire...

But more, much more, remained to be done. A survey had shown more people trapped on a top floor at the rear of the hotel. A TL [turntable ladder], extended over a projecting flat roof, reached a window and a woman was helped on by others inside. But the TL was at its maximum safety limits. The woman was afraid and could not be left to make her own way down the ladder in the choking smoke and past the raging fire. Quickly the ladder was housed and a fireman this time raced up to the woman and led her down. Again the ladder was extended. This time a man was helped on to the ladder and again it was housed and the man helped down. But yet another cry for help was heard and, below the very window from which these two rescues were performed, in the thick smoke, another man could be seen at a window, calling, pleading for help. Once more the ladders were extended. Now the smoke was so thick that the operator of the TL could not see the head of the ladder he was controlling. Coolly, magnificently, he persisted, and although the projecting flat roof prevented a direct pitch to the window at which the man was trapped, a pitch to the flat roof was achieved.

The fireman at the top the ladders jumped off on to the flat roof and then crawled to a parapet at the side from where he was a little above, but only two to three feet from the trapped man. Here he was joined by another fireman. Together they reached over towards the man. Struggling and holding his arms, they helped him on to the roof. By now the man was almost hysterical. 'My wife is in that room,' he cried out frantically, time and time again. One fireman climbed the parapet to enter the room, but could not make it without help. The other fireman tried to calm the man, but recognising the difficulty got him to the ladder, assisted him down and ran back up to rejoin his colleague.

Conditions on the flat roof were atrocious. Flame belched from windows overlooking it and the heat and smoke from the fire beneath them made the atmosphere scorched. Yet again they tried to enter the room. Helped by his team-mate, one of the firemen got over the parapet into the room. The heat and smoke made it impossible to move far into the room, but reaching down he felt a bare ankle of a woman and, pulling her towards him, managed to get her head near the window before having to get back out into the air for respite.

Now they were joined by a BA fireman, summoned by the TL intercom, and they felt the cooling, refreshing water from a jet directed at them from ground level to protect them. Over the parapet and into the room went the BA man. Fire was actually curling round the door edges of the room, but though the heat was intense the BA man lifted the woman until her head and arms were out of the window. Then his two colleagues, reaching over the parapet, grasped her arms, swung her out over the drop beneath and pulled her on to the roof. She was unconscious and had to be lifted on to the back of one of the men who had already mounted the ladder to be carried down to safety. Subsequently, it is pleasing to note, she recovered completely.

For this particular act there is only one sad note to record. One of those who had worked so hard on the roof to effect this rescue complained; 'I was so glad they put the jet on us 'cos I've never been so hot outside a building before, but they wet my last four bloody fags!'

The aftermath of the Hills Hotel fire, showing the fire-scarred window openings the following morning. (Permission of the London Fire Brigade.)

'. . .the black scorch marks above the window openings bear witness to the rage of fire . . .'

Hook ladders

While these rescues were going on yet another old lady had been seen sitting on a window sill, clinging desperately to a drainpipe at first floor level. Beneath her was a drop of some thirty-five feet to a rear basement area which was enclosed by a one-foot wide, twenty-feet high brick wall. Crews with hook ladders made their way to her. Negotiating adjoining premises, intervening roofs and a variety of minor hazards, they reached the top of the basement area wall. From here they pitched their hook ladders to the window and, mounting them, helped her on to the ladder. With two hook ladders pitched side by side so that a man on one could assist the other man with the woman, she was gradually helped down to the top of the wall. Then, it all proved too much for her and she collapsed.

Now the real struggle. Somehow they got her off the wall, then precariously inched their way along the top to the rear. A distance of no more than ten feet, but every foot fraught with difficulty and no little danger. Hesitating none, they pitched a hook ladder. One of the men put the woman across his back and, assisted as much as possible by the others, carried her up the hook ladder to the roof. From there she was carried through adjoining premises to safety.

The deeds, as must be, are described in isolation, but of course the general operations were now in full swing. Reinforcing appliances were arriving in their numbers and jets were increased. Escapes and extension ladders festooned the faces of the building and crews struggled upwards with heavy hose, moving into the windows to begin extinguishing the fire.

In the main entrance crews attempted to use the stone staircase and narrowly escaped serious injury when, en-bloc from the ground to fourth floor, it collapsed with a resounding crash. But the staircase was replaced with scaling ladders built up gradually to each floor in turn and jets were taken in. From adjoining roofs jets of water were directed through the collapsed roof of the building involved into the holocaust beneath. A TL, in use as a water tower, added its power from the side street.

At the front of the building one of the saddest tasks of all had been accomplished. After a prolonged struggle the unfortunate girl who had fallen on to the railings had been cut free. Showered with sparks and falling debris, the crew had stuck to their task and, aided by a medical team, hoped their effort would be rewarded with success. But now, with the girl en route to hospital, they joined in the general fire-fighting.

Smoke to steam

An hour or so had passed and then the flames were beaten. Here and there a little flicker, a glow. Smoke has turned to steam. Inside the building the men carefully pick their way, avoiding weakened sections of floors, bridging the gaps where collapse has occurred. Cold, wet and so bloody tired now that the adrenalin has drained from their systems they push on. Damping down a smouldering ember here, a burning mattress there, they seek and search for those who may have perished and, finding them, wrap the sad remains in sheets to carefully lower them to the street outside where ambulances wait to receive them.

Crew by crew they are released from various tasks and given short respite at the canteen van parked in a nearby road, where a steaming cup of tea or Bovril, a biscuit and a quick smoke helps put the world back in shape. Then, back again into the now cold, dank, steamy atmosphere of the building, the depressing smell of charred wood tinged by the occasional whiff of acrid smoke in their nostrils. For ages, it seems they work on until a new, fresh crew of men come to them and say: 'We're relieving you.'

Outside again, dawn is beginning to break. In the light the tall gaunt walls of the hotel look forbidding and the black scorch marks above the window openings bear witness to the rage of the fire that once tormented it.

Still, elsewhere around London, all is not at peace. The calls still come in. F Division, in the East End of London, now take their share when a paper warehouse is involved in fire and a priority call for more assisting pumps comes over the air; and the night's totals mount as the operators in the controls receive the calls and dispatch the necessary aid. But with all things there is an end. At nine o'clock in the morning a new watch reports for duty. The men who have worked throughout the night go home, unless they happen to be out on a call or with one of the many relief pumps still attending the scene of the night's major fires. Even these will go home soon. They will walk indoors and the wife will say, 'Have a cuppa?' and then tell of Alfred's cut knee.

A little later home than normal will be the few casualties among the firemen of the night's battles. They will have had their treatment at hospital and not been detained, but will be late enough for families to have been told so that undue worry will not arise. Soon, however, they will all be there. Back with the missus, the kids, the people next door and they'll worry about the rent, about food prices, about the holiday. Then at varying times before six o'clock on the evening of the 11th May, 1971, according to the distance they have to travel... oh! and if they are lucky they can buy the evening newspaper and see a picture of a fireman lying injured on a stretcher. The caption reads: 'A policeman, having played his part is carried away.'

Notes

1. The 'stop' message:
'Hotel 2 and 5 floors and basement, 50 by 80 feet, all floors damaged by fire, roof off. 12 jets, Breathing Apparatus. 1 woman jumped before arrival, 1 person rescued by extension ladder from 1st floor, 2 persons by extension ladder from second floor. 2 persons by escape ladder from 3rd floor, I man and 1 woman via escape ladder from 1st floor, 2 men and 2 women rescued by TL from 3rd and 4th floors. I woman rescued by hook ladder from 3rd floor – burned-overcome. 7 bodies found. All persons accounted for.'

2. The Gallantry Awards;
The highest accolade for bravery in the London Fire Brigade then, and still is, is a **Chief Officer's** *(now Commissioner's)* **Commendation**. *The Chief Officer, Joe Milner, issued* ten *Commendations following the serious and fatal fire at Hill's Hotel, Kensington in May of 1971.*

The commended men were: Temporary Station Officer David Ellis and Fireman Bernard Cannon of North Kensington fire station. Temporary Sub Officer Colin Livett, Firemen Leslie Austin and Thomas Richards of Kensington fire station. Leading Firemen Ray Cleverdon and George Simpson, Temporary Leading Fireman Howard Winter and Firemen Ken Salmon and William Willis of Paddington fire station.

Leading Fireman Simpson and Winter brought a man and woman down an escape ladder from the second floor. After climbing along a narrow balustrade Leading Fireman Salmon reached a trapped woman on an adjacent window ledge and brought her down to safety via an extension ladder.

Leading Fireman Cleverdon brought down separately a man and woman from the window sill of the fourth floor. Then with Firemen Richards and Willis he rescued a man and wife from a third floor room in extremely punishing conditions. Having assisted the man down the ladder Fm Willis returned to the room wearing BA, where conditions were very bad, and managed to drag the overcome wife to the window. Fireman Richards carried the woman down the ladder to safety.

Temporary Station Officer Ellis & Temporary Sub Officer Livett and Firemen Cannon and Austin, using hook ladders together brought down a woman trapped on an upper window sill at the rear of the hotel and having collapsed had to be carried down.

Fireman Salmon skilfully operated a turntable ladder, even beyond its limits of safety and made possible a number of rescues.

Leading Fireman Ray Cleverdon and Fireman William Willis, and Fireman Thomas Richards were subsequently all awarded the British Empire Medal for Gallantry.

The Chief Officer congratulated all the crews that attended the fire on their efforts.

3. Nine people died as a direct result of this fire. However, although the conditions were appalling, ten were brought out to safety by the Brigade.

4. The fire was started deliberately: an arson attack.

HORSES

READY, AND WAITING.

Horses had been pulling the fire engines to fires for quite
some time prior to the creation of the Metropolitan Fire
Brigade (MFB) in 1866. First, for London's Insurance
fire brigades, then followed by the London Fire Engine
Establishment. Horses were usually kept stabled at the rear of the
station, close by the engine house, and brought to the engine, to be
harnessed, when the summons for assistance came.

Both organisations had provided their own horse to pull, first, the
manual pumps and then later the steam pumps that were gradually replacing the manual, and man-power intensive, fire engines.

However, these were usually any horse that a local livery company could supply to the fire brigade and had no special training for the work involved.

Captain Eyre Massey Shaw, the new Chief Fire Officer of the MFB, changed all this within a year of taking command of London's enlarged and progressive fire brigade. He turned to one Thomas Tilling, who ran many of London's horse-drawn buses, to supply these specialised fire engine pulling horses. From 1867 Tillings held the contract to supply the MFB and later the renamed London Fire Brigade (LFB) with horses trained just for fire brigade work.

The Tilling Company traces its origins to 1846, when Thomas Tilling started in business. Thomas Tilling was born in 1825 at Gutter's Hedge Farm, Hendon, in Middlesex. At the age of 21 he went into the transport business in London working as a 'Jobmaster,' the provider of horse, carriage, tack and driver on a rental basis, rather like a car hire firm of today, in Walworth using a horse and carriage which cost him £30. By January 1850 he had progressed to purchasing his own horse bus, together with the licence, to run four journeys a day between Peckham and Oxford Street. By 1856 he owned 70 horses which he used for bus and general carriage work. Tilling won the contract with the London County Council to supply the Metropolitan Fire Brigade. Tilling was also contracted to train the horses to haul the fire engines. These horses, Tilling trained to respond quickly and, prior to their handover to the fire brigade, they were employed on the bus services (primarily the Peckham route) to gain experience of heavy London traffic. Tilling eventually became the biggest supplier of horsepower and vehicles in London, having a stable of 4,000 horses by the time of his death in 1893. Thomas Tilling was buried at Nunhead Cemetery in south London.

Once in the fire brigade the horses served about eight years and like the firemen themselves some stood out as characters in their own right, and they won themselves a place in the firemen's, and Londoners', hearts as these magnificent animals sped through the streets in urgent response to the call for help.

At the very start of his book Fifty Years of Fire Fighting in London *(see also page 78), the author **JACK WHILE** captures the moment.*

• •

'Hi hi hi!' Clang, clang, 'Hi hi! Hi hi! Hi hi!' Splendid horses galloping at full speed through crowded streets, dragging a steam-engine behind them. Half a dozen brass-helmeted men on the engine shouting themselves hoarse. Steam and smoke belching from the funnel; myriads of sparks dropping from beneath the boiler on the roadway, horse-traffic clearing out of the way on either side; pedestrians stopping on the pavements to watch with eager eyes the flying and rapidly disappearing mass of men and metal; a dull glow in the sky ahead; and then again; 'Hi! hi! hi! hi!' as another engine rapidly follows the trail of the first.

By the mid-1880s the previous methods of bringing the horse from their stables was abandoned in favour of having the horses kept in 'duty' stalls adjacent to their respective engines with a loose harness already fitted to which the engine could be speedily attached. (Captain Shaw had visited some fire brigades in the United States previously and had brought this American system back to London, together with adopting the 'sliding-pole' into his London fire stations.)

The stories about the horses were endless. Just how true all of them were is open for debate. However, some are still worth repeating, even if over the passage of time a degree of exaggeration has crept into the tales.

Tilling's 'fire' horse Kruger, at Islington fire station, Essex Road, N1 in the station stables at the end of the nineteenth century. (Mary Evans 10535281.)

There was, they said, one pair who were so intelligent that when the call came they looked across to the watchroom where a disc would fall as the street alarm was pulled, showing the point at which it had been given. These two were so astute that, according to the location of the alarm, they would turn left or right out of the station without any direction from the fireman 'coachman' on the box.

The horses would also regularly stamp their hooves if they were kept 'on watch' for more than their requisite two hour stint in the stalls. One pair were believed to have known before any of the other firemen at the station that their fireman 'coachman' was losing his sight. The horses covered for him, galloping round obstacles and sensing their way to the fire long before it was discovered that he was doing very little to help them. Several newspapers reported on a fire horse from Deptford fire station and his antics on the way to a fire. Called to 'Fire in Globe Street,' the occupiers of the house had already extinguished the fire before the reinforcing fire engines could be prevented from attending the call. Still en route, Deptford fire engine was galloping down Deptford High Street when the horse suddenly stopped. No amount of cursing or cajoling by the firemen on board, and particularly the coachman, would make the animal move. It was then the firemen realised why, the house they had stopped outside was on fire too.

By the late 1880s five pairs of horses were kept at most stations, with two always 'on watch' and ready to go. The horses on watch had their collars hooked to the ceiling of the engine room, by a rope, to ease the weight on their necks. Additionally other ropes were attached to their blankets so that when the alarm sounded they could speedily be removed and left hanging in mid-air with the horses ready to trot to the shafts of the engine.

Whilst every engine was clearly marked LCC-Metropolitan Fire Brigade the horses themselves carried the initials 'T.T.' on their blinkers. The 'greys' supplied by Tilling's were a conspicuous colour. It was considered that the greys were, apparently, more fortunate than the others in getting a clear road, and do well in an engine. Although the engine-horses were rarely troubled with burns, and appeared quite heedless of the sparks which could sprinkle on to their backs from the unguarded funnel, they were not free from other accidents. Tilling's had to replace horses, by night or day, on receipt of a telephone message from a fire station, so that sufficient horses were held in readiness at the station yard for emergencies. Given the vast stock of Tilling's animals it paid to maintain infirmaries to which the sick and injured animals were sent and even a farm for their convalescence.

Opposite: An enlargement of a glass plate negative shows the coachman holding onto the fire engine's horses during a drill display at Southwark, the headquarters of the London Fire Brigade. (Permission of the London Fire Brigade.)

Below: Horse drawn steam fire engine and its crew at Greenwich fire station, south east London. (Mary Evans 10535377.)

By 1902 Tilling's had over 300 horses stabled at fire stations in London. No horse was supplied until it was five years old. Having already been used to pull Tilling's buses in the capital's traffic, they were then specially selected: sufficiently strong to pull a heavy steam engine, yet not too heavy to break into a gallop. Now carefully trained, with splendid feeding and veterinary supervision, the life of a fire brigade horse was a good one. These sure-footed animals were much admired by the public and held in high regard by the brigade.

However, the days of the horse-drawn fire engine were already numbered. In 1903 the Metropolitan Fire Brigade introduced a small motor tender that was fitted with a tank of water which was expelled under pressure with carbon dioxide gas. The fire brigade at Tottenham, then outside the London County Council boundary, had acquired a self-propelled steam fire engine and a motor escape carrier, and built a new fire station with no stables or provision for horses.

Firemen and horses in the stables of Knightsbridge fire station. (Mary Evans 10535270.)

The Stables Knightsbridge L.F.B. Station

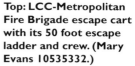

Top: LCC-Metropolitan Fire Brigade escape cart with its 50 foot escape ladder and crew. (Mary Evans 10535332.)

Centre: 'The First Arrival'. Metropolitan Fire Brigade clear their route by calling 'Hi! Hi! Hi!' (Courtesy of the London Fire Brigade Museum.)

Bottom: 1904 and a Fire King self-propelled steam fire engine at the Whitefriars fire station in the City of London. (Mary Evans 10535992.)

1921 and the last horse-drawn fire engine (turntable ladder) is withdrawn from service from Kensington fire station, west London. (Mary Evans 10536001.)

One year later, and a re-branded LCC-London Fire Brigade had twelve of the new generation Fire King self-propelled fire engines. Each weighing approximately five and half tons, it had a maximum speed of 25 miles per hour and could pump water, at maximum pressure, for two hours on its paraffin fuel.

The London Fire Brigade bade farewell to the last horse-drawn fire engine in 1921, when Kensington's horse-drawn turntable ladder was withdrawn from service and the horses retired.

INCIDENT AT ST JOHN'S

A Christmas Tragedy by Gordon White

I f she had not been seven months pregnant at the time, my sister would surely have died on 5 December 1957. As long as I could remember my sister was always in a hurry, always running when others chose to walk. Why stroll to the station when a last minute dash would achieve the objective?

Such was the case on that fateful, cold and murky day when most of London lay shrouded in one of those distinctive yellowish fogs that preceded the dawning of the smokeless-zone age.

My sister worked as a receptionist for a London advertising agency just off the Strand. Her lunchtime had been spent dashing, as usual, from shop to shop searching for and buying Christmas presents. There was an added dimension to her urgency since it was to be her last Christmas at work and she planned to buy gifts for close colleagues as a farewell gesture. The baby, her first, was due in February.

Her regular train home to the south London suburbs was the 5.18 p.m. electric service from Charing Cross to Hayes in Kent, which she would board at Waterloo (now Waterloo East). Her breathless arrival on the platform invariably coincided with the train's imminent departure which meant standing room only in one of the last two carriages before the throng of commuters thinned out as the train made staccato progress to its final destination.

Clutching an assortment of bags and parcels my sister was, as usual, late leaving the agency building in Brettenham Place. The fog was thick enough to blanket the view of the vast Shell Building, which then dwarfed Waterloo Station, from the north side of the bridge.

Five minutes would normally have been enough time for my unencumbered sister to catch her train. Now, weighed down with her unborn son and her clutch of parcels, she lost the race. It was to be the saving of her life. She arrived breathless on the platform just to see the red tail light of her train vanishing rapidly into the foggy gloom towards London Bridge. Her long wait on the cold platform at Waterloo began.

The fog had disrupted the British Rail train services. Not severely, but enough to throw the already hectic rush hour timetable into disarray. Particularly badly hit were the longer distance commuter trains to and from the Kent coast, which in those days were hauled by stream locomotives. Lacking the acceleration of the electric trains the steam engines found it virtually impossible to regain time lost through a series of signal checks which accompanied the fog.

The steam express locomotive 'Spitfire' was barely ten years old and capable of hauling the coastal trains with consummate ease. It was scheduled to pull the 4.56 p.m. service from Cannon Street to Ramsgate. Already arriving late in London on the inward journey the steam engine was well behind on the days schedule when it reversed onto the carriages waiting at Cannon Street. There was no time for the engine's fireman to fill up the tender with water. The crew were told to take on water at Sevenoaks, the first scheduled stop. With no sign of the thick fog lifting Spitfire got under way from Cannon Street, easing slowly round the curve into London Bridge and then off across the viaducts of Bermondsey towards New Cross.

Some two miles ahead of Spitfire, the Hayes electric train had set off again, through the murk, after a stop at New Cross. This train was not booked to stop at Lewisham and after passing through St John's station it was switched to the down main line. It would follow this for a short distance, before veering off at Parks Bridge Junction to regain the Hayes line, just before Ladywell station. A red light brought the Hayes train to a halt on the main line just before the junction.

With its brakes applied fully, to counteract a slight incline, the ten-carriage Hayes train trailed back to a point where its two rear coaches stood beneath an overbridge that carried the railway line from Nunhead to Lewisham. The scene was now set for a tragedy.

Despite the poor visibility the crew of the Spitfire had built up speed on the long, straight run from London Bridge to New Cross where it passed through the station at something like 40mph. For many years this stretch of line had been equipped with multi-coloured signalling, in theory, was far easier for a train driver to read that the conventional semaphore signals that were mounted on posts or gantries. Tragically the driver of Spitfire powered his train, first, past a double yellow signal light, and then a yellow signal. This should have warned him that the next signal would be RED and require him to bring his train to a standstill. Instead only after Spitfire, the Ramsgate express, had passed the red signal at St John's was there a brake application. It was too late.

Spitfire and its train, several hundred tons all told, ploughed into the back of the still stationary Hayes train. The force of the impact was catastrophic and deadly. With its brakes on, the Hayes train offered a dead weight resistance. Its rear carriages were smashed beyond all recognition. The leading coaches of the Ramsgate train buckled and the locomotive hit the pillars supporting the overbridge with such force it caused the structure to collapse on the wreckage below.

(Permission of the London Fire Brigade.)

The one glimmer of fortune to shine on an evening of carnage came moments later when the driver of the train approaching on the line from Nunhead, that would take him over the bridge towards Lewisham, saw through the fog that the line suddenly disappear in front of him. Applying the brakes for an emergency stop he brought the train to a jolting halt just yards from the precipice where only minutes before the bridge had been. An even worse disaster had been averted by only the narrowest of margins.

A characteristic of fog is that it muffles sound. Residents from nearby streets would later recall hearing only a 'dull thud' at the moment of impact. Fortunately some who had telephones had the presence of mind to realise that something had happened and summoned the emergency services. Others scrambled up the embankments flanking the lines to see what could be done. The driver of the Hayes Train which had been catapulted forwards by the collision, staggered from his cabin to the signal box at Parks Bridge Junction to report the crash. He found that the signalman had already set all the signals under his control to red.

In 1957 major accident procedure did not exist. But it was very apparent to the three emergency services that the crash was of catastrophic proportions. Access to the crash site was extremely difficult. It could only be made, initially, by means of an extension ladder pitched, to form a bridge, from the roof of an appliance to the top of a 12ft high brick wall. Also a steep embankment had to be negotiated to reach the permanent way.

The sight that met the first fire engine crews from Lewisham, and then surrounding fire stations, was almost impossible to comprehend. The impact had thrown many passengers from the trains and they were lying, some already dead and others with life-threatening injuries, on both the permanent way and the embankment. The death toll was the most severe, however, in the rear coaches of the Hayes train. These had been packed to 'standing room only' capacity. Miraculously, some passengers in this part of the train had survived the crash itself but now lay entombed in the midst of the entangled remnants of the carriages.

(Permission of the London Fire Brigade.)

Emergency tender crews were to the fore – there were only two then in the London Fire Brigade – and set about the task of extracting the trapped and moving away the bodies of the dead. Alongside London's firemen, doctors and nurses also moved among the injured administering morphine to those in pain.

The Brigade control unit, from Lambeth, was located in the adjacent Thurston Road, and four advanced control points were established around the scene of the wreck making use of the walkie-talkie equipment. Extra cutting equipment was brought in as rescue work continued through the evening and into the night.

The cold, grey light of dawn revealed the true scale of the disaster. It was as if a giant had plucked the trains from the track, crumpled them in a rage and hurled them back to the ground. The last remaining bodies were removed to a make-shift mortuary at Lewisham Hospital. Grim faced police officers gathered up the array of personal belongings that littered the scene whilst British Railway workman busied themselves with the task of shoring-up the overhanging sides of the overbridge.

(Permission of the London Fire Brigade.)

The death toll was initially 'officially' listed as 90, although subsequent records would show a slightly higher number due to the victims who succumbed to their injuries.

The communities of Hayes, West Wickham, Elmers End and Eden Park, where my family lived, were hard hit by the tragedy and as a schoolboy I recall the seemingly endless processions to the local crematorium. We all seemed to know at least one family affected by the crash. The inevitable inquiry into the 'Railway Accident at St John's', not Lewisham as it was, found that the colour light signals had been installed at a time when most locomotives were right-hand drive. Conversely Spitfire was driven from the left-hand side which, coupled with the length of the engine's boiler, made the sighting of the signal less easy. However, the point was made that given the weather conditions the train driver should have asked the fireman to assist with the observation of the warning signals from the right-hand side of the cab. Comment was also made on the pre-war, WWII, rolling stock of the electric train, which offered little protection to passengers on impact. The inquiry concluded that the sole blame for the accident rested with the driver of the Ramsgate train. Yet public opinion was divided when the decision was made to charge him with manslaughter. Many felt that little could be gained from prosecuting a man who was never going to wipe from his memory the event of that fateful day. A broken man, he died within a few years.

'JOE'

Chief Officer Joseph Milner's talk to the Brixton Rotary Club

Joseph 'Joe' Milner.

Asea change happened in the London Fire Brigade in 1970. It came in the form of a new Chief Officer; *JOSEPH MILNER*, who was aged forty-seven. He had previously been the Director of the Hong Kong Fire Service. Many would soon discover him to be a forthright man who did not mince his words. He was in stark contrast to the outgoing Chief who, although a man of his time, had given the impression of being particularly uncomfortable in the company of the Brigade's lower ranks. In fact he came across as rather a snob. As Chief he was rarely seen on the fire ground unless it was politically expedient for him to be there. In 1965, to his credit, he had brought together the amalgamation of the Brigades that made up the enlarged London Fire Brigade. He was nevertheless old school, distant from those riding the engines, certainly from the 'firemen's' perspective anyway. The retiring Chief had been a 'toff' and his look as he walked occasionally across the headquarters' drill yard at Lambeth let you know it.

Joe, as he was to be affectionately called, was not tall and was slightly built. He had the appearance of a marathon runner although he was in fact an avid walker. On nights, when on duty in the watchroom, firemen might see him leaving the Headquarters' front lobby around 5 a.m. for his regular six-mile constitutional with his favourite pipe in his mouth. He would return some ninety minutes later, occasionally popping into the watchroom to chat with the dutyman: a practice that would have been a complete anathema to the previous post holder.

In the profile produced for the **London Fireman** magazine, Joe's war record was akin to something taken from the Boy's Own *annual*. Joining the Army before the outbreak of the war, aged seventeen, he ended up in the King's Regiment and in 1942 became one of Wingate's Special Forces. He served in Burma and China until the end of the Japanese war. During his time with the Chindits Joe Milner fought in some of the war's most hazardous operations such as the crucial blocking of the Mandalay railway. His unit flew into Burma in gliders of which only half reached their objective.

His UK Fire Service career had started in 1946 but five years later he transferred to Hong Kong as a Station Officer. He rose through the ranks serving in all branches of the Hong Kong Brigade and as its

Chief brought forward radical changes to the Force, including introducing its Search and Rescue Division, which comprised about ten per cent of the total force.

His tenure as London's Chief Officer would bring about radical change, change set against the background of the industrial unrest so characteristic of the 1970s. That said, Joseph Milner was seen as a firemen's Chief Officer, a respected leader of men and operationally astute. He would depart the Brigade prematurely in 1976. He was made a Commander of the British Empire in 1975 and died at the age of 85 in 2007.

On the evening of 30 October 1971 Joe Milner gave an address to the Brixton Rotary Club, at King Georges House, Stockwell Road. A flavour of this man's belief in the role of the London Fire Brigade and the value with which he held his officers, men and women of his Brigade can easily be seen from the content of that moving and heartfelt talk. His address was later repeated in a special supplement to the **London Fireman** magazine.

An escape ladder in use at a serious blaze in North London. (Mary Evans 10535637.)

When I am invited to address distinguished groups such as this, I am usually pressed to preach about some aspect of fire prevention. On this occasion, however, Mr Jack Westbury made no stipulation about my subject. With so much being preached about the pay of public servants, busmen, policemen and the like in London, I couldn't resist the temptation to speak about the business of a fireman. I therefore asked one of my staff officers to draft me a skeleton talk about the subject. Within an hour or so, he put an almost complete speech on my desk.

My first reaction was that it was too melodramatic, perhaps childishly so, in fact; on reflection, I thought – 'No, dammit, this is the stuff of a fireman's job. This is what it is all about!' This portrays what the TV cameras and journalists cannot portray. It indicates why there is no fire service equivalent of [the TV series] *Softly, Softly* because the fireman's prime tasks are cloaked in the choking anonymity of smoke in which neither TV cameras nor journalists can effectively operate. It tells of the wet rumps and scorched faces which firemen learn to live with.'

So, almost word for word, here is the talk drafted by my staff officer. It starts off with two quotations:

First –

'We conclude that the job of the basic grade fireman is broadly comparable with industrial jobs in the top semi-skilled categories of the lower ranges of the skilled trades…'

This comes from the 1971 Cunningham Report on which Fire Service salaries are currently based.

Lambeth fire station's pump escape in Lambeth Place Road returning from a call. (Mary Evans 10535839.)

Second, a rather older quotation:

'A fireman, to be successful, must enter buildings, he must get in below, above, on every side, from opposite houses, over back walls, over side walls, through panels of doors, through windows, through loopholes, through skylights, through holes cut by himself in the gates, the walls, the roof; he must know how to reach the attic from the basement by ladders placed on half burned stairs, and the basement from the attic by rope made fast on a chimney. His whole success depends on his getting in and remaining there and he must always carry his appliances with him, as without them, he is of no use.'

Semi-skilled, gentlemen?

Those are the words of Sir Eyre Massey Shaw, who commanded the London Fire Brigade from 1861 to 1891, and I repeat, does that sound like semi-skilled work? Massey Shaw's words are instilled into every fireman but in reality, what do they mean? Just what is it like to be a fireman in London today – a fireman, that quite average bloke who lives in the next street, who kisses his wife goodbye, pats his children on the head and having put on his uniform, becomes the emergency man, expected to deal successfully with all manner of crises and at times to put his life in jeopardy to preserve lives and property?

The fireman commences each tour of duty by parading in full firefighting gear and is given precise direction about which fire appliance he is to 'ride' for the shift. He is rigged that he may be inspected to ensure that his personal equipment is in good order. Subsequently, he places his gear on the fire appliance to which he is assigned and exactly in the right position so that when the calls come there can be no confusion, no hesitation, no questioning – straight to the correct appliance, to the correct position and all equipment ready to turn out.

His routine continues with the checking of the appliance and its equipment. Engines to be run, pump tested, ladders checked, breathing apparatus fitted and adjusted and his life support gas cylinder checked for quantity. Lockers on the appliance are opened up, contents checked, position of individual items noted so that instant collection is possible in emergency, whatever the time of day or night and whatever the foulness of the weather. Then there will be continuation training. Drills will be repeatedly practised until each man instinctively knows his part and the team works efficiently, speedily and virtually without directive. Only thus will crews react together under great stress, when the 'chips' are down. But over 87,000 times per year, the London firemen, whether at drill, lecture, meal or rest, have to race to their appliances. The drivers rev up impatiently, while the teleprinter clatters out the address of the emergency. Brief directions are given to the driver, the appliance room doors swing open and the appliances turn out.

Now the often hair-raising drive through dense traffic – speed is vital but so is safety! Two tone horns and flashing lights help to clear the way and serve also to reassure those in trouble that help is on the way. Whilst the driver is concentrating on his roadmanship, the remainder of the crew are completing their dressing and checking the hydrant locations for the area. The officer-in-charge is mentally summoning up his topographical knowledge. What kind of property? What peculiar operational problems does the property present? The adrenalin is pumping through each man ready for some yet unknown demand on his system.

Often their arrival is an anti-climax – a false alarm, an insignificant incident – important to attend but still an anti-climax for men keyed up to action, and then the adrenalin drains away. Incredibly, men feel washed out, lethargic, yet no real effort has been expended.

Bottom left: Typical roll call at a London fire station. (Permission of Mike Pinchen.)

Bottom centre: Hook ladder drill from the head of an escape ladder during the 1970s. (Permission of Mike Pinchen.)

Bottom right: BA (breathing apparatus.) firemen exiting from a smoky blaze in central London. (Permission of the London Fire Brigade.)

Many times, however, the adrenalin is needed, some super-human effort is demanded of them and always, thank God, is forthcoming.

Fire in a local supermarket

Perhaps it's a fire in a medium sized supermarket of four floors and a basement, all of which may be smoke logged. The officer-in-charge will not yet know exactly where the fire is located within the building. His first task will be to radio for reinforcing appliances and to organise teams of breathing apparatus wearers to search for and locate any casualties and the seat of the fire. These teams will grope their way forward. Members of each team will keep close together so that they may aid each other if trouble comes. They must remember each door they pass through, each turn they make, so that there can be no confusion about the way out. Each foot must be placed carefully forward lest floors, weakened by fire or rot, give way and plunge men into an inferno.

Always they sense the heat, for its intensity tells them whether they are approaching the seat of the fire, yet they must always be alert for a sudden general build-up of heat for it might indicate a developing flash-over when the super-heated gases detonate into flame to scorch all in its path.

As the search progresses, it may be found that the fire is in a basement into which the crews must force an entry. Tugging with them their heavy charged hose, they must find and move down the stairways to the basement. On their rumps or bellies now, they will be hot and sweaty, their clothing will be covered in filth and saturated with water. First they must go through the heat band, that band of high temperature gases which builds up at ceiling level, toasting their exposed skin. Totally blinded by the thick smoke, they must feel their way down each step carefully testing each stair tread before trusting their full weight on it. Spraying water to cool the atmosphere as they go, they will reach the base of the stairs. It's possibly a little cooler at the bottom but still thick with smoke. Now they may be confronted with a confusion of passageways. These they must penetrate and explore, conscious that fire may flash over above them but comforted by the confidence they have that there are others behind to support them. At intervals they must check the gauges which show the quantity of oxygen left in the cylinders of their breathing apparatus – they must always have enough left to make the journey back to safety.

A child is rescued from the uppers floors of this blaze in Brompton Road, Fulham whilst an anxious mother looks on. (Mary Evans 10795542.)

Then suddenly the fire flares up somewhere in front, jets of water are directed at the flames and a dense cloud of hissing, scalding steam envelopes the men. Isolated from the outside, knowing only their little part of the whole affair, they hang on trusting that others are playing their part also and that their means of retreat are being securely held. Soon, although the minutes seem like hours, they know they are winning. The scalding heat begins to lose its sting. The air at the lowest level is cool and by wiping your goggles and tucking your head low, you can begin to see, even though the smoke and steam still lingers in a thick layer above. They move on, searching for the small lingering pockets of fire, but now they are tired, that remarkable something that drove them on has evaporated. They are wet, beginning to feel chilled even and will be glad to see the outside again. When they are relieved, they drag themselves back through the smoke and heat stained passages and up into the open air. Once there, they will be cold, very cold, very wet and very worn out. They will take off their breathing sets and be sent to the canteen van for a cup of hot tea. As like as not, an onlooker to whom nothing seems to have been going on, will suggest in a loud voice that the firemen should be putting water on the fire, not lolling around with cups of tea. But they have done well, they will know they have done well and they will have that sense of satisfaction that comes from achievement.

Multiple rescues from this 1960s office building blaze in West London. (Permission of the London Fire Brigade.)

Dead of night and no light

Ladies and Gentlemen, try to imagine what it's like – think of yourself in your own home, dead of night, not a light on and remember how difficult it is to grope your way around even in your own familiar surroundings. Now recall the day you burned some rubbish in the garden and an unkind breeze blew smoke towards you and you coughed and choked so you had to move away. Imagine switching on the electric fire and trying to hold your face about 12 inches away, even for a few seconds. Then imagine all these things happening to you at once, with you in your heaviest overcoat that is saturated with water. Yes – it feels something like that – except, of course, you wouldn't be in much danger.

Such a fire as I have tried to describe could, of course, be complicated by people being trapped. Frequently, rescues can be a quite straightforward operation if people are at windows. A mere pitching of a ladder and bringing the people down; fire, heat and smoke make for some difficulty but for the well trained crew, a routine procedure.

Sometimes, of course, the rescue effort is well beyond routine procedure. At one hotel fire, a number of rescues had been effected when one man, himself just rescued, reported that his wife was still in a back room on the third floor. Direct access for ladders of any type was impossible. The nearest approach was from a projecting roof of a rear extension to the hotel at third floor level. From this roof, it would be possible to reach the window sill of the room in which the woman was reported trapped, by negotiating a four to five foot gap. Below, a sheer drop of fifty feet. On the projecting roof, firemen were subjected to heat from flames which belched from windows immediately above and below. One fireman made the attempt, he stretched out across the gap, climbed through the window into the thick smoke. Reaching down, his hand touched a bare foot.

Tugging hard, he drew the body towards the window but heat and smoke were too much and he had to withdraw and be pulled back to safety by his colleagues on the roof. By now the heat was intense and from the ground a jet of water was directed on the men to keep them cool. Still they persisted. A fireman in breathing apparatus made the attempt. Encumbered though he was by his set, he stretched over the gap and entered the window. Fire was now entering the room but he found the woman, pulled her to the window, lifted her head and arms clear of the smoke. From there, his colleagues on the roof reached out to take her hands, then dragging her through the window, held on to her arms and swung her across the gap then on to the roof. Now the fireman had to be helped back over the gap before they carried the woman down the ladder to safety.

The lady spent some weeks in hospital with severe internal burns to the throat, breathing tubes and lungs – an indication of the severe heat experienced in that room. Elsewhere at the same fire, men carrying hook ladders balanced for 15 feet along the top of a 9-inch wide wall to reach an old lady trapped on the first floor. Having reached her, they carried her back by the same route. The penalty for slipping? – a twenty foot drop to concrete paving below.

There are, of course, hazards which are lesser known to the public. Stone staircases, when subjected to heat then sudden cooling, will almost certainly collapse without warning. Tons of stone crashing down is no nice prospect. One fireman was on a third floor landing of such a staircase when collapse occurred. He had just enough time to fling himself forward, grasp a window sill and was left clinging by his fingertips.

The Smithfield meat market fire in 1958 that tragically cost the lives of two London firemen. (Mary Evans 10535602.)

Thirty feet below the pile of masonry was all that remained of the staircase he had stood on just a second or two previously.

Then there are the gas cylinders heated up to explosive potential, the chemicals which produce deadly gases, the radiation risks, the compressed air workings all adding their own complications to the fireman's problems.

And above all, there is the human canvas – so much does the fireman see of human tragedy. Of homes destroyed – it is easy to read but less easy to take when those to whom it was home are all about you. The burns, the injuries, the children suffering. These things matter to the fireman who so closely shares these personal tragedies with those who suffer them. Sometimes we are too late or perhaps help was never possible and then the sad task of lifting the part-consumed charred remains of some unfortunate, of wrapping in a sheet and taking it to a waiting ambulance.

'He's alright, my dear, we've got him'

But there are those moments of sheer satisfaction. To snatch a child from peril and breathe back life into a seemingly lifeless body. To take to a whimpering child the pet she prematurely mourns. To whisper to a distraught wife: 'He's alright, my dear, we've got him, he's alright'.

There is another role for firemen not connected with fire, which we term the 'special service call'. I suppose it was inevitable that events would dictate that the fire brigade, capable of carrying heavy rescue equipment and ready for instant turn-out around the clock, would eventually develop into the emergency service able to deal with situations which are beyond the capabilities of other services.

So firemen find themselves waist deep in flood waters to rescue people or to pump out flooded premises. They find themselves with the problem of rescue at train crashes, where casualties suffer terrible injuries. They risk injury to release animals being sucked down in sewage pits or bogged down in a muddy river bed threatened by rising water. They climb ladders to release birds entangled in overhead telegraph wires. They crawl beneath underground trains to release the luckless who have fallen under. They cut, pull, and push at metal to release people from their crushed cars. They wander in clouds of ammonia fumes, explosive corrosive fumes, seeking the valve to close off the leak. They climb untoward precariously and talk, cajole, persuade some temporarily deranged person from jumping to death and they wait patiently for that moment when the opportunity will come to lunge and hold and bring them safely down. They will even release the child whose head is stuck in railings, a position which seems to infect all and sundry to a point where gales of laughter emit – for everyone except the poor, frightened little kid.

Then there are the lifts, those which break down and leave the occupants firmly imprisoned between floors until the fireman comes to work his magic and wind the lift by hand to a landing. And in the factory, people get limbs enmeshed in machinery and again comes Mr Emergency to get them out.

So it goes on, each day it seems brings new hazards, new challenges. Today, serving in my brigade, are many who experienced the Canvey Island Floods, the Harrow train crash, the Lewisham train crash, the Southall air disaster, the great and tragic fires of Broad Street, Covent Garden, Smithfield, and a thousand lesser tragedies between.

May I close with two short examples of the true life drama as seen by firemen. The first, a great success story, the second, one which demanded the ultimate sacrifice from two firemen who took part.

In 1969, the brigade was called to a fire in a hotel in the Bayswater area. On arrival, the officer-in-charge saw a hotel of six floors, about 200 feet in length. Smoke was issuing from all floors in the centre of the building. Three people at third floor windows were calling for help. A ladder was pitched to effect the rescues and a hasty message was dispatched seeking reinforcements. At that moment, as if in response to a command, scores of windows opened at all floor levels.

Chief Officer Joe Milner talking to his firemen during the extended and difficult extrication of the dead at the Moorgate disaster. (Permission of the London Fire Brigade.)

From these windows smoke began to billow and frightened faces appeared, calling, screaming for help. And so a massive rescue operation began. As reinforcing appliances arrived, so the face of the building was festooned with ladders. Hook ladders, escape ladders, extension ladders, turntable ladders. More and more firemen clawed their way up the face of the building to the rescue, others entered the building to fight the fire inside.

One by one the trapped people were reached – one by one they were brought down. Panic was averted by firemen calling reassuringly to those who waited their turn, though indeed, there were moments when illogically, people began throwing out suitcases and hysteria seemed likely to take over. Quite how many were saved was never determined, but conservative estimates gave fifty. The important thing is that no life was lost.

A few short months before that a fire raged in the basement of a restaurant. Two firemen in breathing apparatus crawled into the ground floor. Seconds later those outside heard a great roar, saw a flash of flame engulf the ground floor, belch out into the street and then quickly subside. In seconds other firemen

The fifty pump fire in Tooley Street, Bermondsey in 1971 and an injured fireman, burned in a 'flashover', is placed in an ambulance prior to his removal to hospital. (Mary Evans 10535862.)

had dragged their friends into the street. They were burned – severely burned. Taken to hospital, they were suspended above the beds for there was no unburned skin upon which to lie. For three days they suffered and then, one shortly after the other, they died. They paid the full price – some might say, plus some.

Right: Her Majesty the Queen arrives at the Brigade Headquarters in 1975 to pay her thanks to members of the London Fire Brigade who were involved in dealing with the aftermath of the IRA's bombing campaign in London. (Mary Evans 10576438.)

Opposite: A major blaze near the Elephant and Castle, south London that involved twenty pumps before it was finally brought under control. (Mary Evans 10535235.)

Lest you feel I quote a few isolated examples to dramatise, may I just quote some facts and figures?

Since 1965, nine London firemen have been killed and 748 injured in the exercise of their duties. In 1972, the London Fire Brigade attended 87,406 calls; they rescued 222 people from fires and 192 animals from the same hazard or other; 257 people were extricated from crushed vehicles. 3,226 people were released from lifts and, on average the number of calls increased by 10 per cent each year.

Forgive me for deviating from the normal type of talk. I felt you would like to know what you get, as ratepayers, from your fireman. By fireman, I mean every uniformed man in the London Fire Brigade from the rank of fireman upwards. Behind the operational activities I have described, there are, of course, support elements whose sterling work, though less spectacular, plays a significant role in keeping the London Fire Brigade second to none and better than most. These unseen elements include the control room staffs, who mobilise the brigade's resources to deal with the 87,000 incidents and the non-uniformed staff of clerks, secretaries and administrative officers and workshops personnel who deal with all our multifarious logistic problems. I wish time permitted me to talk to you about their work.

KLEINMAN

*PAUL KLEINMAN started his fire service career at Lambeth fire station in the 1970s. He was a regular contributor to the **London Fireman/Firefighter** magazine, providing a wealth of amusing and intriguing fire brigade tales. When his operational career ended he took up a non-operational position in the Protective Equipment Group, based at Croydon. Still he was the purveyor of wonderful stories, so it would be remiss not to include one of his yarns in this anthology.*

The Quiet Man

My name is Tom. I have been the mess manager at this busy inner London station for more years than I care to remember. I've seen lots of people came and go, had lots of guvnors and met all types of people. Albert was one who was different, a one off. I doubt if I'll ever see the like again.

Albert was unknown to us when he first joined the watch. He was a turntable ladder (TL) driver at another station and had spent most of his career at the far end of the division. Our only TL driver had recently retired and as there was no one willing to take his place, Albert was transferred, reluctantly, onto our watch.

Of course, those were the days when the TLs were open to the elements, and the crew was at the mercy of the weather. Not for nothing was this particular fire engine known as the 'pneumonia wagon'. Mind you it looked like everybody's idea of a fire engine, with its gleaming long bonnet, polished bell and shinning brass work. The local street kids stood at the open station doors and cheered when the mighty engine roared into life and the machine charged off down the road.

Albert's driving was a style all of its own. As far as he was concerned there was only one gear and that was third! He would start, stop, go up hills, and down them all in the same gear, almost like an automatic, except that they weren't in common use back then. But he did have one good point. He was a walking atlas. A Mr A to Z. He hadn't been on our ground five minutes before he knew every side road, back alley and obscure courtyard. He knew which way the house numbers ran, where the hydrants were, the entrances to every major risk, all the one-way traffic systems, not only on our ground but neighbours stations grounds as well. This made him very popular with the guvnor as valuable seconds could be gained when the driver knew exactly where to go all the time. (Not that we didn't, but before Albert arrived we did have to consult a street map sometimes.)

Albert settled down, upset nobody and soon became a popular member of the watch: except for one thing – his almost unnatural silence. He would turn up for a tour of duty, always at exactly the same time, mutter a 'Good morning' or 'Good evening, folks' and that was all you would hear from him till the end of the shift, when it was 'See you, folks' and he was gone.

He worked well, never shirked and never tried to dodge anything unpleasant. It was just his eerie silence that nearly drove us mad. He never laughed at a joke, no matter how funny, and never made one up either. He never joined in any of the watch's badinage, took part in any of the 'wind-ups' or said anything about his personal life. He never said where he lived, whether he was married or single or even if he had any family at all.

We did hear on the grapevine that Albert was a hero. But never a word of it was breathed to us by Albert. It seems that one day Albert and the officer in charge of the TL turned up at a fire in a large old factory on a neighbouring fire station's ground. The building was five storeys tall and flames were seen coming from the first four floors. The firemen were just about to take the first lengths of hose into the blazing building when there was an almighty explosion and the main entrance and staircase inside disappeared in a pile of rubble. Fortunately, the people inside the factory had all evacuated when the fire alarm sounded, or so was thought. Suddenly however, screams were heard coming from the fifth floor. Looking up, a man was seen at one of the fifth floor windows, frantically waving his arms and shouting for help. The only way to reach him was via the TL.

Quick as a wink Albert pitched the ladder perfectly into a position for his colleague to rescue the desperate man. The brave colleague climbed to the top of the ladder and used his axe to clear the broken window glass so the man could clamber through. But the man was too large to get through the window unaided, and out onto the ladder. There was no option but for the fireman to climb into the building, via the window, and try to shove the man out onto the ladder. This he did and the man gratefully clambered onto the top of the swaying ladder and started to climb down the ladder towards the ground. Albert had shot up the ladder to help the man down, expecting his colleague to be close behind. Looking up, Albert saw he was in a lot of trouble. The fire had finally broken through to the fifth floor and a sudden blast of hot gases had caused the window opening to collapse leaving the colleague jammed in the distorted frame. Without hesitation Albert clawed his way past the descending man to the top of the ladder. When he got there flames were licking around the trapped fireman. Using a combination of his bare hands and an axe, Albert pushed, hacked and tore the twisted window frame apart, even though his hands and face were severely burned. Eventually by sheer guts and dogged perseverance he pulled his semi-conscious mate clear, and half carrying, half guiding brought him safely back down to the ground, although they were both badly burned.

When Albert was eventually discharged from hospital he refused any kind of gallantry award or recognition of his heroism. 'I was only doing my job' was the best anyone could get out of him. And that was that.

Even the guvnor gave up trying to get Albert to say something. Once when Albert was in the station office putting his fire boots in for repair the guvnor asked him how he was enjoying his new station. Albert merely shrugged his shoulders and muttered it was alright but not as good as his old one. Then he clammed up and refused to say another word.

Station life carried on until the morning Albert failed to report for duty. You could set your watch by Albert. Without fail, exactly half an hour before the start of the shift you could hear Albert's battered old motorbike chugging into the station yard. Never a moment earlier or a moment later. Except that morning it didn't. Shortly after we found out why. The police were on the phone to say a fireman from our station had had a nasty accident and was in a serious condition at the local hospital.

When we got to see him his leg was in traction and you could hardly see his face for bandages. Not that he seemed particularly pleased to see us but he was a mate and we kept up our visits. We found he was married but had no children.

His wife was a nice friendly woman but as she didn't drive and Albert, like most firemen at that time, didn't own a car, visiting him was difficult. NO problem. The Brigade provided transport. We provided transport. Hardly a day passed without one of us visiting him or taking his wife to see him. He was well looked after by Welfare and the Fireman's Benevolent Fund and of course we carried on doing our bit. We even collected his motorbike and repaired it for him.

Eventually the time came when Albert was again fit for duty. Now don't get me wrong, firemen, as a group, are the kind of people to do someone a favour and not expect thanks. It is our inbuilt instinct to help others or we wouldn't be in the job. But when Albert reported for duty for the first time after his accident, not a word. Alright, he didn't drink so he wouldn't be expected to stand us a round at the local at the end of a day shift. But one word of thanks would have been nice. Not on and on you understand – just once. But no. Not a word!

We just shrugged our shoulders and carried on. We would have done exactly the same again, if needs be, anyway, Albert, for his part, carried on exactly as if nothing had happened, Just, 'Morning folks', 'See you folks'. And that was that.

Then a bit of a bombshell! Albert was sent to standby at another station as our TL was under repair and there was no spare. The next we heard was he had hit another fireman from that station and had flattened him with just one punch. Now that wasn't like Albert. Quiet yes, aggressive never. It turned out that the person he had hit didn't want to press charges. He had said something out of order, apologised to Albert and as far as he was concerned the matter was over.

But it wasn't as far as out guvnor was concerned. As soon as the news of the incident reached his ears he ordered Albert into the station office. So there was Albert, dressed in his best bib and tucker, seated in the old man's inner office. 'Now Albert,' said the guvnor. 'Like any responsible Station Officer I can't allow one of my firemen to go around hitting people. Unless you can give me a good explanation I may be compelled to take this matter further.'

Albert said not a word. Our guvnor was now starting to get a bit rattled and said to Albert in a raised voice. 'Albert, this is your last chance. You either tell me exactly what occurred when you hit that bloke or you'll be on a fizzer for dumb insolence for starters. Now, for the last time, what happened?'

Albert looked at his feet, then muttered in a low voice, almost audible. 'I heard him say something nasty about my new station.'

LONDON SALVAGE CORPS

By Gordon White

The London Salvage Corps tenders attending this major fire at the Leinster Towers Hotel in West London in June 1969. Multiple rescues were performed by the London Fire Brigade at the incident, many via hook ladders, whilst the Salvage Corps worked inside the building minimising the damage from smoke and water. (Permission of the London Fire Brigade.)

In 1973 and around 3,500 times a year the appliance room doors at London Salvage Corps headquarters in Aldersgate crash open to allow the salvagemen to speed their way to all parts of the capital.

The Corps, with just 112 uniformed personnel, obviously cannot follow the Brigade to every incident and the decision whether or not they do turn out is left to the officer-of-the-day. Because of the high risks involved in Central London and the dock areas, as in the latter case, this is in a state of rapid decline – the Corps invariably responds to the initial call in these instances.

For incidents in the outer London boroughs and districts the Corps will normally wait for the informative message to be sent back by the Brigade. The Corps has both full 'listening in' and teleprinter facilities – before deciding what action, if any, to take.

'Operating from just one station we have to bear in mind the time it will take us to get there and what action we might be able to take when we arrive,' said the Corps' deputy chief officer, Mr T. L. Plumer.

Many people, when informed that the Corps is independent from the fire brigade and is paid for by the insurance companies, believe mistakenly that the salvagemen will only set to work at insured risks.

There is no such discrimination and salvage work is carried out without regard to insurances. Thus, much of the Corps' work is of a 'public service' nature, particularly with regard to calls to Government buildings.

The equipment carried on a standard salvage tender is comprehensive enough to cover virtually every aspect of salvage work, and includes salvage sheets, roof covering, and pumps. Deodorising apparatus for clearing the smell of smoke, heaters, brooms, squeegees, mops, scoops, buckets, keys, saws, hammers, ladders, lamps, padlocks – you name it and the LSC more than likely carries it!

Naturally enough one of the Corps' major tasks is to restrict the amount of damage that can be done to property by the water used to extinguish the fire. This is done by the construction of intricate channels and dams with salvage sheets, strategically placed trays to catch dripping water, removing objects to dry areas and ensuring that water already spilling about can drain away. Fans can be brought in to ventilate premises, corrugated sheets used to secure broken windows and doors and roofing sheets used to keep out the elements.

'It is virtually impossible to estimate the amount of money that is saved by this work, but what is important is that in many cases the Corps' attendance means firms can soon be back in business,' said DCO Plumer.

The treatment of the contents of a building after a fire is vitally important and where possible the Corps makes full use of its heating apparatus for drying-out purposes. Where machinery and tools have become soaked these are dried and oiled to prevent rusting, furniture is leathered and dried, sprinkler systems are reinstated and the premises properly secured.

London Salvage Corps attending a major fire in Eversholt Street, west London. (Mary Evans 10535664.)

The causes of the incidents it attends are also investigated by the Corps, and any important details are brought to the notice of the insuring company and loss adjusters, who have the ultimate responsibility for the recovery, custody and disposal of salvage.

Much, if not most, of the Corps' valuable work goes unheralded and unnoticed by the public, and this is the way that Chief Officer Mr R. V. Seels likes it. 'If people are kind enough to thank us for our work we are satisfied, but we will not go out to seek praise,' he said. The Corps may only get a handful of major incidents in a year, but the total amount of money saved by restricting damage to a minimum certainly runs into many, many thousands of pounds.

At a time when fire losses are soaring to sky-high proportions there may well be a case for the insurance companies to consider setting up a couple of 'satellite' stations for the Corps in other parts of the capital.

Food for thought anyway.

Footnote

That never happened, quite the reverse in fact. Whilst, by the 1980s, the London Salvage Corps attended all fire calls in the City of London and its local surrounding fire station areas, and all significant fires and floods in the Greater London area, it was not to last. Despite the fact that they worked successfully alongside the London Fire Brigade, controlling damage by protecting contents from the firefighting operations, pumping out, ventilating and drying out, then temporary roofed and offered security protection including post fire and security watching duties, serious concern was being raised about the cost of the service.

It was in the early 1980s that meetings took place between the Insurance Office representatives, Central Government and the London Fire Brigade with a view to incorporating the services under-taken by the Corps into the London Fire Brigade. As a result an agree-ment was reached and the Corps was disbanded in April 1984. All of its equipment, vehicles and Headquarters premises were offered to the London Fire Brigade, much of which was accepted and used. The staff were not as lucky: due to reasons of age, recruiting condi-tions and staffing costs, very few of the general staff were trained and absorbed into the London Fire Brigade. Those remaining were offered early retirement (depending on their age and service) and the rest were made redundant.

Salvage Tender at work in the City of London. (Courtesy of Gerard Paul.)

LONDON'S FIRST: BRAIDWOOD

By Gordon White

Britain's first properly organised municipal fire brigade was that of Edinburgh, in 1824. Chosen to lead this brigade was a 23-year-old surveyor named James Braidwood. He had under him eighty firemen, all part-timers, who were chosen from trades associated with methods of building construction such as masons, slaters, plumbers, etc., as it was felt that the knowledge of men working in these trades would help them in their new job. Braidwood trained and drilled his brigade until they became the most proficient in Britain. He encouraged his men to attack the fire at its source rather than just pour water into a building which was alight and to creep low to gain the benefit of the layer of relatively fresh air drawn in from outside by convection from the blaze.

James Braidwood, the first Superintendent of the London Fire Engine Establishment, established in 1833. (Permission of the London Fire Brigade.)

The Braidwood black leather fireman's helmet of the LFEE, later replaced with the brass helmets by Captain Massey Shaw for his Metropolitan Fire Brigade firemen. (Permission of the London Fire Brigade.)

In 1833 the leading London insurance brigades decided to amalgamate into a combined unit and it was agreed that Braidwood should head this establishment. His salary was £250.00 per annum, a respectable sum in those days.

The London Fire Engine Establishment, as this new force was called, comprised the brigades of the Alliance, Atlas, Globe, Imperial, London Protector, Royal Exchange, Sun, Union and Westminster insurance companies. The LFEE had eighty full time firemen and nineteen fire stations. Conditions were severe; two men were always on a 24 hour watch while the remainder had always to be within the station building in readiness for call-out at any time. Each man was officially on duty 168 hours a week, leaving just four hours of spare time. The pay of £1.0s.0d was good, however, and Braidwood had no difficulty in finding recruits, mainly from men used to working long hours for little pay on the rivers and waterways.

The growth of London was too much for the insurance firemen and the City of London demanded a new force after a series of disastrous large fires found their firefighting skills seriously wanting. With just his whole-time 'professional' firemen, Braidwood started structured fire training, established a duty system and brought new ideas and original techniques into fire-fighting. Getting 'stuck in' would be the hallmark of future

The 1861 warehouse fire in Southwark that would bring about the demise of James Braidwood. (Courtesy of the London Fire Brigade Museum.)

generations of firemen who followed these early practitioners of their craft. His men were trained in the dark, and made to get near the source of a fire, crawling low on their hands and knees, and below the rising hot gases. He also insisted that no fireman enter a building alone, stating that there should also be a 'buddy' or comrade to assist in the case of an accident or if a man collapsed in the heat or fumes.

In 1834 Braidwood's LFEE attended a fire at the Houses of Parliament and despite the efforts of sixty-four men and twelve engines only Westminster Hall was saved. The buildings were not insured and the proprietors of the London Fire Engine Establishment petitioned the government to set up a proper organised firefighting force. The government, sensing considerable expenditure, declined, leaving the fire protection of central London in the hands of the insurance companies. They did, however, agree to the provision of buckets, hand pumps and a few fire engines for use at important places, but when the Tower of London Armoury was destroyed by fire in October 1841 the firefighting equipment there was found to be in a sorry state.

Occasionally the insurance companies' brigade was powerless to act, even though their equipment was kept in first class order. One such incident occurred in a particularly cold January night in 1838 when the Royal Exchange caught fire. The wooden fire plugs in the street mains were frozen solid and when alternative water supplies were found the engine froze solid too.

Some private concerns formed their own fire brigades and often fought side by side with the LFEE. One such brigade was that of Frederick Hodges, who owned a distillery at Lambeth. Hodges claimed that his brigade, in relation to its size, was better equipped than Braidwood's, and thanks to a specially built 120 foot high look-out mast, his brigade could often reach the scene of the fire before the LFEE, who then missed the reward paid to the first engine to the scene of a blaze.

Though he was always seeking ways to improve the efficiency of the brigade, Braidwood was basically opposed to steam fire engines as he felt the powerful jet with this type of engine would encourage his men to revert to the old 'long-shot' method of firefighting instead of tackling the fire at its heart. He did, however, introduce a floating steam fire engine to deal with waterfront fires and a Shand horse drawn steamer was being experimented with in 1861.

But in that year, 1861, a six-storey warehouse, full of highly flammable goods, including hemp and cotton, caught fire in

The funeral procession of James Braidwood in 1861.

James Braidwood's funeral procession.

Tooley Street, near the River Thames in Southwark. Braidwood took command of the fire and decided to investigate one of the burning buildings. He paused to lend his red-spotted handkerchief to a friend whose eyes had been affected by the smoke. He had just taken a few more steps when the red hot brickwork of a tall warehouse wall bulged dangerously outwards and collapsed onto Braidwood. It was three days before his body could be recovered from the debris.

London's first fire chief was given a hero's funeral, one befitting the high regard that he had secured in London's population. His funeral cortège was one and a half miles long, and all the church bells in the City of London tolled a farewell to this brave fireman.

Braidwood's plaque, Tooley Street. (Courtesy of Stephen Jacob.)

MASSEY SHAW –
THE MAN

by R Wheatley, BSc (Econ.)

M

n the library at headquarters is a bronze statuette of the first Chief Officer of the Brigade – Captain Eyre Massey Shaw. It stands about two feet tall, and shows a tall, slim, bearded man, bare headed and in uniform. I'm not competent to judge it as a work of art, but it seems very fine – rather aristocratic, perhaps. It affords, I'm sure, an excellent insight into the character of a very remarkable man.

The statuette of Captain Eyre Massey Shaw, First Chief Fire Officer of the Metropolitan Fire Brigade. (Mary Evans 10795014.)

Two of Shaw's Metropolitan Fire Brigade escape conductors at the Southwark headquarters. (Permission of the London Fire Brigade.)

Shaw was born in Ireland in 1828 of a Scots-Irish family which had settled in Ireland in the seventeenth century. George Bernard Shaw, the playwright, was another member of the family. After attending Dr Coghlan's school in Dublin, he studied at Trinity College and took his MA there in 1854. It was intended by his family that he should enter the Church, but when the time came for him to take Holy Orders, he couldn't face it, and bolted to America.

This is so unrepresentative of Shaw, to run away from some-thing – that it deserves examination. Why should a serious minded, intellectual type of man like Shaw refuse to enter a profession which seemed likely to prove congenial and where his family could secure him preferment? The answer might lie in family letters, but these do not exist, to my knowledge; and I can only speculate as to the true explanation.

The years of Shaw's childhood and early manhood though they may have been happy enough for him personally, as the third son of Bernard Robert Shaw of Monkstown Castle he is unlikely to have suffered any material hardship, were far from kind to Ireland. The years between 1840 and 1850 were the years of the famine. I believe as many as eight million people died from starvation in Ireland or emigrated to avoid it, approximately half the population. Villages and towns were emptied, and corpses lined the roadsides. The effect on a sensitive boy from riding home from school through villages where death and disease had carried off half their inhabitants, where starving women shook their fists at anyone on a horse, or were even too apathetic to protest, must have been disturbing. He might even have doubted the benevolence of his Maker, and the value of the Protestant Church for which he was intended.

Anyway, Shaw took ship to America and stayed there several months. One incident occurred which is worth comment. While staying in a hotel in New York, the hotel caught fire and the guests had to evacuate the building. There is little doubt that the incident made an indelible impression on Shaw. He returned home, on the understanding that he might choose another career.

In 1855, a commission was obtained for him in the North Cork Rifles, a militia regiment – and he married a Portuguese lady from Lisbon. By 1859 he had risen to the rank of Captain and was the father of two children, but he had still to find a profession that suited him. In 1860 he left the Army to become Chief Constable and Superintendent of Fire Services in Belfast and was at once a success. He quelled the riots between Sinn Feiners and Orangemen without forfeiting the respect of either party, and reorganised the Fire Services which had been in very poor order. It was this latter achievement which led to his appointment to succeed James Braidwood as Superintendent of the London Fire Engine Establishment after Braidwood was killed by a falling wall in the disastrous warehouse fire at Tooley Street in 1861.

The years from 1862 to 1865 were Shaw's years of apprenticeship when he acquired a detailed knowledge of every aspect of firefighting. The London Fire Engine Establishment was a small and vastly overworked force paid for by the insurance companies. It never numbered more than 130 men or 19 stations, but it was well trained and completely professional. Under its first Superintendent it had won a remarkable reputation for efficiency and considerable popularity.

The Tooley Street fire, however, had persuaded the insurance companies and the public that the defence of London against fire should not be a matter for private enterprise, though the Duke of Wellington had thought it should, and the Metropolitan Fire Brigade was established on 1st January 1866. Captain Shaw was the natural choice for its first Chief Officer. The men from the London Fire Engine Establishment formed the core of the new Brigade, and added to them and their stations and equipment were the escapes and conductors of the Royal Society for the Protection of Life from Fire. Later, Shaw persuaded his employers, the Metropolitan Board of Works, to buy those fire engines of the London parishes which were in good working order.

The Brigade at this time was composed exclusively of seamen, from the Royal Navy and the Merchant Navy, who were used to irregular hours and living in confined quarters. Shaw was a stern but fair martinet, rising at 3 a.m. to drill and train his men when the streets were empty, but there was no doubt of his personal popularity. When men refer to a senior officer formally by name or rank it implies a lack of acceptance, if not of active dislike or disrespect. Shaw was universally known among his firemen as the 'Skipper' or 'the Long 'Un'.

At a fire in the basement of a big warehouse in Upper Thames Street, a fireman was struggling to drag a hose towards the centre of the fire when dimly through the smoke he noticed someone behind him. He suggested quickly and coarsely, that the long person behind him should give him a useful hand with the heavy hose instead of aimlessly standing about doing absolutely nothing. Shaw merely told a fireman with him to take up the hose as suggested. There was no further outcome to the incident.

This story contrasts nicely with that of a subsequent Chief Officer who very early in his Brigade career arrived at a fire and angrily demanded of the officer in charge why the firemen were not formed up on parade and awaiting his orders. I don't know what the officer said in reply, but I imagine his expression would have been sufficient indication that London firemen don't wait to be told what to do at a fire.

Perhaps a better clue to Shaw's personality lies in the care he showed for his men's safety at fires. Warehouses at that time presented a particular risk. They were commonly built of brick with unprotected steel or iron girders to support the floors and roof. In a fierce fire the girders would expand with the heat and push out the walls of the building. The floors, in turn, are liable to collapse. A fireman directing a hose through a lower window from the street is particularly exposed to danger from falling brickwork. Shaw took the greatest pains to see that his men were posted in positions where they would be safe.

On one occasion in the 1880s, at a very big fire at the King and Queen Granaries, Shaw was superintendent of firefighting operations when there was a crash of brickwork. The huge walls, bulging under the weight of swollen maize and tons of water, looked as if they were going to collapse. One of the firemen who was directing a jet from the centre of an escape, dropped his hose, slid down the escape, and started to run. Shaw caught him by the arm as he ran. 'Don't run,' he told him, 'you run into danger. Go and pick up your hose and carry on. I'll tell you when to run.' The fireman looked at the bulging walls, looked at his Chief Officer, who stood quietly on the very spot where the walls would crash if they did collapse, picked up the nozzle and resumed his work. The walls did collapse, but not till three days later.

Finally, Shaw backed his men on every occasion when they made representations for improvements in their pay and conditions. For three shillings a day when he joined, a man was required to remain continuously on duty, fully dressed in uniform, boots, belt and axe. If he took off his boots, he was liable to be fined the best part of a day's pay. Leave was allowed for a few hours during the day with the station officer's agreement, but beyond this, or after 10 o'clock at night, Shaw's personal permission was necessary. When recruiting was poor and men fell ill, firemen might be on duty for six days at a time, never shifting out of their clothes.

In 1884, the position at last improved, and Station Officers could grant leave for 24 hours, District Officers could grant leave for 48 hours, but this was a special privilege, not a right, and the firemen were still otherwise employed on continuous duty. The strain on the men was enormous. Shaw could ensure that few died on active duty – there were, in fact, only ten deaths in the 30 years he was Chief Officer – but he could not prevent the breakdown in health and early retirement to which many were forced.

It is difficult to estimate how much these conditions arose from public parsimony – the Metropolitan Board of Works ran the Brigade on a very cheap shoestring – and how much from the defects in Shaw's own character. There is a modern tendency to look for feet of clay on every idol, and I think it likely that Shaw had his faults. If nothing else, he had some of the defects of his many virtues. His powers of leadership almost certainly surpassed those of any other fireman in the world at that time, but he seems to have been quite unable to secure the backing of any elected body or committee with whom he had dealings.

He was an aristocrat by birth and an autocrat by nature. He expected implicit obedience from his subordinates. I don't suppose he ever forgot for a single moment that he was a gentleman on the friendliest terms with Royalty. The statuette I spoke of at the beginning was made by Prince Victor of Hohenlohe-Langenburg, a son of Queen Victoria's half-sister, who was a very talented amateur sculptor. When Shaw was

Captain Massey Shaw, officers and men of the Metropolitan Fire Brigade waiting on the Prince of Wales and his Royal party as they visit the Brigade's headquarters at Southwark on 23 October 1883. (Mary Evans 10536017.)

Photographic portrait of Captain Massey Shaw, who was knighted upon his retirement from the fire brigade. (Permission of the London Fire Brigade.)

injured at a fire in 1883 which left him with a permanent limp – he collected several injuries in the courses of his firefighting career – the Prince of Wales, his close personal friend, together with other members of the Royal family, drove in open carriages to the Brigade's headquarters at Southwark where Shaw was convalescing, through streets lined with cheering Londoners. There can be very few people who have belonged to quite so many clubs – besides The Carlton and Pratt's, there were at least five others. He was very much a member of London Society.

His was very much a character to admire, rather than to love. Throughout his life, apart from the single lapse when he preferred flight to America to Holy Orders, I doubt if he ever flinched from the path of duty even in the full glare of publicity. He wrote of a fireman's work – 'If he wants to do it well, he must show moral as well as physical courage; in short, he must harden his heart and act as if no one were looking on.' I have a nasty nagging suspicion that Shaw may have enjoyed disdaining public approval and flexing his moral muscles: and it would probably have served his own interest and those of the Fire Brigade better if he had on occasion showed that he cared even a little what other people thought and felt. One would have thought, for example, that when the Metropolitan Board of Works gave way to the London County Council in 1889 he would have used his immense influence and personal authority, and his great popularity with the general public, to have persuaded the Fire Brigade Committee to expand the Brigade and improve working conditions for firemen. The financial restrictions which had bedevilled the Metropolitan Board of Works had disappeared, and money could be found quite easily. Instead matters went from bad to worse.

Two years after the London County Council was formed, Shaw abruptly retired. It is difficult to know exactly why. The Committee Clerk was notably discreet, and nothing of the true facts was allowed to infiltrate the minutes. The Committee, as a whole, was genuinely surprised, and expressed their pain to see him go. They may also have secretly been relieved. He had become an institution, and institutions are obstacles to evolution. But he departed with the Committee's thanks, an inscribed marble clock from Queen Victoria, a fine silver tea service from the insurance companies, and a knighthood.

He became managing director of the Palatine Insurance Company, and Chairman of the Metropolitan Electricity Board. He was even appointed Deputy Lieutenant of Middlesex, but these are peripheral to his real achievement. He was the creator

in his own time of the finest fire brigade in the world, and when he died in 1908, a legless old man approaching eighty years old, this was remembered by the thousands who followed his funeral cortege from Pimlico to Highgate Cemetery where he now lies buried with his wife and children.

He remains a potent influence even today in the London Fire Brigade. His memory is perpetuated in the fireboat bearing his name which showed some of his indomitable courage in 1940 off the beaches of Dunkirk, but his was the moral fervour which makes firefighting in the London Fire Brigade more than a way of earning one's livelihood. It brings membership of one of the most tightly-knit, morally-motivated groups of men in the world.

The London funeral of Sir Eyre Massey Shaw in 1908 in London and preparing for the procession to drive to Highgate Cemetery. (Mary Evans 10536581.)

The Massey Shaw fireboat heading down river alongside London's Victoria Embankment. The fireboat was named after, possibly, the London Fire Brigade's most famous Chief Fire Officer. (Mary Evans 10534847.)

M2FH OUT

The Closing of Lambeth's Fire Control Room

By Station Officer Sid Snell BEM

After a life span of over thirty years the end of an era came recently when the shutters at Lambeth Control were pulled down for the last time. In a way there was possibly a similarity between us and the old Windmill Theatre ('we never closed'), famous for its nudes and comedians.

Although we cannot claim any distinction for the former. We had, over the years, our fair share of the latter, like the radio operator who added 'jumping sheets in use' to a stop message, which was duly circulated but not very favourably received.

London fire control room as it looked prior to the 1966 refit and modernisation. (Mary Evans 10536726.)

Up to 1939 mobilising in the old London County Council area was conducted from four Superintendents' fire stations at Clapham, New Cross, Manchester Square and Whitechapel where the dial 'O' or 2222 emergency calls were received. These controls would mobilise up to 12 pumps (Distant call) and the control room on the first floor at Lambeth would assume command of all incidents requiring assistance above this level.

In 1939, in view of the impending war, an underground control room was constructed on the present site which was formerly known as 'Stiffs Dock'. On the outbreak of hostilities the existing Superintendents' stations assumed a major mobilising role by becoming responsible for the mobilising of large numbers of Home Office emergency appliances, which were housed in vacated schools and other large buildings, to incidents within their area. Requests for assistance from these areas were passed to the underground control at Lambeth for mobilising of the region's resources.

Armed fireman guard on London's fire brigade headquarters control room at Lambeth during the Second World War. (Mary Evans 10536730.)

The fire raid on the city of London on 29th December 1940 resulted in over 2,000 fires which were mobilised by Lambeth

Control. On the formation of the National Fire Service the Lambeth Control was not only responsible for the No. 5 London region, but also acted as a liaison centre for the other regions and the Home Office control. As well as providing reinforcements to other regions, it also acted as a central information centre providing situation reports of the region's activities.

In 1948 the Fire Service reverted to local authority control, and the Lambeth Control continued in its underground form to mobilise the London County Council Fire Brigade area. The Superintendents' stations ceased to function as mobilising centres, and Lambeth Control, after considerable modification, assumed the role as a reception center for the receipt of emergency calls in the London postal area.

These arrangements continued until the formation of the Greater London Council in 1965, the enlarged brigade consisting of 620 square miles as compared with the 117 square miles of the former London County Council area. Again, this meant a re-appraisal of the brigade's communications system, and a completely new control room was devised for the existing site. While this was being rebuilt and refurnished the control room was moved to a temporary site in the basement at brigade HQ.

Lambeth Control Room in the 1950s. (Permission of the London Fire Brigade.)

The new control room was re-occupied in mid-1966 and officially opened by Her Majesty the Queen in November of that year, which was also the centenary of the London Fire Brigade.

Her Majesty Queen Elizabeth formally opening the London Fire Brigade's Lambeth mobilising control room in November 1966. (Permission of the London Fire Brigade.)

The function of the control room was mobilising the Central London area, as well as being the general communications centre and coordinating control for the whole brigade. During its lifetime the control room has known many stress periods including the largest peacetime fire mobilised by Lambeth Control, the 60-pump fire at Eldon Street, Broad Street, City of London in December 1951.

Example of a teleprinter message sent from the Lambeth control to all fire stations on the 'make pumps 30' message being received by radio. (Permission of the London Fire Brigade.)

```
TO ALL STATIONS   ALL DIVISIONS   ALL CONTROLS   OPS ROOM   LSC
A C O WATKINS
AT
No 9 SHED     KING GEORGE 5th DOCK
MAKE PUMPS 30
ADDITIONAL APPLIANCES TO CARRY BA
TOO 0717


SGT


0729
```

The brigade, as a whole, for the period 1966–73 attended annually calls in the region of 75,000 to 85,000, culminating in a record total of 93,000 last year [1974]. As will be appreciated, Guy Fawkes Night was always a busy period, and the year which will be remembered by most will be 1970. It was when Lambeth Control dealt with a total of 1,902 calls in a 24 hour period, and during that October, 1970, which coinciding with an industrial dispute involving refuse workers, 7,464 calls were received in Lambeth Control over a period of 21 days.

A popular feature of the **London Fireman** magazine is the 'Behind the Stop' stories. Perhaps, it is appropriate now that Lambeth Control should add a little gem of its own: Called to explosions at the Royal Albert Hall. The 'Stop' message was sent, 'Alarm caused by the rendering of the 1812 Overture by the London Symphony Orchestra.'

Finally, with the closure of Lambeth Brigade Control, and the subsequent dispersal of personnel who have served the brigade so well and efficiently, every good wish goes out to them in their new postings.

Two firemen, from West Norwood fire station, working in their Proto BA sets at the King George VI dock blaze. December 1974. (Mary Evans 10793971.)

Night Shift

By Caroline Siggs

Fingers of light swept the rain-soaked night as the car braked
  in the park.
The car door slammed, then the sound of hurried footsteps in
  the dark.
A fireman going on duty, a man just doing his job.
Early for eighteen hundred hours to join that friendly mob.
'Hi there,' shouts a friendly colleague's voice. He's grinning
  with delight.
'I thought I'd come in early. It's a beastly, filthy night.
I remembered it's your wife's birthday and you're taking her
  out to dine.
Well! Now I am here, you can go off. Have a wonderful time.'

There are lots for firemen to do before the night's parade.
Nothing's ever left to chance in an efficient fire brigade.
Every little detailed task must be done with care and pride.
They read the 'riders' board' to know which vehicle to ride.
In the gear room they collect tunics, helmets, belts and axes.
Get waterproof trousers, check their BA, before they can
  relax.
'Four bells.' The shift is now officially changed, and in their
  fire gear,
The firemen stand and wait in a line for the officer to appear.

The roll call's read, the orders given, everything's checked and
  it's right.
The gear is put in its right place and the men settle down for
  the night.
There's a lecture on radiation that everyone must attend.
New knowledge to be absorbed, and notes that must be
  penned.

Time passes. Soon it's supper time. Tonight it's Fireman Jeff
Who does the honours, prepares the meal and is the night
  shift's chef.
Tonight, it's bacon, eggs and sausage, served up as a mixed
  grill.
Oh! The ecstasy of the cooking smells. The men settle down
  with a will,

To the delicious supper delivered on their plates. But they
 barely begin,
The teleprinter's high pitched ring says a message is coming
 in.
The firemen freeze and listen, not one of them has any doubt,
That teleprinter's the first signal for a shout.

They scramble as the bells go down, each man ready for his
 role.
They leave their food uneaten and then slide down the pole.
The great doors open and they're gone, 'two tones' and 'flash-
 ing light',
As they race off in the darkness through the wet and chilly
 night.
But it's a call of nuisance value, no one's come to any harm.
A surreptitious smoker triggered off a fire alarm.
Back to the station, the supper spoiled, congealed in grease on
 the plate.
This is one price they have to pay, a fireman's supper is often
 late.

The evening passes in good companionship, but each man is
 aware,
That any second could bring some 'unfortunate's' nightmare.
Ten thirty, the witching hour starts when pub barmen all call,
 'time.'
The men keep looking at the clock as eleven begins to chime.
Then it happens. This is it. The bells go down again,
The teleprinter's ringing as if it's quietly insane.
The tension-riddled silence freezes, each man is on his toes,
And leaps to action for the pole-house as the urgent signal
 goes.

They scramble in their gear for the second time that night.
The 'Christmas tree' is lit up with a blaze of coloured lights.
First red, then the green, and blue coloured bulb lights up too,
And somewhere the teleprinter is still beating its tattoo.
Bent on a mission of mercy once more, out into the night and
 rain,
And then they come to the accident that blocks the driving
 lane.

Ghostly white, the ambulances gleam wetly in the night,
Shadows are working desperately in the emergency floodlight.

'God, what a mess!' their first reaction is as they take in the
    scene,
A shattered post and broken bodies where a bus-stop once
    had been.
An upturned car, like a blazing torch, was there beside the
    road,
Trapped and struggling the driver dies as the petrol tank
    explodes.
The awful, cloying, sickly stench of burning flesh in the air,
Of that burning human being who was still trapped in there.

The fire's put out, but the firemen get a glimpse of sheer hell,
When they are able to see inside that burned and twisted shell.
The Cengar pistol rattled as it cut the tight jammed door,
If only it had been possible to open it before.
The Porto power pries wide the jagged metal vice,
That trapped a man to die in there like a heathen sacrifice.
The firemen put the burned out corpse on a stretcher sheet,
His cindered shoes just fall off, inside are his cindered feet.

Somebody quietly brings a bucket for the cinders in the car,
To think this was once a man, stretches the mind too far.
By now, all the shattered bodies are covered by a sheet,
Their whiteness soon stained red, and drenched by rain and
    sleet.
Revulsion, horror and distaste flicker on the face of every
    man,
Is this the way for anyone to end their earthy span?
This is the time of the witching hour, had these people been
    on a spree?
Was that last happy call, 'A drink for the road', a drink to
    eternity?

Had those shattered broken people just been laughing in some
    bar?
Had that cinder of a human been fit to drive his lethal car?
But what a hell of a way to die! What a price to pay for a drink!
Hold on! Blot it out! It's just a job! Better by far not to think.
Mundane clearing-up jobs now. Like sweeping up the glass,
And laying all the pieces of the bus-stop on the grass.
Back to the station for a rest and a well-earned cup of tea,
To 9 a.m. when this shift ends now seems an eternity.

The fatal Covent Garden fire at Langley Street, W2, that took the lives of Station Officer Frederick Hawkins and Firemen Arthur Batt-Rawden and Carles Gadd. (Mary Evans 10535516.)

The station's quiet, the men deep in thought,
But the angel of death's in the dark,
And the rain batters down on the roofs of the cars,
That are left in the station's car park.
Unquiet silence fills the air, recent memories are gnawing and
  cling,
Reaching to archives deep in the mind to record these terrible
  things.
The teleprinter rings again, with a clang the bells go down,
This 'shout' will be a ringer, and its way beyond the town.
The 'Christmas tree's' lit up again, a blaze of coloured lights,
'Two tones' sounding; flashers flashing, once more they're out
  that night.

A baking factory's ablaze, flames turn the night sky red,
The air is filled with the acrid fumes of burning cakes and
   bread.
The place by now is well alight, flames shoot high in the air,
And somewhere in that holocaust we're told. 'Two men are
   there.'
Sucked open by the fierce blast the rubber doors swing wide,
The flames are leaping through the roof and it's hot as hell
   inside.
BAs are donned and jets of water from the fire hose
Are turned upon the rescue men to saturate their clothes.

Their safety line adjusted and their tallies handed in,
The rescue party goes inside, well trained and disciplined.
They seek out foxholes on the way, to shelter if there's need,
And push the fire forward in order to proceed.
They disappear in the choking smoke, silhouetted in the glare,
In that tremendous heat their well-soaked tunics steam in
   there.
They watch with care the needles of their BA pressure gauge
Searching for the men trapped by the fire, in this fiery war
   they wage.

Like packs of cards, the cardboard flats are whipped up in the
   draughts,
And launch themselves to feed the flames, like storm-tossed
   crazy rafts.
One injured man has just been found, but the other one is lost,
Too often some unlucky devil has to pay the cost.
They've all been in there long enough, it's time to turn about,
There must be air enough in the tanks to see them safely out.
They back away, retracing steps with the weight of the injured
   man,
Marking their foxholes, feeling their way, where the safety
   lifeline ran.

As roof creaked and shuddered, they dive in holes that each
   had found,
Then the blazing rafters splinter and comes crashing to the
   ground.
Someone sounds his DSU in that fiery wilderness,
The top priority call goes out, 'There are brothers in distress.'
Now the greatest risks are run in a battle to control the fate
Of these conscientious firemen who started back too late.
Superhuman efforts are made, but the flames in triumph won,

The silent tally board will count the cost that has been run.
Each smoke-grimed tired hero takes his tally off the board,
But one is still left hanging there in that grim episode.
'It's Jim's.' A fireman moves towards the flames, others hold
   him down,
'There's not a hope in hell in there,' says someone with a
   frown.
Distressed and tired, numbed with grief, the men are all
   appalled,
'Make pumps twenty', 'Make pumps thirty' had long ago been
   called.
Fresh crews are here; the rescue party take a well-earned
   break,
This is the job they chose to do, they know the risks they take.

All through that long dark winter's night the fire fight went
   on,
A fortune lost in smoke and flames and two precious lives are
   gone.
Back at the station, time to go home, weary with little to say,
Someone brings them all back to earth, 'Men, don't forget
   your pay':
Pay! Who thought of payout there? Pay doesn't come to mind,
If someone's hurt and needs your help, your smoke-filled eyes
   are blind.
You don't see 'Pay' in the human cinders of a man burned in
   his car,
There's no connection with money, when things ''ave gone
   that far.'

But at the end of the night shift, in the early morning light,
The fireman becomes a 'dad.' His heroics fade with the night.
Pay day. He starts planning how the money must be spent,
There's groceries, rates and mortgage payments, or perhaps
   the rent.
He starts his ancient car and drives along the shortest route,
A fireman who is going home in a damp and crumpled suit.
Still mentally budgeting his pay, he's pulled up with a jerk,
Red lights ahead. In all the corners of his mind a red still lurks.

His exhaustion and worry over pay, had someone given him a
   'biff':
His wandering mind, driving home, could make him the day
   shift's 'stiff.'
Jim! A pathway cleared in his mind. Jim won't be going home,

His pretty wife will have to bring their girl up all alone.
Don't think about that too much, shut your mind and put up a
  screen.
The man in the car in the damp crumpled suit, waited for the
  lights to go green.

**Stamford Street, SE1.
Lyons Ice Cream
factory fire. Crews
replenishing their
breathing apparatus
sets in the street. (Mary
Evans 10793486.)**

OUT OF THE ORDINARY

O

Rescue by a Hook Ladder

By Paul Kleinman

There was something odd about the stand by. You know how you sometimes get the feeling that something is not quite right, but you can't put your finger on it. Well this was one of those occasions.

Let me explain. My name is Rob, I have served at Brixton for more years than I care to recall. Brixton is a busy station, of that there is no doubt. Never one for promotion I did rise to the exalted position of mess-manager, looking after the culinary needs of the best watch at the station, my own watch. One night many years ago I was in the kitchen preparing the usual fry-up when I had the feeling I was being watched. Looking up from the sizzling chip fryer I saw this fireman standing just in front of me.

'Good evening,' I said. 'I'm afraid I didn't hear you come in. Can I help you?' 'Yes,' said the unfamiliar face. 'I'm standing by for the watch. Can you tell me where the officer in charge is please?' 'They're all out in the station yard doing drills,' I replied, 'but first would you like a cup of tea?'

The stand-by, who looked in his early thirties, shook his head and said, 'No thanks.' When I looked at him more closely I noticed a ruddy complexion that signified he might have been a sailor at some time. Of course in those dim and distant days the majority of firemen had been in some kind of service, our own guvnor was ex-Grenadier Guards, so I didn't think that all that unusual, but he had a slightly old-fashioned air about him that was a bit different.

'Please yourself,' I said with a grin. 'Would you like me to do you a supper, though?' Once again the stand-by shook his head. 'No thanks very much, but I don't have much of an appetite.' He still shook his head when I asked him if he wanted breakfast, so reluctantly giving up on the food score I asked him what station he was from as I wasn't aware we were actually short-handed that night. He said he was from a station that is now long since closed, but when I said I hadn't come across him before he said he was from the other watch, just transferred over, which explained it.

Hook ladder drill.
(Permission of the
London Fire Brigade.)

Hook ladder drill. (Permission of the London Fire Brigade.)

We were suddenly interrupted by another member of the watch entering the kitchen. 'The old man wants you down in the yard for hook ladder drills,' he said. 'I'll look after the cooking while you are down there.'

'Bugger it,' I said. 'Just when I thought he had forgotten all about me.' 'Come on. You know what the old man is like for hook ladder drills. Don't know why, it's not as if we ever use them in anger. But there it is. If you've got to do them, you have got to do them.'

Now, as anyone who remembers hook ladders will tell you, firemen had a love hate relationship with the things. If pushed, most who are reasonably fit could climb an escape or extension ladder, climbing hook ladders is a real skill. It requires a good sense of balance, strength, a cool head and, most important of all, guts. Some recruit firemen never did master them and had to resign as a result. Much to my surprise the stand-by, on hearing this, jumped in with both feet. 'Mind if I join in?' he asked. 'Hooks ladders are my favourite drill.'

When the guvnor saw the pair of us appear in the yard he was also surprised. 'I didn't know we needed a stand-by tonight. Still, as you're here you can make up the next pair.'

We both took up our positions at the foot of the drill tower in front of the two hook ladders suspended by their hooks from the first floor window sill. 'Hook ladders to the fifth floor,' barked the guvnor. 'Scale the building.' And up we went. I was number one, so I climbed to the first floor, connected the snap-hook on the specially strengthened hook belt I had put on through the metal ring at the top of the ladder, shouted out 'Hooked', swung round to face the other ladder, picked it up and pushed it up to the second floor sill, where it was again suspended by its hook on the wooden sill. I then unhooked myself and climbed foot-hand-hand-foot onto the bottom of the other ladder.

The stand-by then climbed his ladder to the first floor sill. Leaning back on his arms, whilst keeping his backside well below the hook, as a hook ladder relies for its stability on keeping the weight below the point of suspension, he put one leg over the window sill and sat astride it, keeping his outside leg parallel with the face of the drill tower. While he was doing this I climbed to the top of my ladder and hooked on again to the metal ring bolt, shouting 'Hooked' and keeping one foot on the ladder, I jumped round so I was facing the ladder below me. The stand-by then lifted that ladder and leaning out, passed it up to me, where I took it and pointing the hook away from me, pushed it to the next floor, hooking the ladder on the sill above my head. We repeated this process until we reached the fifth floor and both climbed into the tower.

It sounds dangerous. It is, and there have been instances of firemen losing their lives at hook ladder drills though no accident has ever occurred because of a faulty ladder. But our stand-by was mustard. I have never before, or since, seen anyone perform so well on hook ladders. Even the guvnor was impressed, and he hands out compliments like they cost a fiver each.

When we finally came down the guvnor said the stand-by could ride the pump escape as we had a spare seat. So he put his fire gear on the appliance, booked in at the watchroom, and drill period for the night was over. For the rest of the evening our stand-by said hardly a word. He didn't eat a thing and every time someone tried to engage him in conversation he just clammed up. He didn't even want a game of snooker, and when time came for lights out he lay on his bunk and stared at the ceiling.

We all thought it was going to be a quiet night for a change, but it was not to be. About three o'clock in the morning the bells crashed down and we were ordered to a fire and explosion in a street of four storey Victorian tenement houses, not far from the station.

On our arrival the job had all the makings of a nightmare. The house, which had long seen better days, was divided into four different flats, but each sharing the same front door. It appeared that a main in the bottom flat had exploded and the doorway and entrance hall was a blazing inferno. While the rest of the crew were getting stuck in laying out a jet, donning breathing apparatus and setting into a hydrant, the stand-by and I grabbed a hook ladder and went through to the rear of the blazing house via the house next door which was, for us, standard procedure.

Like most houses of that period it had an addition with a flat roof. Although the ground floor was ablaze the rest of the house was so far untouched, but suddenly through the crackling of the flames we could see a child screaming from the third floor window.

There was nothing else for it, it was a no-brainer. First the stand-by, then myself used the hook ladder to climb onto the flat roof, then pulling the ladder up behind us. The stand-by unfolded the hook and noticed the second floor bottom sash window had been raised slightly. Without hesitation he pitched the ladder, with the hook over the sill, into the room. Although the bottom of the ladder was several feet from the top of the flat roof the stand-by pulled himself up the ladder using his hands until his feet touched the bottom rung of the hook ladder. Then he shot up the ladder to the second floor, carrying a lowering line on his back, and telling me to stay put so I could pull the child away from the building, using the guide line attached the lowering line, when he lowered her back down. Shouting to the distraught child to mind the hook he pushed the ladder up to the third window and again hooked onto the sill. He swung onto the ladder and was racing up at a rate of knots. Once he got inside the room, the stand by used his axe to smash the glazing and clear the wooden frame. Then, placing the child, who was a little girl about six years old, in the lowering line and threw me the guy line and carefully lowered her onto the flat roof where I was waiting to receive her.

I then thought the stand-by would come back down the way he got up, but for some reason, probably because he thought there might be more to be rescued, he disappeared back inside the room.

Only a fireman really knows what a cunning, vicious enemy fire is. One minute there can nothing but heat and smoke, but get the right combination of heat and air and next you have an inferno and that is what happened now. With an almighty roar the whole of the room where the child was only moments ago was a mass of flames. There was no way he could escape from that direction. His only hope was to go higher and to reach the top floor and be rescued himself by the rest of the crew.

Inside the blazing building the stand-by made his way on to the landing that led to the top floor. He could see pale tongues of fire at the top. The smoke wasn't heavy and by squinting he could just see a way out into a room as yet untouched by fire. Heart pounding he gingerly made his way up the final staircase which creaked under his weight, but just before he reached the top and comparative safety the windows of the rooms of the fourth floor exploded outwards and the fire eddied in a sudden change of draughts, roaring up the staircase and engulfing it from floor to ceiling.

The stand-by was hurled backwards. Trying to grab the bannister he missed it and lost his balance, ending up on the fire ringed landing below. He tried to get to his feet but a blazing lump of timber fell onto his chest pinning him to the floor. The fire steadily increased in its all-consuming roar and the stand-by shivered as he felt tides of heat washing over him. Now gagging for air he desperately tried to free himself, but it was impossible. For a few seconds he clenched his teeth, trying to hold his breath, but it was no use. As his mouth filled with bitter acrid smoke and he could feel the pain as the heat burned its way to his lungs the wooden joists supporting the landing collapsed and he plunged, with the other debris, head first into the flames below and was no more.

Whilst all this had been taking place, the guvnor had made pumps six and reported people involved in the fire, whilst directing his crews in desperately trying to control the blaze and enter the building. The child's parents were both rescued by escape ladder from the front of the building, another occupant jumped from the second floor before the ladder that was being extended towards him, reached the window. I was brought to the ground, with the child still in my arms, by a fireman from an adjoining station. With the report of the missing stand-by a roll-call was held and the search of debris in the gutted house started, now that the fire was brought under control.

But there was no sign of the stand-by. We searched and searched again the hot remains of the smouldering building. Try as we might there was no sign of the stand-by's body. Eventually our Divisional Officer, who had taken charge of the fire, ordered us back to the station, vowing that the body would be found even if the house was taken apart brick by brick.

We were just backing the machines into the engine room when there was a screech of brakes. It was the Divisional Officer who rushed from his car, dashing into the watchroom and frantically started to pour through the station log book.

Now this particular officer was noted for his rather ripe use of Anglo-Saxon vernacular and now it was in full flow. It seemed that no-one knew the stand-by's name. The dutyman, with a worried look swore he had entered his name in the log book and placed it on the nominal roll board, carried on the appliance, but now there was no trace of them anywhere.

The rest of us were milling around the watchroom racking our brains. After what seemed like an eternity, but was really only a few seconds, the dutyman himself thought he remembered the stand-by telling him his name as he wrote it in the book but he couldn't be sure.

The Divisional Officer dived for the phone and called the stand-by's base station. We could hear the staccato tones of the Station Officer speaking. 'No Sir, we didn't send you a stand-by tonight, we are riding minimum riders as it is. Anyway there is no one of that name on our watch, in fact at the station. Although, I must admit the name does seem a bit familiar. Hang on a minute. Hanging on the wall above me is the station's Honours and Awards board and the name you mentioned is on there. Lost his life performing a hook ladder rescue rescuing a child shortly after the end of the war.'

The watchroom suddenly became filled with an eerie silence. The only sound to be heard was the ticking watchroom clock as it suddenly became clear. 'That's what was strange about the stand-by. Ghosts don't need food, do they?'

Prose and Poems

I am a Fireman

by Kevin Wright

How many times was I asked? 'I bet you've seen things as a Fireman?' Yes I Have! I've seen, life in the raw and just how precious it is to most.

I've seen death in all its horror and the lengths that some go to achieve it.

I've seen laughter so contagious that it's drawn me in and left me with sides fit to split and gasping for breath.

I've seen tears shed by hundreds, many of joy, but far too many through sorrow and pain.

I've seen parents lose their children, siblings lose each other, children lose parents, and so so many lose pets.

I've seen children saved, siblings save each other, parents saved and beloved pets returned to fretful owners.

I've seen mouths open wide, but no noise heard, where some poor soul is just empty.

I've seen grown men acting like children playing and joking only to see the same men later coughing and choking!

I've seen the dawn come up through a smokey haze more times than I care to remember.

I've seen those that you wouldn't look twice at when passing in the street do things that in any other instance they would be called heroes.

I've seen my mates receive injuries time and time again, some so bad they never returned.

I've seen the tearful uniformed lines formed as we've gathered to pay our respect, to those that have paid the highest price.

I've seen, actions by others that have made me hold my head high with pride.

I've also seen the actions of a few where I wish I could hide!

I've seen the hands of so many being held in the wee wee hours as they and their passengers are being cut free.

I've seen the looks of relief and heard the 'Thank you' so many times, knowing that this is the one and only time we will meet!

I've seen the lost hollow looks in searching eyes; their mournful screams, as they realise their companions have not made it.

I've seen myself holding the hands of too many as they've slip away trying so hard to hold on, always fighting to preserve their dignity!

I've heard questions being asked, by those in need, 'Is my mother; my father; my child OK?'

I've heard the answers given that will haunt the givers to their graves.

I've seen all of this and so much more with some of the greatest people I've ever met in the best job in the world!

I've heard this question asked a thousand times and the reply given is the same every time, with the shrug of the shoulders 'yeah a few!'

So I have seen. But it is virtually impossible to answer this question. You can only live it and experience it! I AM A FIREMAN!

· ·

Divisional Officer Charles Clisby leading the efforts to save Temporary Leading Fireman Michael Lee; tragically it was too late. Goswell Road, Shoreditch. (Permission of London Fire Brigade.)

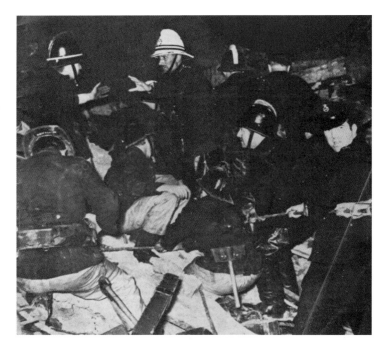

Poems by Charlie Clisby

*One of the most prolific contributors to the **London Fireman** of verse was **CHARLES (CHARLIE) CLISBY**, a senior officer in London's 'C' Division that covered the City of London, east to Whitechapel and north towards Kentish Town and Holloway. This well-spoken, and highly educated, chap could easily be taken for a proper 'dapper' gentleman. However, he was a fireman's fireman and believed in leading from the front. In an iconic image of the late 1960s, Charlie Clisby is captured (with a pained expression on his face) leading the frantic rescue efforts to save the life of Temporary Leading Fireman Michael Lee, buried under debris following a building collapse. Tragically it was too late to save Michael, he was already dead. Rising to principal rank Charles Clisby was awarded both the MBE and the Queens Fire Services Medal (QFSM) for distinguished service. He was credited as one of the originators of the now widely used Hazchem Coding for toxic and hazardous materials, pioneered by the then Greater London Council.*

'Charlie' Clisby's poems were recognised by the BBC and he was commissioned to write for them. A special programme featuring the work of the firemen's 'Bard' was broadcast in May 1975 on Radio Four. A selection of his poems follow...

Control Room

We wait and we watch through the long nights which are long.
We spring into action when something is on.
We feel for the crews who are out on a shout.
That they are hard at it we are in no doubt.

There's no one as proud of their efforts as we.
Who commit them to jobs we never shall see.
But we can imagine the problems they face.
For instance, when death and they are having a race.

Because gap between calls allows for no pain.
Study Peter and Tom as much as they can.
While Joyce proves the same way that women are worth;
A bar on their shoulder and place here on earth.

Though Anne sticks to knitting, she's best we have got.
Stay's cool as can be when the going is hot.
Calms down ev'ry caller; elicits the facts.
Which basis provides for all subsequent acts.

Sometimes on the air sad affected is pride.
A child has been burned or a mother has died.
How proudly is detailed the saving of life.
When a fireman is killed, news cuts like a knife.

We know we are part of a team out to win.
To say we are not is the worst kind of sin.
For we would if we could stand fast at the sides.
Of the gallant who scorch, but rescue besides.

We wait while they curse when they're in a blind spot.
Forgive some for viewing as easy out lot.
The greatest reward by our watching is earned.
A 'Thank you Control', when the tide has been turned.

The London Fire Brigade's Lambeth control room, circa 1970. (Permission of the London Fire Brigade.)

The Recruit on the Drill Tower

**LFB recruit firemen
at hook ladder drill at
Lambeth fire station.
(Mary Evans 10794652.)**

All right for him to shout at me.
I'm shaking like a leaf.
He's on the ground, I'm three floors up.
It's me, not he, will come to grief.

'Go on, go up. Don't hesitate!'
I can't. I'll fall. I daren't look down.
I hear a thumping, tower shakes.
A hook goes past me, round by round.

He comes aloft, he wears a grin.
'Suppose you thought that I'm too old.
That only young like you can climb.
All men can climb if they are bold.'

And on he climbs. I follow suit.
Feel sure a fool, his help I spurn.
My squad will laugh; I too will laugh.
For in a moment comes their turn.

205

The London Players

Along the road towards us a woman starts to run.
Bathed in spots and headlights bright, how well the thing is
  done.
She trips upon her nightdress and falls dramatically,
But struggling up, a heroine, she gestures frantically.

The dance of flames has started at window of a room,
In wings the crowd arrangement is one of deepest gloom.
Female lead cries 'Save my child,' off goes the message fast;
For ambulance, all sorts of help, a full supporting cast.

Guvnor is the first on stage, round him this story's spun.
At forty he's a heavy, our age not twenty-one.
There sounds the catgut music of fast revolving reel,
We race the hose paid out because a snag the scene would
  steal.

On stairs in heavy smoke we stumble on a man,
Who'd lost his chance as stand-in for only training can?
Produce a great performance the run of which will last,
He's breathing well, we let him lie and quickly wriggle past.

We slide along the landing, our heads upon the floor.
See against a brilliant set a fully open door,
And legs of cot still standing, now comes the cue to pray.
As Guvnor kneels to reach in it we wet him down with spray.

The final act commences, asides are all in oaths.
He moans in desperation and flings aside the cloths.
The steam which rises from him is no CO_2 effect.
We let him have the full discharge, switch nozzle onto jet.

Never seen an act like this, frustration is the spur.
The award that's due to him no critic can defer.
We rise to him but hide our heads, 'Jesus it is hot.'
Forgive our blasphemy good Lord, this is a thorny plot.

He's down again. 'I've got it.' His voice a throaty rasp.
Rolls upon his back with infant firmly in his grasp.
We drag him out. On each stair, he's braced to meet the jar.
For, safe within his tunic front is loud complaining star.

On the 13th December 1974 Fireman Hamish Pettit, from Paddington fire station's Red Watch, was tragically killed at the fire at the Worsley Hotel, Clifton, W9.

The then Divisional Officer Charles Clisby was detailed to travel to Rochester, in Kent, to break the news to Hamish's wife. Ironically, 10 months before that fateful fire, 'Charlie' Clisby had written a poem entitled 'Breaking the News', and it was Paddington's Red Watch who had been chosen for a 30 minute TV documentary about Clisby's fire poetry.

The Worsley Hotel fire in December 1974. (Permission of the London Fire Brigade.)

Breaking the news

I spoke as calmly as I could,
'Do please sit down, I've brought your mum',
At this the girl then understood.
'Oh No!' she cried, 'Oh God, Oh God!'
Picked up their infant from its cot.
'He's dead,' she said. I simply nod.
'By how? A fire?' I nod again
Her thoughts are for the little one.
'The roof fell in, he felt no pain.'
The fewest words, two moves of head.
My task is done, her's has begun.
The going's hard, tears will be shed.

Shoreditch

A Shoreditch blaze in London's East End in the 1930s. (Permission of the London Fire Brigade.)

Was once a ditch ran from the Thames
Which when 'twas foul was filled.
Elizabeth was more concerned
That odours poor men killed
Than that an unused merchant's way
From rich to rich was willed.

Today the problem's here again
For dirt and odours rise,
And though I live up sixty feet
My views are no surmise,
For motor cars produce an air
Tall buildings can't disguise.

'Tis said that soon a flyover
Will rise to window height.
And bring with it most deadly fumes
To worsen this our plight.
Perhaps Elizabeth will note
And put the wrong to right.

Would-be rescuers

We are weary, sad at heart,
Never had a chance from start,
Far too late we got the call,
Gave us wrong address and all.

Broken in was large front door
Giving vent to fire in store.
By the time we did arrive
No one there could be alive.

Child was found at head of stairs.
All the rest lay dead in pairs.
Can one say to those who try,
'Have you never reasoned why?

The Tales of a Single Night

Dejected stands the little crowd
Before the smoking shell
Of what was once their place of work
Each one has tale to tell.

'I made the tea for thirty years
Where else is place for me?
In single night my life has changed
And I am sixty three.'

'I wonder, oh! My darling Frank
Will you remember me?'
Each at a different place will work.
Love thrives on constancy.

'To whom am I to sub-contract?
I made most special things,

From nothing built my business up
With love which owning brings.'

'I live alone. Part of my life,
Most probably the best
Was here as one of family.
I walked to work with zest.'

'I can apply most anywhere
For work at bench or lathe,
But living close I took job here.
A lot of fares to save.'

To those who pass by unconcerned
These tales are just a bore,
But let me warn you everyone,
For you the same's in store.

The Hold-up

My God! It can't be true. Another traffic jam.
What's it this time, the roads get worse.
I'll never get my load to Birmingham.
Hullo! Fire bells. A person come to harm.
No smoke about. I'll have a look.
I suppose it's just a bloody false alarm.
A Copper! Pointing down. There the firemen go.
'Bus off the road, what they got.
A jack it is, they're pushing it below.
Doctor! With his gear. He's bending down.
He's listening, with his stethoscope.
Looks like a dog with hair so dark and brown.
Not a dog! A child. Her head askance.
Fireman's lifting her, he holds her tight.
Kissing her he walks towards the ambulance.
Doctor done! Picks up his bag. To leave.
Shakes his head, the fireman weeps,
The Copper and the bus crew stand and grieve.
Ambulance men! Take the child. The fireman's load.
He speaks to me, he quotes her words,
'Don't tell my mum I ran across the road.'

QUEEN ELIZABETH
THE QUEEN MOTHER

O n Saturday 4 May 1991, Her Royal Highness Queen Elizabeth, The Queen Mother attended St Paul's Cathedral, London, to attend a special service and to unveil a statue. It was no ordinary statue. This national monument, named **The Blitz**, was originally the concept of Cyril Demarne, and was commissioned by the Firefighters Memorial Charitable Trust that had been set up in 1990. It was sculpted by John W. Mills. The statue was a much awaited tribute to those men and women who fought so gallantly against fire on the streets of London during the Blitz of World War II, when the city was struck by bombs on 57 consecutive nights in a sustained campaign of bombing. It also served as a national monument to commemorate the service of the nation's men and women firefighters, who, throughout the Second World War gave their lives in the line of duty on mainland Britain.

The statue, composed of three bronze statues, depicted firemen in action at the height of the Blitz. Originally positioned in St Paul's

Her Majesty Queen Elizabeth arriving at the London Regional National Fire Service Headquarters at Lambeth in 1944 to review the work of firewomen of the NFS. (Mary Evans 10576422.)

Churchyard in later years the statue would be relocated but still in the shadow of St Paul's Cathedral. It also became the responsibility of the Firefighters Memorial Trust and was renamed the **National Firefighters Memorial.** Today, located on the Jubilee Walkway in the City of London, it is the focus of an annual Remembrance Service to fallen firefighters. The statue is approachable from the south bank of the River Thames via the Millennium Footbridge.

Her Royal Highness Queen Elizabeth the Queen Mother was no stranger to the London Fire Brigade. Together with her late husband, King George VI, she had officiated at the Royal opening of the new London Fire Brigade headquarters in Lambeth in 1937. Her Majesty had had regular contact with the London Fire Brigade throughout the war years, and only the year prior, 1990, HRH The Queen Mother had visited Chelsea and Paddington fire stations on official visits.

At the commemoration and unveiling service, conducted at St Paul's Cathedral, and attended by Her Royal Highness Queen Elizabeth The Queen Mother, The Right Honourable Kenneth Baker MP, Secretary of State for the Home Department (then responsible for the Fire Service) gave a reading. His reading was taken from a piece by **RICHIE CALDER** in The Home Front: An Anthology of Personal Experience, 1938–45, edited by Norman Longmate (Chatto & Windus, 1981). Calder's words were reprinted in a later edition of the **London Firefighter** when covering the story of the unveiling. This extract provides just a glimpse of the harsh conditions experienced by those facing the London Blitz from September 1940 to May 1941.

The sculptor and artist John W. Mills showing the Queen Mother the Blitz statue maquette in St Paul's Cathedral prior to her unveiling his bronze statue. (Permission of the London Fire Brigade.)

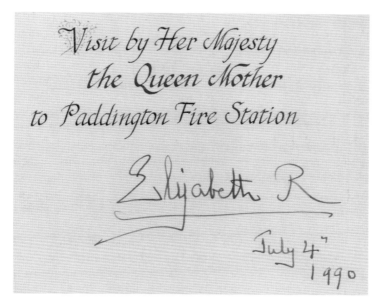

Visit by Her Majesty
the Queen Mother
to Paddington Fire Station

Elizabeth R

July 4th
1990

Extract from the London Fire Brigade's VIP visitor's book from 1990. The Queen Mother was also the first to sign this book, together with her late husband, King George VI, on the occasion of the formal opening of the Brigade's new Lambeth Headquarters in 1937. (Permission of the London Fire Brigade.)

The typewriter is treading flakes of soot into the paper as this ... is being written. Every now and then, like the opening of an oven door, as the wind changes, a gasp of hot breath comes in through the seventh floor window, a breath foul with the reek of burning London. At three in the morning (of Monday, 30 December) with the curtains drawn back and the light turned off (although no warden could notice if it were not), it is possible to see to type in a light as bright as an angry sunrise. Fiery confetti spatters the papers on the desk with singe-marks. A spindrift of fine spray from the firemen's jets follows them reassuringly. Now there is another muffled roar, like the blowing of a Bessemer blast furnace, and a fountain of flames, crested by a plume of sparks as vivid as the fire-belch of a Roman candle, leaps to the high heavens; another building has been clean-gutted. Something flutters like a stricken bird against the window, hovers burning, then sizzles on the spray-damp sill; it is a charred form, delivered by the fire from a near-by printers; it says 'Last Will and Testament'.

The Second Great Fire of London is raging furiously. Over the stricken city hung dense clouds of smoke, lit up as the smoke of a railway-engine is from the fire-box... And upon us descended a blizzard of snow-fire-flakes that stung and scorched. Familiarity with the district added to the dread... One suddenly realised that the building threatened by a change in the wind was a paper warehouse, or a varnish works, or a celluloid store, or a photographer's wholesaler stocked with film... And as each in succession caught, there was a kind of routine. Flames licked round the walls as though they were sampling a fresh tit-bit; then thrust through the windows and attacked the stores hungrily. Beams caught alight. The roofs slowly sagged as though they were gelatin, and then crashed with a roar. A container would explode and add fresh fuel to the flames. Floors would be eaten through and collapse in succession, and then, with each new gift of stores, the fires would leap up. The wind from the south-east acted like a forced draught, and a fountain of fire, with a jet of sparks, would spout fifty feet or more and then suddenly subside. Gradually, the flames would be confined with a lantern-effect within the walls of the building... 'A nice tidy job, if I may say so,' said one AFS man, ex-motor-salesman, talking ... about the fire he and his mates had just put out...

'Has it gone midnight yet?' asked another Auxiliary as he wrestled…with a serpentine hose-pipe. I told him it had. 'Then it's me birfday,' he said… And with that he darted up an alley with the length of hose – I watched him disappear into what looked like a furnace door, and had not the nerve to wish him many happy returns of such a day.

The Queen Mother meeting firefighters at Chelsea fire station. (Mary Evans 10793360.)

REQUIEM FOR THE OLD FIRE BELL

R

by Kevin McDermott

Silent now ye harbinger of hope,
But London's streets still echo from your note.
A note that once did bounce of city walls
And stirred excitement in the hearts of all
Who listened as the wrists of 'number ones'
Knocked out its beat in different rhythmic runs.
Through years of war and many tragic things,
That 'ding a ding' did help and solace bring
To Londoners who in a time of fear said,
'There's the bell, the fire brigade is here.'
For when burning buildings sent the people running
That bell tolled out the message that 'We're coming'.

Then two-tone horns and sirens became the thing
The Fire Bell had forever lost its ring.
Now as I walk the streets of London city
I hear the horns and think 'O what a pity,'
That even I, a fireman from the past,
Can only guess at what is travelling fast.
And as I sigh and go upon my way
Those sirens make me think I'm in LA.

(Mary Evans 10794576.)

S SIDNEY STREET SIEGE

"The Battle of Stepney"
The Fire

A little known fact about this famous London siege, in the early part of the twentieth century, is the involvement of the London Fire Brigade. For one of its number that January day in 1911 would have fatal consequences. This is the account of Station Officer **ALBERT EDMONDS**, *the officer in charge of the second Brigade attendance to Sidney Street.*

Some of you no doubt have heard of what has been described as the Sidney Street Siege. A number of very desperate men one night were robbing the safe of a diamond merchant named Harris, in

Houndsditch, when they were disturbed by the City of London Police. The men did not intend to be captured if they could help it and they shot one or two of the police: one, I think, being killed outright. The men got away; one severely wounded, he was very soon found and died.

You may be sure there was a great hue and cry for the others. Two there was supposed to be, one going by the name of Peter the Painter.

They were eventually run to earth in a house in Sidney Street, a turning out of the Mile End Road about half a mile from Bethnal Green fire station.

I was just about going to have dinner when the bells rang and our engine was ordered to 'Trinity Almshouses, Fire Alarm.' This alarm rang into the Mile End Road station, my station being the next nearest. When we got to the Mile End Road I was surprised to see a crowd of people who cheered us as we came along and they pointed to Sidney Street. I thought perhaps the Mile End firemen were carrying out some good rescue-work and thus causing the excitement. We got a little way into Sidney Street when I was met by the Assistant Station Officer of the Mile End station, the Station Officer being away. He said, 'It's only an alarm, Sir, caused by the police smoking out the burglars of the Houndsditch diamond robbery.'

I walked a little further down the street and away ahead I saw the smoke coming from the house. I saw at once the inside of that house was on fire. 'Why, man,' says I, 'that house is well alight. There is more than just smoke there.'

Rifles

A line of police was drawn across the road. In advance of the police, soldiers were lying on the ground watching the house with rifles to their shoulders. Soldiers were also stationed on the roofs of adjacent houses; waiting to get a shot at the men if they left the house. I got as far as the line of police when an inspector stopped me.

'You can't go any further officer,' says he. Now by Act of Parliament the Chief Officer of the Fire Brigade, or his representative for the time being, at a fire, has very great powers. He takes precedence over all other officials and I knew what I was about when I demurred and said, 'That house is on fire. It's my job to put it out.' The inspector also knew what he was about when he said, 'There is the Home Secretary, Mr Winston Churchill, over there. Perhaps you would like to talk to him.' 'That's my man,' says I. So up I steps and touches Mr Churchill on the shoulder. 'I represent the Fire Brigade, sir. Just arrived. That house is on fire and it's my business to put it out. But of course I don't want to run counter to anything you are having done so I place myself and my men at your disposal.' 'I am afraid if you go to that house at present you will be shot,' he says. 'Those men inside will stick at nothing, but stand by with your engines and men and we will advance as soon as possible.' I sent a message away that soon brought up the higher officials of the Brigade.

Surrender or shooting

I had hose coupled up to hydrants and flaked ready to rush up to the house, made the best dispositions I could and stood by, expecting every moment to see the men driven out of the house by the fire and either surrender to the police or do as much shooting as they could before they themselves were shot down. If they had shown themselves before poking out a white flag they would not have stood much chance.

For a while I stood watching, a curtain blew out from the first floor window and for just a moment in the smoke, it looked like a man's leg coming out of the window. Bang, bang, bang went the soldiers' rifles and the curtain was riddled with bullets. However, no men appeared, the fire got hotter and hotter and by and by the flames shot through the roof. It was then decided to advance.

Our men seized the hose and we rushed the house, back and front, in case they had found a comparatively cool place within. The police came also with revolvers.

We worked and got the fire under control and as soon as we could got inside and started to search among the debris for the bodies, for the police were very anxious to know for certain whether they were still there (dead) or by some mysterious manner got away. However, we soon found one body terribly burned, quire beyond recognition. It was removed and we started to search for the other.

There were several of us in the back room, or what had been the back room, turning over debris, when I said, 'There are too many of us here, we are in each other's way.' I stepped out. As I did so down came a hearth stone weighing over a hundred-weight, from the floors above, severely injuring several men and pinning one, Assistant Superintendent Pearce, down. He was a fine, powerful man, but he never walked again, dying six months later in a nursing home.

When the fire brigade arrived at Sidney Street, Winston Churchill, then Home Secretary, refused them access to the building until the firing from inside stopped. With the robbers shot dead they started to extinguish the fire. (Permission of the London Fire Brigade.)

The body of the other man, also terribly burned, was found soon after, also the automatic pistols with which they had done their shooting. They were splendid weapons, so made that they could be fixed on a stock and used like a rifle.

I had to attend the inquest on the bodies and explain why the Brigade did not do its duty on arrival at the fire, because really these men were left to be burned with the Fire Brigade making no attempt to save them. It was tried to keep Mr Churchill in the background, the police taking all the responsibility, but my evidence could not corroborate and Mr Churchill attended on the third day and admitted that he practically ordered me not to attempt to put the fire out as he was afraid we should be shot. It was never explained how the house came to be on fire. My own opinion is that these men deliberately started the fire, hoping to escape in the confusion they thought would ensue, or else choosing that horrible death rather than fall into the hands of the police.

The fire brigade moves in to start fighting the flames. The Sidney Street Siege would claim one more life, that of Assistant Superintendent Pearce of the London Fire Brigade. (Permission of the London Fire Brigade.)

SMITHFIELD MEAT MARKET FIRE 1958

By Anon

The coldest day in all the year,
It was a Thursday morning,
And the hottest place in London town.
Was Smithfield market burning?

It burnt four days without a pause,
It melted all the snow,
And two brave men were choked to death,
Trapped in the smoke below.

It was down there underneath the ground,
The fire started burning,
It blazed along each storage hall,
And round each passage turning.

The melted grease flared in the fire,
And filled the air with smoke,
The firemen wearing gas masks,
For fear that they would choke.

Ten minutes was the longest time,
That they could work down there,
The heat and fumes and burning fat,
Were more than they could bear.

The funerals of Station Officer Jack Forte-Wells and Fireman Richard Stocking, departing from Clerkenwell fire station in January 1958. (Permission of the London Fire Brigade.)

223

But two men lost their way below,
And lay down there to die,
The searchers found them but too late
To lead them to the sky.

Another day had passed,
When an explosion rocked the town,
Then broke out into the air,
And Smithfield tower came down.

One hundred feet into the air,
The greasy flames leapt high,
From Clerkenwell to London Bridge,
We saw them in the sky.

From every London Fire Brigade,
They came to fight the flames,
A thousand firemen heroes,
We didn't know their names.

But two men died and two wives cried,
And three young children too,
Remember them and all the men,
Who fight the fires for you.

Coverage of the Smithfield fatal fire in *Fire* **magazine, March 1958. (Courtesy of** *Fire* **magazine.)**

592   *FIRE* March, 1958

CROWDS PAY TRIBUTE TO LONDON FIRE-FIGHTERS

They died at Smithfield

THE funeral of Station Officer Jack Fourt-Wells and Fireman Richard Stocking who lost their lives at the Smithfield blaze was held at Streatham Crematorium.

The coffins were borne on a turntable ladder from Clerkenwell fire station and was followed by a long cortege.

The Brigade provided a guard of honour at Clerkenwell fire station, Brigade Headquarters and at Streatham Park Crematorium.

The service was conducted by the Rev. D. F. Strudwick, who is a serving member of the London Auxiliary Fire Service, and Mr. W. T. Kent, the Fire Brigade's missionary.

As the funeral cortege passed Smithfield Market firemen were still damping down the ruins of the smouldering building.

The wreath-laden turntable ladder bearing the bodies of Station Officer Fourt-Wells and Fireman Stocking passes Smithfield Market.

SOUTHWARK

The former Metropolitan Fire Brigade and London Fire Brigade Headquarters 1878–1937

by Gordon White

One hundred years ago last month [1978] an impressive ceremony marked the opening of the new headquarters of the Metropolitan Fire Brigade in Southwark Bridge Road, Southwark.

Although the headquarters building was demolished nearly a decade ago, the centenary provides a timely opportunity to look at the history of the site and its buildings. The land on which the current Southwark Training Centre, Southwark fire station and Winchester House stand first came to prominence in 1770

The original frontage of the Metropolitan Fire Brigade Headquarters in Southwark Bridge Road in about 1920. The arch frontage was demolished in the late 1960s by the Greater London Council following years of neglect after bomb damage during the Second World War. (Mary Evans 10535440.)

when one Thomas Finch inherited a house on the adjoining St George's Fields. He noticed that on a nearby plot of land, which formed part of the Winchester Park Estate, there was a spring. Finch, an enterprising individual, saw business potential in the spring and bought the land at a knockdown price. He then claimed that the spring had medicinal qualities and, to attract customers, laid out gardens, built an octagonal shaped house, installed an organ and provided orchestral music.

An artist's impression of the horse-drawn fire engine pulling away from the Metropolitan Fire Brigade headquarters' fire station, opened in 1878. (Permission of the London Fire Brigade.)

It became known as 'Finch's Grotto' – something of a miniature Vauxhall Gardens – and was remarkably popular. In due course Finch sold the business to a Mr Williams who added costly firework displays and other attractions. Over-ambition is said to have been the cause of Mr Williams' eventual bankruptcy and the closure of the grotto, although the location nearby of two open sewers may have had some bearing on its demise!

The land was bought by the Parish of St Saviours who built a workhouse on the site. Most of the original fabric of the north-west corner, which today leads into the Southwark Training Centre yard, was the original entrance. The north and west blocks around the drill yard are the old workhouse buildings.

The only other remaining evidence of the workhouse is a tablet to the memory of a Mr Pilgrim Warner which lies beneath one of the lecture room floors. The inscription reads: 'Sacred to the memory of Pilgrim Warner Esq, who died on the 7 March 1807, aged 45 years, whose remains lie here. Mourned by all who know how to estimate abilities of the secretary, politeness in a gentleman and fidelity in a friend.' Warner had been secretary to the Winchester Park Estate and must have had much to do with the running of the workhouse.

His death marked the end of the workhouse's days and the property was bought by Mr Rawlinson Harris, MP for Southwark. He was a hatter by trade and converted and used the old workhouse buildings as a hat factory.

In 1820 Mr Harris built what we know now as Winchester House. This was originally a pair of houses, one for Mr Harris and his family and the other for Robert and Arthur Pott, two brothers who leased the house from Mr Harris. The houses were fronted by sweeping lawns but the surroundings were spoiled to no little extent by the remaining presence of the open sewers, one of them where Southwark Bridge Road now runs. Not until nearly 30 years later, when Henry Daulton had invented stoneware sanitary drainage pipes and the Public Health Act was passed, did the last of the open sewers cease to poison London's air.

The London Fire Brigade headquarters' watchroom and control room at the Southwark headquarters.(Mary Evans 10793337.)

Drills at the London Fire Brigade Southwark headquarters, circa 1905. Firemen using hook ladders on the building whilst the engine's coachman controls the Tilling's horses. (Mary Evans 10535082.)

In 1866 the entire site and its buildings were purchased by the Metropolitan Board of Works who wished to build a headquarters for the newly-formed Metropolitan Fire Brigade. On a macabre note, while contractors were digging out for the foundations of the new building they unearthed a vast quantity of human remains and it was thought at the time that this must have been the site of a burial pit following the Great Plague of London in 1665. In truth, however, the area immediately to the front of Winchester House had been the burial ground for the inmates of the workhouse.

When the new headquarters were opened in 1878 Winchester House became the home of the Chief Officer, Captain Eyre Massey Shaw. It had been one of his requirements that he should be provided with a house of not less than 20 rooms; hence the two original dwellings became one.

Winchester House continued to be the home of successive Chief Officers up to 1937 when the new, purpose built Brigade HQ was built at Albert Embankment. The Chief Officer's quarters moved to Lambeth.

Winchester House housed several fire officers and a number of officers during the war.

The old headquarters building sustained extensive damage as a result of German bombing in the attacks on London during the Second World War. It remained derelict until 1969 when it was finally demolished, thus opening up Winchester House to public view once more.

Left: Presentation of the London County Council's Long Service medal to officers and men of the London Fire Brigade at the Southwark Headquarters. (Mary Evans 10793579.)

Below: Learner fire engine drivers outside the London Fire Brigade headquarters in Southwark Bridge Road. SE1. (Mary Evans 10535916.)

Below is **FRANK MUNDELL**'s *description of Southwark station from* Stories of the London Fire Brigade *(1894).*

A horse-drawn escape cart leaving the headquarters fire station in Southwark and speeding down Southwark Bridge Road, in the direction of the Elephant and Castle. (Permission of the London Fire Brigade.)

The LONDON FIRE BRIGADE at work

WINCHESTER HOUSE, Southwark, the headquarters of the Metropolitan Fire Brigade, is one of the sights of London, though it may not have a place in the Guidebook. We can, however, assure our readers that it is well worth a visit, on account of the many interesting and ingenious appliances which are contained within its walls.

When the visitor is ushered into the office, he finds himself surrounded by what appears to be, to his inexperienced eyes, a bewildering mass of tubes and bells. Here are fixed the telephones, bearing the names of the various stations, by means of which immediate communication with the various parts of the metropolis can be obtained, and the particulars of a fire promptly reported.

Not the least interesting feature in this room is the Roll of Honour. This is a large oak frame, to which are attached brass tablets, bearing the names of heroic firemen who have met their death at the post of duty. Among these may be seen James Braidwood, Joseph Ford, and Joseph G. Jacobs.

As we pass through the various rooms, we are struck with the air of quiet and order which pervades the establishment, contrasting strongly with the hoarse noises of the busy city outside. Though strict discipline is maintained, the men, as they move about attending to their several duties, have the free and easy bearing of sailors.

In the repairing shop we find quite an exhibition of fire-extinguishing machines of one kind and another. Some are standing ready for use, others are being repaired, and others again are being tested. The boilers of the steam-engines are examined every six months, and subjected to very high pressure, that there may be no risk of explosion while on service. No detail is too small and no labour is considered too great to ensure the safety of the firemen and the public.

In the stables we see the same perfect arrangement, accompanied by cleanliness and neatness. Horses are standing facing outwards in their stalls, with collars round their necks, while above their heads is the harness, which, by means of a simple apparatus, can be let go at a moment's notice. No sooner is the

The London Fire Brigade headquarters in Southwark Bridge Road, showing the original fire station and the horse drawn fire engines heading southwards with people on the streets stopping to stand and stare. Circa 1905. (Permission of the London Fire Brigade.)

signal given than the trappings fall on to the animal's backs, and they are in the shafts as quick as winking.

The horses are fine-looking animals, and are selected with great care, but the work is so trying that they do not last many years. They are trained by the firemen, and they learn their duty in an astonishingly short time. The jingling of bells seems at first to bewilder them, but in a few days they become accustomed to the sound. The whip is never used in teaching them. Kindness and little presents of an apple or a lump of sugar are found to be more effective.

One of the strength tests for potential recruits wishing entry into the London Fire Brigade. Firemen demonstrating how to raise the escape ladder into an upright position by means of a line and pulleys in the drill yard of the headquarters station at Southwark, SE1. (Permission of the London Fire Brigade.)

In the yard the new men are drilled and put through the work which they will afterwards be required to perform. Each man is taught how to manage a fire escape alone, and how to jump on and off the engine in the most expeditious manner. The rescue drill, as it is called, is very interesting, and tests the strength and smartness of the men to the utmost. All the details of a fire are thoroughly worked out. The man ascends the ladder, and leaps upon the parapet, while another represents the unconscious figure of a suffocated person, whom he promptly seizes and carries down the ladder to the opening of the shoot of the escape. In a moment the supposed victim is placed in the net head downwards his rescuer following in the same position. The fireman uses his elbows and knees as breaks, to prevent a too rapid descent. The feat of lifting a grown-up person into the position necessary for carrying him down the ladder, amid all the terrible surroundings of a fire, requires great nerve and strength.

The expedition and the wonderful promptness with which the firemen respond to the call of fire is remarkable, and would not be possible but for the splendid organisation of the Brigade, and the thorough training to which they are subjected. Ever on the alert, like the sentinels of an invading army in an enemy's country, they never forget that a moment's delay, or an act of carelessness, may result in disaster to themselves and to those who can only be rescued by their assistance.

Suddenly the silence of the night is broken by the most terrible cry which can fall on human ears – a cry which often paralyses those in danger, and renders them incapable of clear thought or prompt action, when both are of the most vital importance. Charles Dickens writes: 'Of all the rallying words whereby multitudes are gathered together, and their energies impelled forcibly to one point, that of "Fire!" is perhaps the most startling and the most irresistible. It levels all distinctions; it sets at naught sleep, and meals, and occupations, and amusements. It turns night into day, and even Sunday into a working day. It gives double strength to those who are blessed with any energy, and paralyses those who have none. It brings into prominent notice, and converts into objects of sympathy, those who were before little thought of, or who were perhaps despised. It gives to the dwellers in a whole huge neighbourhood the unity of one family.'

When the alarm reaches a fire station, there is heard at once the sound of hurrying feet and the clattering of horses' hoofs. In a few seconds the animals are harnessed to the engine, the men are in their places fully equipped, and almost before a passer-by has had time to ask the meaning of the bustle, the engine is gone. As the horses gallop through the streets, covered with foam, with the engine with its swaying forms and bright-helmeted attendants, the only wonder is that it reaches its destination in safety.

A loud shout from the multitude announces its arrival at the scene of the fire, and a ringing cheer is heard as the first jet of water is thrown on the flames, In an incredibly short time, the firemen make their way to every coign [corner] of vantage from which they may, effectively, direct their hose. Occasionally a glimpse is caught of the helmet of a fireman standing on some tottering wall, but the next moment clouds of smoke hide him from view. Suddenly a sea of white faces is upturned, as a loud, shrill cry is heard from the figure of a woman, who is now seen wringing her hands and imploring help from an upper floor window. A deafening shout goes forth as the huge fire escape is placed in position, and a nimble fireman hurries up the ladder, springs through the window, and disappears. A deathly silence falls on the watchers below; the blood in a thousand hearts runs cold. The unspoken questions, 'Will he be in time? Will he return?' are in every mind. Ah, there he is, back at the window with the woman in his arms, and the pent-up feelings of the multitude are relieved by an outburst of cheering. A moment later, and a fresh deed of heroism has been added to the brave annals of the Fire Brigade. Sometimes human strength and human endurance are all too little to effect a rescue. Both perish in the flames, and another name is added to the 'Roll of Honour'.

The scene at Southwark headquarters after a 'district call' (requiring all the engine of the district to respond urgently to a fire.) A new style, self-propelled, Fire King horseless steam fire engine can be seen toward the rear of the picture and these engines were introduced into the London Fire Brigade in 1904. (Mary Evans 10536549.)

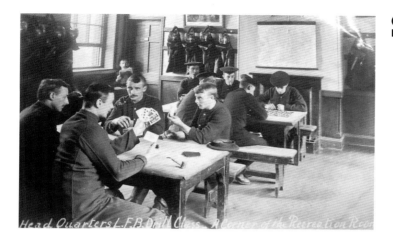

Footnote

Frank Mundell's book Stories of the Fire Brigade *has appeared frequently in this anthology. Mainly published by the Sunday School Union, he was a prolific author whose other books include* Heroines of Daily Life *(1896) and* Stories of the Victoria Cross *(1895). Here is Mundell's description of fire itself.*

· ·

Fire is a good servant but a bad master. We know only too well the truth and wisdom of the old proverb. It is indeed the best of all servants, because it is the most useful; and the worst of masters, because it is the most tyrannical. As a servant, 'Fire is a companionable friend, who meets your face with welcome glad, and makes the poorest shed as pleasant as a palace;' but as a master it is the most frightful and destructive of enemies.

T TURN-OUTS

The Fireman's Wife

by Mrs Jean Johns, Tottenham fire station, London N15

Turn out from Lambeth-LFB HQ station, circa 1964. (Permission of the London Fire Brigade.)

It's not a bad job – quite well paid,
The Station's become his second home,
I'm pleased he joined the Fire Brigade,
Well, who am I to moan and groan!

His work is exciting – his interests are many,
He's got hundreds of new friends, so look,
Now tell me, why is it I who have not any?
My social life ruined by a Rota book.

'No we can't come – he's on duty that night
No not Sunday either, he's on days then,
You'll let us know – yes, that's all right,
He can always try for a "PH" again.'

We could get together, us Fire Brigade wives,
Just a small hen party perhaps one night.
I bet we could have the time of our lives,
But one husband is on Blue Watch, another is on
   White.

So we'll just have to wait and worry alone,
All through the Day Shift then the fifteen hour
   night,
Yes we'll still be here when you come back home,
To welcome you back for your brief respite.

So when you set out, your fires to fight
Your two-tone Klaxon deafening the sky,
Think of your wives alone in the night.
Remember after you'd said your goodbye,
Didn't she say, as she always does,
'God bless you, and bring you home safely
   my love'?

The Call of Duty

by Station Officer Joseph Elliott

The bells go down and duty calls
Another shout to Wren's St Paul's
Over the railings, through the grill
All the firemen know the drill.

Grab the keys, illuminate,
Unlock the door, and then the gate.
Man the phone; known as main stairs,
Doing it quietly during prayers.

O-I-C, like well-trained gnome
Sets off with keys to search the dome.
Round numerous voids, with nostrils set,
He smells no smoke or fire yet.

Crews arrive from over the river,
Junior bucks just stand and quiver.
Search the crypt and main church floor
Just like you've done, ten times before.

The unit comes with two tone blaring,
They gaze to see if dome is flaring.
Nothing visible from outside.
Let's go in, and try to hide.

Deputy stands fast at main stairs
Where he is, he has no cares.
All deserted and alone,
He waits for calls upon the phone.

Back come the messages: nothing found.
St Paul's will not burn to the ground.
Crews return with lungs all tight,
We've saved it for another night.

On the search we've given our all,
To protect this monument to St Paul.
The Cathedral stands there yet again,
'*This* masterpiece by Mr Wren.'

Cannon Street's pump escape pictured at St Paul's Cathedral, on whose fire station ground St Paul's was located, 1964. (Mary Evans 10794385.)

The Message of the Bells

by Anon

(Dedicated to the men of the London Fire Brigade)

A turn out from the London Fire Brigade A Divisional headquarters at Paddington on London's Harrow Road, in the late 1960s. (Mary Evans 10795013.)

To those beleaguered by the flame.
Wherein the fire god Vulcan dwells.
Distant on the morning breeze, came
The brazen clangour of the bells.

Promise of succour drawing nigh.
Ever louder the sound is borne.
And hearts sore troubled lift up high.
By hope of rescue in the dawn.

The bells loud clamour seems to cry
We're coming, wait, and take a breath
Of hope, and pray for those who'll try,
To wrest you from the hand of Death.

Rescue of a burned woman from a Peckham flat in December 1991. (Permission of the London Fire Brigade.)

A shout. 'They're here. Now don't jump':
The call, heard above the flames' roar.
'Slip and pitch, get ready the pump,
People are trapped on the third floor.'

The escape's pitched and in they go,
On Mercy's work with Death to beat:
In time? Ah, yes. See in the glow?
And thankful murmurs fill the street.

Down the escape the rescued go,
Skilful hands bear them on their way;
While fiercer the relentless foe
Strains after its escaping prey.

Then, 'Water on!' And the attack,
By dauntless crew with branch and hose,
Drives the devouring furies back,
And smothers their expiring throes.

Ready. Aye, ready, is their claim.
These firemen, and, doing their best
To pit themselves against the flame,
Dare all, no less, whate'er the test.

Uniformed Fears – The Mind Lockers

by Kevin Wright

U

When thinking of a story for inclusion in the London Fire Brigade magazine's 'Letters to the Editor' I naturally thought of the various fires and other emergencies I've attended over many years. But on reflection I considered that there would be plenty of such tales written, and recounted by others, relating to a vast array of operational incidents, some of which I may well have attended. It was then that 'lockers' came into my head and my very own mind locker was reopened.

When firefighters join the London Fire Brigade, in fact probably any of the UK's fire brigades, they quickly learn that lockers are going to play a big part in their fire brigade life and their vocabulary. I know I did. We were given a personal locker at training school, and then at the fire station. Somewhere for the safe storage of your personal possessions, your civilian clothing, and fire brigade uniforms. The inside of locker doors would soon be adorned with pictures of loved ones, or pinups, or even a favourite car and motorbike.

All fire engines have lockers too: offside lockers, nearside lockers and foot lockers. Here a variety of necessary front line emergency equipment is stored. It ranges from the all-important rolls of 25 metre lengths of hose to the ancillary small gear such as hose beckets (that can secure a line of hose to a ladder) and hose bandages (that can stem a burst in a water filled hose line). Everything has a place, standardised within Brigades, so that whether it's your own fire engine or another station's, you know exactly where everything is!

As a young probationary firefighter I was constantly quizzed by the 'older hands' (qualified firefighters): where is so and so stowed on the engine? Then to go and fetch this and that without hesitation. You learn quickly through these practical tests and the constant questions and answer (Q&A) sessions. Lockers and what is stowed in them even plays a part in the probationary exams!

These are the fire service's physical lockers. You have your personal locker, you are allocated one. No matter where you are stationed, or how your career progresses, (albeit through promotion or transferring from one station to another station) you will always have your own locker. It is something, which over the years, sees a gradual accumulation of different clutter, both personal and fire brigade, which for some reason is stashed away in your locker. The necessary items always easily at hand, whilst the unnecessary is hidden away under something else, lost in the locker's darkest corners and only seeing the light of day when you have a clear out, or it's your time to move on to your next posting or eventually retire from the service.

But there is one other locker. It is the one that nobody really talks about. The locker you can do nothing about, that is unconsciously forming in the darkest corners of your mind. This one you keep until the day you die. This I call the 'mind locker'. Stored in this one you will file away everything from your first shout to your last and so much more in-between! Your memory may fade with age, faces remembered but names forgotten, but there will be a word, a colour, or a smell of something that will suddenly unlock the mind locker door!

Just like your personal locker this one in your mind has everything nicely in place, all the wonderful memories easily to access. But you still have dark, out of the way, corners. In these dark corners, and hidden away amongst all the good, are your ghosts. The memories you wish could be taken away but never can. Again something quite simple, yet clearly related in your memory banks, will bring them back to haunt you in an instant!

I, like nearly every other firefighter, have these personal ghosts that stay, mostly, neatly locked away inside my mind locker until they are suddenly bought back by some unwanted trigger, whilst never knowing when or where this may happen. I'm lucky, I seem to be able to cope with my ghosts' well enough. Sadly other colleagues have been less able to cope. Some have suffered so badly that they have been prematurely medically retired because their brain lockers are full to overflowing. Their only hope in exorcising their personal ghosts is with the aid of specialist help!

However, I do have one ghost that regularly haunts me. Maybe the telling will provide me with an opportunity to see it exorcised, banished, and gone? Perchance the person involved will even get to read this and understand that at the time I found myself alone, without the aid of colleagues to help, and left panicking to frame a suitable reply, but without the luxury of time to think my answer through.

It was just before Christmas 1989. I had been ordered to go to another station, a stand-by duty to Hayes fire station, a fire station close to Heathrow Airport. Standing-by meant that I was covering a station that was short of firefighters to crew the station's engines. I made up the required number of firefighters necessary to be on duty that shift. I was working with people I knew but not from my own watch at Heston in West London. As I recall it was late morning when the call to a road traffic accident (RTA) with people trapped was received at the station. When we arrived at the incident there were two vehicles involved in a serious crash. One of the vehicles looked as if it had exploded on impact. It was immediately obvious that this was a life-threatening accident, with people trapped in one vehicle and the other that had broken up on impact had seen its driver and two passengers thrown from the vehicle and onto the roadway.

I was ordered by Hayes's officer in charge to go to the casualties lying in the road and assess their injuries whilst the remainder of the crew were deployed to extricate those trapped in the vehicle. The three on the roadway were all female. I later discovered that they were a mum and her two daughters who had been going to the local Christmas market to look for those

A road traffic accident (RTA) on the North Circular Road. (Courtesy of Paul Wood.)

last minute Christmas presents. I guessed that the two girls were in their late teens or early twenties.

It was obvious, as I drew nearer, that they were all seriously injured. When I reached the mother it was clear she had received fatal injuries and was already dead. The two sisters were some little distance away, both alive, but from visual inspection suffering from serious leg and head injuries with the possibility of other multiple injuries. Both conscious, they were both in considerable pain and going into shock.

I had taken a salvage sheet, already fearing the worst, and used it to cover the mother's body, thus keeping it out of the sight of the two girls' and the public's gaze. It was whilst covering the body I heard this voice, 'My Mum's dead isn't she?' I turned to see, that even with the terrible injuries she had sustained, one of the sisters had dragged herself along the roadway to try to be with her dead mother. The daughter looked pleadingly into my eyes, a look I will never forget, and even though she feared the worst, I could tell from her eyes and heart breaking voice that there might be hope!

The daughter's question caught me totally off guard. I just looked at her and said, 'No.' It's my answer that still comes back to haunt me. Why did I give her false hope? Why did I say NO? There was no time to say any more. The Ambulance crews now arrived and immediately started to treat her and her sister and to try and stabilise their injuries. There was no opportunity to saying anything else to her, although I stayed with her until she was taken to the air ambulance, a relatively new concept then, although I would work alongside it and its crews many more times in years to come.

I have experienced many similar incidents over the years, some much worse, but this remains one of my ghosts in that locker in my head. One that refuses to leave. I would give anything to be able to turn back the clock. To be able go back in time and to tell this young woman, 'I'm so sorry if I gave you false hope.' Should you ever get to read this then please understand why I said 'No' and I am truly sorry for being weak and not telling you the truth when you most needed to hear it!

VICTORIAN LONDON RESCUES AND FATALITIES

(From Stories of the Fire Brigade by Frank Mundell, 1894)

A big V letter in the top right corner.

A t the headquarters of the London Fire Brigade, there is a room in which may be seen many interesting relics of fiery warfare. Ranged along two sides of this apartment are the helmets, smoke-begrimed, dinted, and in some cases quite shapeless, of men who have been killed or wounded while on duty. To each relic is attached a label, on which is recorded the fate of the wearer, together with the date and locality of the accident. The following is a specimen –

'This helmet belonged to Fireman W. B. Smart, who was killed at Hargrave Park, Upper Holloway, June 10, 1892.'

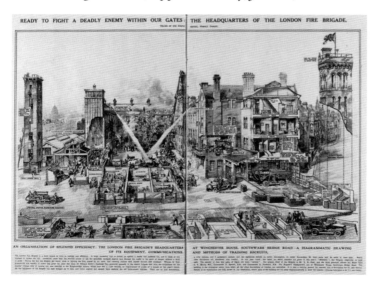

An 'exploded' artist's view of the LFB Headquarters complex at Southwark. Circa 1904. (Permission of the London Fire Brigade.)

Smart lost his life by being buried beneath some bricks, and on this occasion the firemen showed how devoted they are to one another. When the fire had been got under control, Smart's comrades went to the spot and dug out his body. While they were so engaged they were exposed to great peril, for they were working near a tottering wall, which might have fallen at any moment. Had it done so, the workers, twelve in number, would have met the fate of their companion.

A brass helmeted London fireman climbs an escape ladder at an east London warehouse blaze, 1930s. (Mary Evans 10535954.)

In another part of the room may be seen a piece of charred tunic, a small portion of a belt, part of an axe handle, and a few scraps of underclothing. 'These are remnants or the clothing and accoutrements of *Fireman Joseph G. Jacobs*, who was burned to death at a fire in Bell Lane, Wandsworth, on September 12, 1889.' The story of this fire is a touching record of pure heroism.

On the 12th of September 1889, a terrible fire broke out at the large works of Messrs. Burroughs & Wellcome, manufacturing chemists, Bell Lane, Wandsworth. The outbreak occurred in a very high building of three floors. No time was lost in raising the alarm, and soon the engine was upon the scene. A stand-pipe was immediately brought into use, and two firemen, named Jacobs and Ashby, ran the hose up the staircase in order to get at the flames. This staircase was at the farther end of the building, and the men had then to work back again along the upper floor in order to reach the spot where the fire was raging.

The two men stood calmly on the top floor, directing the hose in the midst of a cloud of suffocating smoke, hardly knowing whether they were gaining on the fire, or whether the fire was gaining on the building; suddenly a terrific explosion was heard, and wood, slates, and stones were hurled into the air. At the same time, the staircase was demolished, and the only means of escape for Ashby and Jacobs was thus cut off.

Fireman of the Metropolitan Fire Brigade. (Courtesy of the London Fire Brigade Museum.)

Both men rushed to the window, and the crowd below heard a cry from above, 'Throw up a line.' The window-frames of the room in which the poor fellows were imprisoned were made of iron, with a swing sash in the centre for ventilation. The fire was rapidly advancing on the men while they were endeavouring to break through the stubborn metal. In the meantime, a scene of terrible excitement was proceeding below. Engineer Howard was endeavouring to join his men, and, finding that this was impossible, rushed about to find some means for their escape. Three lengths of the ladders always carried on the engines were joined together, but these would not nearly reach the window. Then a builder's ladder was procured and lashed to the others, but even this fell short of the window by a few feet.

Meanwhile, a terrible struggle had been going on behind the iron bars. Jacobs, who was rather stout, saw at once that escape was hopeless as far as he was concerned, but of this he said not a word to his companion, but bent all his energies to assist him. The crowd raised a cheer when they saw that Ashby, who was a small man, was being pushed through the swing sash by Jacobs. Without a moment's hesitation he dropped from the

Victorian artist's impression of the Metropolitan Fire Brigade at work. (Courtesy of the London Fire Brigade Museum.)

Pen and ink drawing of multiple rescues using escape ladders and their add-on ladders at a London terrace. (Courtesy of the London Fire Brigade Museum.)

window-sill, and in some extraordinary way managed to drop or fall onto the top of the ladder and cling to it. Though almost powerless with fatigue, and dreadfully burned, he got safely to the ground.

All attention was again directed to the third floor, where Jacobs was seen bravely endeavouring to break through. Suddenly, admiration gave way to horror, for he was seen to fall backwards into the flames. As soon as the premises had cooled, his comrades went in and found his charred remains lying face downwards. He had laid down his life for his friend.

Another interesting relic is the helmet of Joseph Ford, who lost his life at a fire nearly twenty-five years ago. Early on Saturday morning the 7th of October 1871, a fire broke out in Gray's Inn Road. The alarm was at once sent to the Holborn station of the Brigade, and Ford, who had charge of the fire escape there, was soon on the spot with his machine.

The flames had then obtained a considerable hold upon the house, and the inmates were imploring help from the crowd in the street. They were at the top storey of the house, and as the fire quickly rose, their deaths seemed certain, and their cries for help became heartrending.

Ford lost no time in pitching his escape against the building, and ascending the ladder to their assistance. With the help of Police Constable George Carter, he succeeded in bringing five persons down to safety. Suddenly a piteous cry from a woman, who had been left behind, was heard. The flames were by this time bursting from the first floor windows, but without a moment's hesitation, and amid the hoarse cheers of the crowd, Ford ascended the escape again. He succeeded in getting hold of the woman, when, all at once, the fire caught the canvas shoot of the escape, and rescuer and rescued were enveloped in flames.

Unable to hold her any longer, he was obliged to let her drop, and she fell to the ground, without, however, sustaining any serious injury. Ford was not so fortunate. While attempting to descend the escape, his axe became entangled in the wire network, and there he hung, absolutely powerless, at the mercy of the flames, and being literally roasted to death.

After struggling for a few moments, he managed by a desperate effort to break through the network. He fell to the ground, but with such force as to double up his helmet, the brass work of which inflicted a dangerous wound on his head. The flames about his burning clothes were soon extinguished, and he was removed in a pitiable condition to the hospital near at hand. He lingered in great agony till about eight o'clock on the following Saturday night, when death put an end to his sufferings.

Thus died Joseph Ford, in the gallant discharge of duty. But for him the lives of six persons would doubtless have been lost. Having previously risked his life in saving five of them, he made a still more desperate attempt to rescue the sixth. In that heroic act, he fell a victim to his own courage. The policeman, Carter, had a wonderful escape. On seeing that Ford was entangled in the wire netting of the machine, and that his own escape by the regular way was impossible, he glided down one of the lever ropes, and, in so doing, rubbed the flesh off his hands.

Period print of the Metropolitan Fire Brigade carrying out a rescue on the escape ladder. (Courtesy of the London Fire Brigade Museum.)

Weird Ship Fire and the Helping Hand...

By Anon

She was a beautiful ship, looming above us at the quayside and throwing her distorted shadow across the quayside and dock buildings. She had seen better days, yet had that air of grace and dignity which somehow seems missing from today's sleek super streamlined liners, which to my eye have as much individuality as mass produced saloon cars.

On the very first occasion this grand old lady of the sea had made her stately way up the River Thames in to London, she had encountered trouble. A great pall of oily black smoke hung lazily above the dockyard, moving lightly in the soft summer breeze, taking the appearance of an enormous umbrella with the handle resting on the ship's funnel. From a distance the column appeared quite solid, but as we had approached I saw that it was a violently gushing stream, giving the funnel the appearance of a gigantic tap from which the smoke gushed

Weird ship fire...
(Permission of the
London Fire Brigade.)

forth as a stream of evil black fluid, defying gravity and spilling on to the blue sky floor above.

The old Merryweather fire engine laboured up a slight incline to park on the dockside behind several other appliances. Over the radio I heard a 'priority' message being sent making pumps up to ten. I might have been a bit of a sprog, but I could see that this was going to be quite a job.

Our Guvnor jumped down from the machine and went on to the control unit to book us in attendance. He came quickly back to get us into breathing apparatus. 'Come on, lads, it's BA and topsides for us.' I took off my belt and axe, and helmet and climbed back into the rear cab.

'Here, Guv, I'll pass the sets down.' I said. 'Here's yours.' 'Thanks, young Dave,' he said. 'What about mine, you snivelling young devil?' Peter, our driver asked, a smile on his face.

I heaved the second BA set off its metal brackets. 'Guv gets his because my probation report's due. It's insurance, see? Why should I get yours?' ''Cos I'll fill you in if you make me get up there.' Pete was big enough to do it too. A really violent character on the volley-ball court.

'That's all I asked for, a good reason.' I said, passing the set down to him.

Then I got my own and started the elaborate rigging procedure.

The BA sets weigh thirty pounds each, but when worn the weight is evenly distributed at front and rear and they seem quite light. The small cylinder, with its one hour supply of oxygen, fits snugly in the small of the wearer's back, the breathing bag rests comfortably on the chest. The only thing I don't care for is the mouthpiece, which when in place is as effective as a gag; it invariably tastes of disinfectant.

BA firemen wearing Proto oxygen sets. (Permission of the London Fire Brigade.)

We would work as a team, and walked together to the control unit to report ready for action. The Sub Officer was attempting to do too many tasks at one time, but that's always the way with control staff on a big job. When he saw us he pointed vaguely along the quayside.

'The Divisional Officer's waiting for you on the deck,' he said. 'Will you take up some foam compound with you?' With a five-gallon can of the smelly liquid in each hand we waddled like ungainly penguins up the steeply-inclined gangway, reaching the deck just aft of the main superstructure. From there I could see the smoke billowing from ventilation shafts as well as the funnel.

We dropped our cans of compound along with a small but ever-growing stock, and I turned to Peter. 'Blimey I don't like the look of that lot,' I said, with feeling. 'This is just what you need for your very first job,' he replied. 'In a really big job nobody notices if you make a mistake. The top brass are so safety-conscious there's no risk, and you will talk about your first BA job around mess tables for the rest of your time.' He smiled and gripped my arm in a friendly manner, but it didn't stop the pounding of my heart.

I had only recently completed my training at the BA school, and had not worn 'a set' at a job before. I didn't actually feel fear, but there was a strange tingling sensation at the base of my spine and a general tenseness which made it difficult to co-ordinate my movements.

An Assistant Divisional Officer was at the main control, and he beckoned us across, taking the Station Officer by the arm. 'As you might guess, it's an engine room fire,' he said. 'From what I can make out the maintenance boys have been at work, and I think they cut a fuel line with a welding set. Before we start to fill her with foam I'd like you to see if you can locate the seat of the fire.' The Guv frowned. 'It looks like a damned sight more than a fuel line to me.'

'It is now. There's been one fair explosion since I've been here. I'd guess it was a gas cylinder going off. There are no ship's officers around yet and the contractors are not reliable. Probably been breaking some regulations to get the job done. Just go in and have a look around. No need to take chances.'

We started up our sets, then followed one of the maintenance men along the deck and into the ships accommodation area. I had never been on a large ship before, and even though there were no lights I was greatly impressed by the splendid saloon and its luxury fittings, looking eerie and deserted in the dim light filtering through the small portholes. We followed our guide along carpeted passageways with timber panelling, then passed on through into the crew's domain, the metal deck and dull paintwork in striking contrast to the passengers' quarters. Our guide halted before us.

'This is about as far as I go, mate,' he said. 'Open the iron door and you're in the machinery space. Good luck to you.' The Guvnor removed his mouthpiece. 'Thanks very much.' He turned to me. 'Nothing to worry about, Dave. We'll stick together like porridge to a blanket. A quick recce and, as soon as we've seen all there is to see, it's a hasty retreat we beat. You keep a hold on my belt. Pete will hold yours.' I gave him the thumbs-up sign and tried to exude a confidence which I certainly didn't feel. He replaced his mouthpiece, turned and opened the big iron door. We stepped across the high metal sill and on to metal gratings, Peter closing the door with a metallic clang which echoed through the surrounding silence.

As in the remainder of the ship, there were no lights, only those of our 'CEAG' spark-proof lamps on our sets. The shadows bobbed and danced around us with every move we made, and I could see smoke thinly drifting in the air. We moved forward slowly, our fireboots scraping softly on the bare metal gratings.

Our intention of holding on to each other was scotched from the start. We were on a high observation platform, and the only way down was by a narrow metal ladder so steeply inclined that we found it necessary to go down backwards, facing the ladder in real nautical manner. Each man was on his own at that point, but there seemed little danger, the smoke was still quite thin, drifting wreathlike in the still air. Now though, I thought I could detect a far-away roaring, just discernible above the soft murmur of the gas circulating in my BA set.

The Guvnor went down first, a couple of dozen steps to the lower deck. At that distance he was enveloped in the smoke, his lamp showing as a light patch in the blackness. The lamp stopped its bobbing motion, and I guessed he had reached the bottom of the ladder. I stepped onto the top tread and began to descend. I suppose that I was within a few feet of the lower deck when there came a muffled explosion. I did not hear a bang, but felt the force of the blast pushing me against the ladder. The hot blast of air found the gap between the top of my tunic and my helmet, not hot enough to burn me, but uncomfortable and extremely disconcerting.

Volumes of black oily smoke surrounded me, dense enough to reduce the glow from my lamp to a feeble glimmer. I held on to the sides of the ladder for grim life, for the moment petrified. I couldn't think. Then after a few moments I realised that nothing was happening. No noise, no fire, nothing. And there I was. Clinging on to a ladder like a big ninny. Well, not much good staying there. Should I go up, to Peter, or down, to the Guv? I couldn't see more than a few feet. No sign of their lamps. What should I do? I was sweating freely.

As I was nearer the bottom than the top of the ladder. I decided to go on down. On reaching the deck I stood quite still, listening for the Guv. There was nothing! I tried to call out, but in doing so I took in a little of the smoke filled air and needed no more than that to realise I must not do it again.

The smoke around me was very dense, and with one hand firmly gripping the ladder I crouched down to see if the smoke thinned out at the deck level. It didn't. Well, I thought the Guv must be there somewhere. I began to circle carefully, swinging my foot out in a wide arc to see if I could find him. I hoped with all my heart he was there. What could I do if I found him? I would never get him up that ladder on my own. And where the hell was Peter? He was only a few feet above me, I had expected him to come down for me. As it was, I felt I had done the correct thing. The Guv was down here somewhere, I felt sure. There was only the one way up that I was aware of, up the same ladder I had descended. He would have to have passed me to get backup.

I had been scrabbling about on my knees for some minutes before I realised I had released my hold on the foot of the ladder. What a twit! I must regain it quickly or I would lose my sense of direction. I took a few paces in what I thought to be the right direction and came upon the rounded steel plates of a boiler. I could make out the rivet heads, in my lamp's dim glow. I followed the boiler around and in a moment was among a maze of dials and pipework. I was going in the wrong direction, getting farther and farther away from safety. I must get back, I thought, and almost running I blundered back the way I had come. In an instant I had caught my foot on a trailing cable and fell headlong, catching one shoulder on a protruding control valve. I was sprawling on the deck, almost panic-stricken. There didn't seem to be enough air in my set. I was gasping, sucking hard at the mouthpiece, unable to breathe properly, hovering on the brink of consciousness.

It was at that moment that I looked up and saw an approaching light. Thank the Lord! It must be another crew I thought. What a relief not to be alone any more. I pulled myself painfully to my feet, my lungs still fighting for air.

A dim figure stood before me, indistinct through the haze of smoke.

He was alone, which I thought odd: BA crews always work in pairs, never alone. I got the impression that he was a tall man and not young at all. But as I peered at him, through the haze, he seemed to draw back a little. However, he was indicating something at the side of my set. Of course! The by-pass valve! No wonder, I was gasping. The amount of gas I had consumed during the past few minutes had exceeded the flow of oxygen from the cylinder into the breathing bag, draining its reserve capacity and leaving the bag flat. I gave him the 'thumbs up' and pressed the by-pass valve, inflating the bag. The oxygen tasted sweet and cool, and I breathed deeply and fully.

There was something decidedly odd about my companion, something in his appearance that had me puzzled. For some moments it eluded me. Then I realised that his breathing set was of a different type. Unlike my own with its Terelyne harness, his was of leather, and I recognised it as an old Mark IV set, the type pictured in old fire brigade manuals.

We had not had that type in London for many years. His uniform was slightly different as well. The transfer on his fire helmet was not an LFB badge, I wondered if he had come in from Essex or Kent. I bet the top brass had made pumps 'Plenty' for this little job I fancy, getting in a load of outsiders! Anyway, whoever he was, I was glad to be with him.

For with him I was. There was no doubt that he was in charge. He indicated that I was to follow him, and follow him I did, without any doubt or hesitation. I realised that we were going farther and farther into the ship, not back the way I had come, yet I felt complete confidence in him. In some strange way I just knew that I no longer need concern myself over my companions, Pete and the Guvnor.

We made our way along greasy and cluttered decks, picking our steps carefully, and passing through several water-tight doors. My companion always led, looking back to me frequently, and always maintaining the same distance between us. I never managed to make up enough distance to take hold of his belt yet, when I slowed to overcome some particular hazard, I would look to find him still that same few steps ahead of me.

We had by now been going for quite a while, and I was feeling some concern. The oxygen in my cylinder was running low. The assurance I had felt was wavering. Doubt was now taking its place. Then before me I noticed the smoke thinning. We were about to enter a long tunnel-like passage – the propeller shaft tunnel. I realised. To my surprise, my companion stepped to one side and beckoned for me to lead on. I hesitated and he waved a hand urgently to indicate that I must continue, yet still I lingered. He was by now becoming quite agitated, and took a step back, away from me. I looked away from him, down the propeller shaft tunnel and saw two other men there. More crews on their way in to the job, I thought. But as they approached, I couldn't believe my eyes. It wasn't possible! It was Peter and the Guv! Startled, I turned my gaze back to my companion, my guide and rescuer. As I watched, he took another step back, and lifted one hand, as if in salute. Then, even as I stared, in the almost clear air and in the light from my lamp, he went back again, back to the solid steel bulkhead and back *through* the bulkhead. I stared, unbelieving, at that spot, my knees weak, my head spinning. I leaned forward to steady myself, just as Peter put a hand firmly on my shoulder. It was the last straw. I passed out and was dead to the world.

They helped me along the shaft tunnel and up the ladder to the deck. We were all much shaken, and rested beside the hatch cover we had emerged from. Our safe working time had almost elapsed and emergency crews were being briefed to go in after us. Their relief at seeing us was only exceeded by our relief at getting out, and as they milled around us, confusion reigned. The Assistant Divisional Officer pushed through to us, and squatted down on the deck.

'How are you feeling, lads? Would you like to go to the hospital for a check-over?' 'I feel OK, or will do after a rest,' Peter replied. The Guvnor nodded agreement. 'I'm all right. I just need to rest up for a while. What about you, Dave?' I nodded agreement. A rest and I would be as good as new. After a few brief questions, we were left by ourselves.

We sat on the metal decking, our legs stretched out tunics unbuttoned, and the BA sets laid to one side. The atmosphere between us was strained and conversation restricted to a few words. The other men were fully engaged with the business of fighting the fire. We were ignored.

The Guvnor got wearily to his feet. 'Come on, let's look for a cuppa,' he said, and we trooped off the ship, dumped our sets in the machine and using the fireman's natural instincts we soon found the dock's canteen. It was deserted, its customers busily earning double-double time on the burning ship.

We sat gloomily at a dirty wooden table, steaming mugs of tea before us. Through the murky windows we observed the scurrying fire crews. It made a change, being a spectator. The Guvnor looked at me. 'How did you find your way out of there, Dave?' I sat back, unsure what to tell him. 'I doubt if you would believe me if I told you.' 'You weren't shown the way, by any chance?' Peter joined in. 'He was in NFS rig, the gear that was worn during the war.' 'Did you notice his set, his Breathing Apparatus?' I said. 'It was an old type, I've seen it in an old manual.' Peter nodded, 'It was a Mark IV set, used during the war and up until about fifteen years ago.'

So, it seems the three of us had been led to safety, separately yet at the same time, by the same man. We came to an agreement there and then not to spread the story around. It would sound like just another of those tall stories which are regularly told around the mess tables in fire stations all over the country. I doubt if anyone would have believed it. Well, there's always someone who might.

WHEN THE SMOKE THINNED OUT

By Anon

Dave Chambers spluttered and coughed as he forced his reluctant body forward into the smoke. His throat was sore and his eyes stung like the devil. Deep inside he felt real fear. How on earth had he become separated from the others in his crew? Well, it wasn't surprising when you stopped to consider. The smoke given off by the burning waste paper and cardboard was dense and acrid. Blasted waste paper! Might as well let it burn itself out!

They had received the call to the warehouse on fire, just after 9 o'clock on Friday 28 April. It was his brother's birthday that day, and they had planned to go to the Duke of Cambridge straight from the station that night. He knew that after this lot

Waiting for news. (Permission of the London Fire Brigade.)

he was going to have a head start over the others when it came to getting a hangover. If he ever found his way out, he thought wryly. Still, no point in thinking that way. Lost in smoke he might have been, but he was not the type to panic. He had kept faithfully to one wall since he had become lost. Follow one wall and he knew he wouldn't waste time by keeping going back over the same ground. Damnation, he had followed that wall for ages, he was surely going further and further into the building.

The warehouse was a pretty big building, three or four hundred feet deep. Apart from all the smoke he had not seen or heard any fire, and it wasn't very hot. He pushed on, left hand groping for the wall, feet warily testing the ground ahead. Every couple of minutes he stopped to listen. He heard nothing above the noise of own laboured breathing. 'Surely,' he thought, 'surely they will have missed me by now. They must have started a search?'

He was about to retrace his steps when he thought he detected a slight thinning in the smoke ahead. Yes, it had become just a little lighter. He looked up and could make out wired glass in the roof allowing daylight into the building. A few more strides and he was up against a brick wall. He realised he must have reached the rear of the building, so in fact he had been getting deeper in all the time!

The smoke had become much thinner, and he knelt beside the wall to regain his breath. After a few minutes he had recovered sufficiently to move on between the wall and the towering bales of waste paper. He had stopped calling some time ago. His throat felt raw, and he realised that his voice would carry only a very short distance. So he carried on slowly feeling his way along the rear wall. He was looking for a window or a door. Anything to get out of this place. Then just ahead a door. Now that was a break. He moved quickly to it and gave it a push. It opened easily, and disappointment instead of open air, he was looking into a small windowless office. A quick look round showed him that there was no other door. He was in a dead end. More than disappointment he felt fear.

He stepped right inside the small room. The door clicked shut behind him. The click startled him and he suddenly felt quite sure he would never leave that office again. He jumped back to the door knowing he would be unable to open it. He grabbed at the door handle and wrenched it with all his might. The door opened easily and he felt rather foolish, but reassured. With a great effort of mind he steadied himself. After all it was only smokey. No real need to worry. At least not yet.

He closed the door and took a steady look round the small office. Someone had vacated it in a hurry. Its only contents were a desk and chair. On the desk was a large mug of tea. a thin wisp of steam still rising from it. Beside it a newspaper. He thought it might have been left there for him and shuddered at the thought. This place was really upsetting him. He opened the office door again and looked out. The smoke seemed to be thickening. It was better to stay in the office, at least there was no smoke in there yet.

He walked back to the desk and sat down in the chair. He watched as the door slowly swung closed. The latch clicked shut. All was silent as the grave he thought, and couldn't help but smile. Then he laughed aloud. His croaky laugh sounded thunderous in the small room and he quickly choked back the sound. His gaze rested on the mug of tea. He stretched out his hand lifted the mug and sipped at the contents. Marvellous! The best cup of splosh he had ever tasted! He drank deeply, emptying half the contents at one go.

He felt much better for the drink and sat back and undid his belt and fire tunic. He took off his helmet. His breathing was much easier now. He reached for the tea again, and in so doing he knocked the newspaper off the desk and on to the floor. It fell at his feet, open at the back page. The headline was 'Oh! What a finish for Millwall.' That was odd. Millwall's last league game was coming up, but that was tomorrow. They had to beat Preston to stay in the promotion chase. He reached down for the paper and picked it up. The front page said it was Saturday, 29th April, classified edition.

It couldn't be! Today was Friday! He turned the paper over. The 'Stop Press' column had the full classified results. He checked the date again. Sure enough. 29th April 1972. How was it possible? How could he have tomorrow's paper? It was impossible!

He looked at the results carefully. He could remember most of the fixtures from filling in his football coupon. There could be no doubt about it. He actually had tomorrow's paper! In the paper, the football results, the racing results, even the dog racing! It was all there!

He was shaking all over. He had to get out as quickly as possible. He had to get to a telephone. He could lay on a few bets and clean up a small fortune. Even clean up a large fortune! He was nearly hysterical by now. He turned back to the front page to see what else was in the future to, what else would happen tomorrow?

Below the football results in the 'Stop Press' column he read 'Fireman killed in waste paper blaze.' He didn't want to read on, but couldn't seem to stop. He read, 'The body of a fireman, named as David Chambers, missing at the paper warehouse since early yesterday was found in the ruins late this afternoon.'

He jumped to his feet screaming. At that instant the whole place exploded in front of his eyes. It was over in a split second. It was quite painless.

WHITECHAPEL HERO

(Extract from Stories of the Fire Brigade *by Frank Mundell, 1894)*

A typical Victorian illustration of London firemen engaged in a daring rescue. (Mary Evans 10536090.)

Few men there are who can lay claim to such a glorious record of humanity as that of Samuel Wood, one of the bravest of the London firemen who, at the risk of his life, saved nearly a hundred men, women, and children from the flames in Whitechapel, in the East End of London. Much of his success, however, is justly due to his faithful and constant companion – a little dog named Bill.

The animal, a terrier, had been given to Wood when he was only a few months old. As he grew up, he displayed an almost human interest in everything connected with his master's calling. When an alarm of fire was heard Bill began to bark with all his might. Wood had no occasion to sound his rattle for assistance, as the policemen all around knew Bill's bark, and they at once hurried up to give help. If the alarm of fire was given when there were but few people in the street Bill ran round to the coffee-shops nearby, and, pushing open the doors, gave his well-known bark, nor would he leave until he had obtained assistance.

On dark nights the lantern had to be lighted, when Bill at once seized hold of it in his mouth and ran on in front of his master. When the ladder was put in position against the wall of the burning building, Bill was at the top before his master had reached half-way. The sagacious animal then bounded in at a window and, amid thick smoke and the approaching flames, began to hunt about for the inmates. When he found anyone he barked loudly, so that his master might follow the direction of the sound.

On one occasion, the fire burned so rapidly, and the smoke in the room became so dense, that Wood and another man were unable to find their way out. Escape seemed hopeless, and they were just about to give themselves up for lost, when Bill began barking. Taking this as a sign that the dog had found a way out, the two half-suffocated firemen crawled after him on their hands and knees. In a few moments they reached the window, and were saved.

On the 29th of April 1854, Wood was called to a fire which had broken out in a lodging-house in Colchester Street, Whitechapel. On his arrival, he found that a number of unfortunate people were in the house, surrounded by flames. In spite of the clouds of smoke that poured out from every window, he made his way up the ladder to the first floor, and there, with the red flames raging all around, and already making their way through the walls, were five poor creatures – father, mother, and three children half-suffocated by the intense heat. Wood snatched the mother up in his arms, and held one of the children by its clothes in his teeth, while he cautiously made his way to the ground.

No thought of danger could keep him from mounting again to the help of the father and the two little ones still left in the room. Taking a child under each arm, he guided the father to the escape, and they all reached the ground unharmed. Before

The Davis street fire escape. (Mary Evans 10795093.)

Wood could ascend a third time, the upper part of the house fell in, burying eight unfortunate people in the ruins.

Several eye-witnesses of the rescue determined that such courage should not go unrewarded. A subscription was accordingly set on foot, and Wood was presented with £20, and a handsome silver watch, on which was inscribed an account of the deed for which it had been presented.

On another occasion Wood was summoned to a fire in Fashion Street, Spitalfields, There were two poor old folks; John Atkins and his wife, in an upper room, in danger of being burned to death. Wood dashed to their rescue, and succeeded in saving them. The manner in which he accomplished the task will be best seen from the following letter: –

> Sir,
> I cannot help but acknowledge my gratitude and thanks for the preservation of my life and my wife's life. The man found me almost stifled. He could find me, only by my moaning, and when he got me on the fire escape, I cried out for my wife. He asked me where she was. I told him she was in the loft next the tiles. Then he got on the top, and took off the tiles, and got her out on his back, and carried her to the fire escape, and put her in, and so saved her life. So, through the mercy of God and the wonderful skill of the man, we are saved.
> Your humble servant,
> John Atkins.

For his bravery on this occasion Wood received a silver medal, and Bill was also decorated with a badge. Bill's last call also nearly cost the dog his life. Springing eagerly in at an open window, in search of someone to whom he might give or call assistance, he fell through a hole burned in the floor into a tub of water in the cellar. The flames had heated the water to the boiling point, and before the poor animal could be rescued, he had suffered the loss of almost all his coat.

During the nine years that he filled the post of fire escape dog, Bill had many adventures, besides the one just narrated. On three occasions he was run over; but with careful doctoring he recovered, and was able to resume his duties. Around his neck the inhabitants of Whitechapel placed a silver collar, on which was engraved the following inscription -

> I am the fire escape man's dog – my name is Bill.
> When fire is called I am never still.
> I bark for my master, all danger I brave,
> To bring the escape, human life to save.

Again and again did the inhabitants of Whitechapel, roused to enthusiasm by his extraordinary daring, present Wood with marks of their gratitude and admiration. He had a truly formidable collection of medals, rewards, and testimonials on vellum. Highly as he prized these acknowledgments of his bravery, the knowledge that he had been the means of saving so many people from a frightful death must have been a still more precious possession.

Yellow bag of Courage

By Anon

Jack shifted his weight on to his right side and tried to reach the by-pass valve on the Proto breathing apparatus set with his left hand. Blinding pain knifed through his back, causing him to inhale sharply. The rubber breathing bag on his chest, already dangerously starved of oxygen because of the weight of his body, collapsed still further and he momentarily panicked as he fought for breath like a drowning man.

His groping fingers found the valve group and sought out the by-pass valve. As he pushed the button oxygen from the cylinder on his back forced its way into the bag and he sucked it greedily into his lungs.

With the fresh oxygen clearing his mind, Jack thought of his next move.

The distinctive yellow bag of the Proto BA set worn by the Emergency Tender crews. (Courtesy of Paul Wood.)

His right hand moved up to his chest and located his distress signal unit. Quickly, his finger found the button and pushed. He was immediately rewarded by a high pitched shriek which continued. With the immediate priorities taken care of, Jack relaxed a little and tried to take stock of his predicament.

He was lying face down on a pile of smoking debris which was all that remained of the floor that he and his crew had been crossing. Something heavy was pressing down on his legs, trapping him, and he guessed that it was one of the floor joists. He knew that he must be in the basement but couldn't see anything, partly due to the heavy smoke but also as a result of his goggles having misted up with condensation. He could hear the crackle of flames somewhere nearby and could feel the heat beginning to build up on the exposed parts of his skin making him sweat and causing the nose clip of his BA set to slide down his nostrils. Hastily he replaced it and tried to assess his chances of survival and rescue.

The fire in the disused cold store in Tooley Street, Bermondsey, had started simply enough. Workmen had been hot-cutting pipes when suddenly one of them noticed black smoke coming from behind the thick cork used as insulation. A bucket of water, kept handy, had proved ineffective and as the smoke got thicker the foreman had ordered everybody out and had telephoned the Fire Brigade. Although only a matter of minutes had elapsed from the discovery of the fire to the arrival of the first fire appliance a vast quantity of thick black smoke was soon pouring from the building. The Station Officer in charge of the first attendance, being a veteran of numerous Dockland fires, knew that this would be a long, hard fight. He radioed back to his control with the urgent message, 'Make Pumps Ten, Breathing Apparatus required' and set his crews to work.

Jack had just put on his plimsolls and was looking forward to the game of volleyball. It was just after 5 p.m. and they always played volleyball then, fire calls permitting. Suddenly the teleprinter bell began to ring followed, seconds later, by the urgent clanging of the call bells. The game was forgotten as the crews made their way to the appliances and began to rig.

At Jack's station, which was also the Brigade Headquarters, there were five appliances – the Pump Escape, the Pump, a Turntable Ladder, an Emergency Tender and the Canteen Van. Plus there was the Brigade Control Unit. Jack was the Leading Fireman in charge of the ET and as the indicator board lit up for all the appliances the dutyman gave Jack a copy of the call slip and a route card. As they followed the PE and P through the rush hour traffic a look at the cryptic writing on the call slip told Jack that this would be a hardworking job for him and his crew.

Heading towards the Elephant and Castle, but still some two or three miles from the fire, the ET crew suddenly saw the huge pall of smoke from the burning building. They began to rig in their Proto BA sets with the distinctive yellow bags which indicated that the wearer was a member of an ET crew as opposed to the blue bags of the BA sets carried on Pumps.

Once at the scene Jack had waited for his driver to finish rigging and then, followed by the rest of the crew, had sought out and reported to the senior officer in charge. With obvious relief at having an experienced ET crew at his disposal he had ordered Jack and his crew to work a jet into the ground floor and seek out the fire. Depositing their tallies at the BA control they had started up their sets and entered the building. Immediately they had become isolated in the dense black smoke and fear began to touch their spines. Inch by inch, in a series of jerky movements, they moved forward, dragging the heavy hose with them.

In the lead, Jack was methodically testing the floor in front of him as well as the air above before moving forward, indicating by a series of mimed touches to the man behind him any obstacles. These mimed touches were necessary as Jack could neither see the man because of the dense smoke nor talk to him due to the encumbrance of the mouthpiece of his set.

Suddenly, there was a deep rumble from in front and the floor beneath Jack sagged. Before he could retreat the floor collapsed, pitching him forward into empty space. The wooden floor above, already weakened by unseen fire, had collapsed on to the floor that Jack and his crew were crossing. Unable to support the additional weight this, in turn, had collapsed, taking Jack with it.

The man behind him was more fortunate. He had managed to grab hold of the hose and was left dangling over the edge until pulled to safety by the remaining crewmen. They were by now thoroughly alarmed and realising what had happened made their way back along the hose to open air and reported what had happened.

Meanwhile, in the basement, Jack tried to curb his rising panic and remember the 'entrapped' drill. It had always seemed so easy at drills but here in the darkness and smoke, and with the fear, he couldn't think properly.

Slowly his head lolled and he slipped into unconsciousness. He came to as pain once again tore through his back. He had no idea how long he had been out and thought he must be dreaming but the shrilling of his DSU convinced him he was not.

Turning his head to try and ease the pain Jack thought he saw a flash of light. He closed his eyes and opened them again, wishing that he could clear his goggles. Once again he glimpsed the light and stared fascinated as it appeared to hover in mid-air then make its way towards him.

As it got closer he was suddenly able to make out, just below the light, a square yellow shape. As the realisation hit him that it was another ET fireman it all became too much for him and Jack lapsed back into unconsciousness. He didn't hear the urgent clapping of the fireman who had found him, summoning the rest of the crew, nor did he feel the strong hands gently carrying him to safety.

It was the next day, sitting up in his hospital bed – with his broken hip in plaster – that he learned how he had been rescued. His own crew, despite the fact that they had had one lucky escape already, had immediately volunteered to enter the basement to look for him. They had found a set of stairs and descended, passing through the heat barrier and into the smoke.

Once in the basement they had heard his DSU and, keeping in physical touch with each other, had started to search. Finally locating him but not knowing if he was dead or alive they had quickly released him and carried him back to open air and safety. Jack had been put in an ambulance and rushed to hospital.

Jack still remembers, to this day, the feeling of sheer relief as he saw that yellow bag in the smoke and fear of that basement all those years ago.

POSTSCRIPT...

And finally. For five decades an important ingredient of the London Fire Brigade's in-house magazine were its images. So how better to finish this anthology than with a last montage of London's fire brigade. Sadly, from 2002 until 2005 only four editions of the **London Firefighter** were published. Its days were clearly coming to an end...

The magazine also contained some remarkable drawings over the years from its London firefighter artists. Two regular contributors were Graham Le Page and Chris Reynolds; both were operational firemen. Sadly, Graham died shortly after his retirement from the Brigade. It would be most remiss not to pay tribute to all those who amused others with their wit and drawing skills.

Opposite: Montage by the editor. (By courtesy of the Mary Evans Picture Library.)

Left, above: Cartoon by Chris Reynolds. (By courtesy of the artist.)

Left, below: Cartoon by Graham Le Page. (By courtesy of the artist's family.)

'My word! . . . they certainly have made our job a lot easier with these new B.A. guide lines . . .'

273

APPENDIX ONE:
FIREMEN REMEMBERED

World War II London Firemen and
Firewomen's Remembrance Group
(Charity No 1091889)

**The plaque to the London Auxiliary Fire Service (AFS) fatalities at the
Wandsworth Fire Station bombing.**

T his is an independent charity established in the year 2000. It is dedicated to recording, and remembering, those firemen and firewomen who served in the London Region in World War II and commemorating those who died.

The charity was set-up in response to conversations with wartime firemen over a number of years. Its aim is primarily to address the sense of neglect that many felt surrounded the memory of their comrades who had died and, by association, their own contribution to the war.

In Greater London alone, over 400 firemen and firewomen died between the years of 1939 and 1945. Many died as a direct result of enemy action, others as a result of accident, injury or illness while in service. Thousands also were injured, physically and emotionally, and carried the scars of their wartime service for the rest of their lives. Not all who died were casualties of war, therefore, but for those who perished in the line of duty, Firemen Remembered is working to create a lasting memory in the form of commemorative plaques in places where deaths, or injuries that later resulted in deaths, occurred.

The unveiling of the plaque to Sidney Alfred Holder in Shoe Lane, City of London.

Today it is difficult for Londoners and visitors to London to imagine that places we pass every day are the sites of distant trauma and loss but when understood as such they are a powerful and significant part of the history of the capital and, when known, they may serve as places for reflection that taken together tell their own story, providing a unique journey into what the artist Susan Hiller has described in the context of her own work as 'the heartland of loss', in this case at the centre of London's experience of war. In time, memories will fade and the nature of these sacrifices will be lost. Through research and commemoration, Firemen Remembered hopes to locate these memories permanently in the communities to which they belong.

Education is thus an important part of what we do. Based on the lives and work of those who served in the Fire Service and other emergency services we aim to explain some of the problems faced by Londoners and how they adapted and endured in time of crisis.

The unveiling of the Firemen Remembered plaque at Plaistow, East London.

Ideas of community and responsibility are explored through the experiences of Londoners at war. Children are also encouraged to take part in dedication ceremonies, enabling them to consider the idea of Remembrance at first hand. Firemen Remembered provides material for schools in the form of worksheets that in some cases may be tailored to the needs of individual schools. We also provide talks to adult groups on a number of aspects of wartime firefighting in London.

Enquiries and donations to **stephaniemaltman@hotmail.com**

Or to: **Firemen Remembered, 23 Thurlow Park Road, London SE21 8JP.**

APPENDIX TWO:
Roll of Honour

The Roll of Honour of the firemen and firefighters of the Metropolitan Fire Brigade and the London Fire Brigade, who sadly lost their lives in connection with their fire service duties during peacetime.

We shall always remember them.

(Not including are those killed as a direct result of enemy action on London during 1914-1918 and 1939-1945. Entries in bold are those killed in action at an incident.)

The Metropolitan Fire Brigade 1866–1904

MFB. 1866.

7th October 1871
Fm. Joseph A. Ford. Grays Inn Road

10th November 1872
Fm. Stanley M. Guernsey. Upper Thames Street.

26th July 1876
Fm. George Lee. St John Street, Westminster.

27th April 1880
Fm. Patrick Fitzgerald. Charlton Street.

7th December 1882
Asst Officer Thomas C. Ashford. Leicester Square.
Fm. Henry Berg. Leicester Square.

20th December 1882 (Fatal illness following fire)
Fm John Bailey. Wood Street. City

Funeral of Fm Martin E Spraque leaving the fire brigade headquarters in Southwark Bridge Road. 1895. (Permission of the London Fire Brigade.)

24th July 1883

Fm. Richard Long. Greenwich Road.

14th December 1883

Fm. Joseph G. Thatcher. Hamsell Street, City.

24th October 1888

Fm. John. C. Barrett. Upper Marylebone Street.

12th December 1889
Fm. Joseph G. Jacobs. Bell Lane, Wandsworth.

18th February 1890
Fm. J. W. Ansell. Westminster Bridge Road.
Fm. Sidney. A.H. Crowe. Westminster Bridge Road.

10th June 1892
Fm. William B. Smart. Hargrave Park, Holloway.
Fm. William J. Abernethy. Hargrave Park, Holloway.

26th November 1892
Fm. Frederick J. Fielder. Agar Street, Strand.

29th October 1895
Fm. Martin E. Spraque. The Strand, Westminster.

29th July 1896 (Died 31st July Fell from engine responding to a fire)
Fm Charles A. Wilcox. Vanbrugh Fields, Shooters Hill.

21st December 1896
Fm Lunn. Bow.

6th February 1898 (Fatal illness following fire)
Fm. John Rees. Jewin Street.

31st July 1899
Fm Smeed. Crayford, Kent.

3rd January 1900 (Fall from roof during training exercise)
Fm. Samuel Esau Handley. Southwark HQ.

15th April 1901
Fm Fredrick George Baldock. Brixton Road, SW.

The London Fire Brigade 1904–2004

LCC-LFB.1904.

3rd January 1911 (Died 9th July 1911 from injuries)
Superintendent Charles Pearson. Sidney Street, Whitechapel.

28th February 1911
Fm John H. Webster. Bankside, Southwark.
Fm George H. Willan. Bankside, Southwark.

18th March 1913
Fm Robert. L. Libby. Pembridge Villas, W11.
Fm William McLaren. Pembridge Villas, W11.

17th September 1913 (Died 18th September-Fell from hook ladder)
Fm William H.E. Martin. Knightsbridge fire station.

21 June 1914 (Fell from engine responding to a fire)
Fm William H. Mott. Vanbrugh Park, Blackheath.

7th May 1915 (Overcome by acid fumes at fire station)
   Sub Officer William Spensley. Whitefriars fire station.

24th August 1916 (Fell from fireboat and drowned)
   Fm George Cobbolt. Battersea Bridge.

26th January 1918 (Died 31st January, Fatal fall at fire station)
   Fm Henry B. Summers. Greycoat Place, Westminster.

**The front page of the Daily Mirror, 28 February 1911, showing the aftermath
of the Southwark blaze that claimed the lives of Firemen John Webster and
George Willian.**

30th January 1918

Sub Officer W.W. Hall. Albert Embankment.
Sub Officer W. E. Cornfield. Albert Embankment.
Fm. K.J. Fairbrother. Albert Embankment.
Fm. J.W. C. Johnson. Albert Embankment.
Fm. W. E. Nash. Albert Embankment.
Fm. A. A. Page. Albert Embankment.
Temp Fm. J. E. Fay. Albert Embankment.

27th July 1918 (Fell into Thames and drowned)
Fm Edward T. Woolf. Cannon Street fire station.

1st November 1920
Fm John Coleman. Oliver's Wharf, Wapping.
Fm Albert Best. Oliver's Wharf, Wapping.
Fm Harry J. Green. Oliver's Wharf, Wapping.

17th April 1924 (Fell into Thames and drowned)
    Fm John Clarke. Pageants Wharf fire station.

27th May 1924 (Fatal injuries from escape ladder drill)
    Fm John Scholes. Southwark. HQ.

23rd August 1924
    Fm Alfred H. Parsons. Kingsbury Road North.

18th September 1925
    Sub Officer Valentine G. Sindon. Finsbury Street, City.

11th April 1928 (Fatal injuries from escape ladder drill)
    Fm Joseph G. Schubert. Stoke Newington fire station

28th May 1931 (Fatal illness after attending fire)
    Station Officer E Dowsett. Peckham fire station.

3rd January 1933 (Died 5th January – Fatal injuries performing hook ladders)
    Fm Arthur J. Stillman. Southwark HQ.

14th June 1934 (Fatal injuries whilst performing drills)
    Station Officer Cecil Dickenson. Southwark HQ.

13th June 1935 Fatal injuries performing hook ladder drills)
    Fm Arthur J. Putt. Edgware Road fire station.

7th July 1935
    Station Officer Deal. Orchard Place. Blackwall.
    Fm Netley. Orchard Place, Blackwall.

4th April 1938
    Fm Charles P. Sweetlove. Camomile Street, City.

NFS.1941.

1946

Fm George Davis. GC. (NFS) Harlesden, NW10.

LCC-LFB.1948.

20th December 1949

Station Officer Charles Fisher. Tavistock Street, WC2

21st December 1951

> **Fm. Edward Harwood. Eldon Street, EC2.**
> **Fm. Leslie Skitt. Eldon Street, EC2.**
> **Fm. Thomas Joy. Eldon Street, EC2.**

11th May 1954

> **Station Officer Frederick Hawkins. Langley St, WC2.**
> **Fm. Arthur Batt-Rawden. Langley St, WC2.**
> **Fm. Charles Gadd. Langley St, WC2.**

29th July 1954

> **Sub Officer John Skinner. King Street, Hammersmith.**

22nd February 1956

> **Leading Fm. Frederick Willoughby. Kensington High Street.**

1st June 1956 (Fatal fall whilst at hook ladder drills)

> *Fm Ronald Stiles. Downham fire station.*

23rd January 1958

> **Station Officer Jack Fourt-Wells. Smithfield Market, EC1.**
> **Fm. Richard Stocking. Smithfield Market, EC1.**

12th February 1962

> **Station Officer Thomas Carter. Wyndham Road, Camberwell.**
> **Fm. James Bardens. Wyndham Road, Camberwell.**

11th March 1964

> **Fm. Daniel O Donovan. Hilldrop Lane, N7.**

GLC-LFB. 1965.

3rd August 1965 (Fatal fall whilst under taking turntable ladder drills)
     Fm Donald Owen. Wembley fire station.

23rd August 1965 (Died 2nd September 1965 – fell at extension ladder drill)
     Recruit Fm Ronald C. Wiggins. Southwark Training School.

4th December 1966 (Fatal fall whilst using firemen's sliding pole)
     Sub Officer Leslie Tucker. Ealing fire station.

8th March 1968
     Fm. Brian O'Connell-Hutchins. Kings Road, Chelsea, SW3.
     Fm. Colin Comber. Kings Road, Chelsea, SW3.

17th July 1969 (see photograph opposite)
     Sub. Officer Michael Gamble. Dudgeons Wharf, Isle of Dogs.
     Fm. John Appleby. Dudgeons Wharf, Isle of Dogs.
     Fm. Terence Breen. Dudgeons Wharf, Isle of Dogs.
     Fm. Trevor Carvosso. Dudgeons Wharf, Isle of Dogs.
     Fm. Alfred Smee. Dudgeons Wharf, Isle of Dogs.

29th September 1969
   Leading Fm Michael Lee. Goswell Road, EC1.

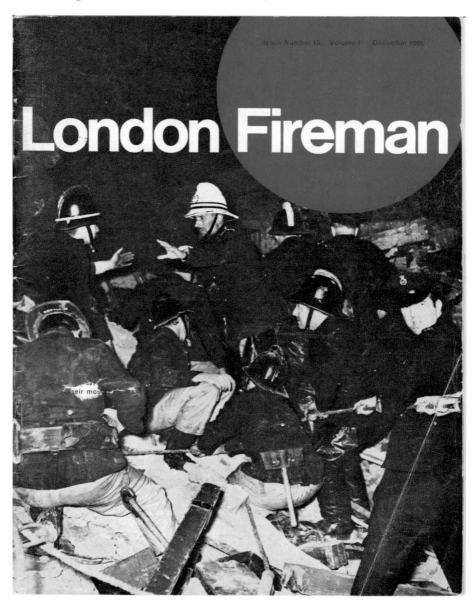

13th December 1974
Fm. Hamish Pettit. Worsley Hotel, Clifton Gardens.

1st October 1978
Fm. Stephen Niell. St Pancras Way, NW1

26th January 1980
Leading Fm. Stephen Maynard. Regent Canal Dock, Mill Place.

30th April 1981
Fm. Anthony Marshall. Broadway, Wimbledon.

27th April 1981
Firefighter Barry Trussell. St Georges' Hospital, Tooting.

27th June 1983 (Died of a heart attack whilst fighting a fire)
Firefighter Derek Potts. Finsbury.

LFCDA-LFB. 1986

18th November 1987
Station Officer Colin Townsley GM. Kings Cross Underground Stn.

10th July 1991
> **Firefighter Terence Hunt. Gillender Street, E3.**
> **Firefighter David Stokoe. Gillender Street, E3.**

30th September 1992 (Died in a traffic accident whilst responding to a fire)
> Temp Sub Officer Kevin Power. Scrubbs Lane, Hammersmith.

10th May 1993
> **Firefighter Michael Hill. Villiers Road, Willesden.**

20th July 2004
> **Firefighter Bill Faust. Bethnal Green Road**
> **Firefighter Adam Meere. Bethnal Green Road**

APPENDIX THREE:
TIMELINE OF LONDON'S FIRE BRIGADES

1666. (2nd September). The Great Fire of London started in Pudding Lane, Eastcheap. 100,000 people were rendered homeless; 13,000 houses were burned plus 44 Livery Companies' destroyed. However, there were only six people reported killed by this fire whilst a great many others were reputed to have died through indirect causes.

1667. The City Council established the first fire insurance company, 'The Fire Office'. It employed a small team of Thames watermen as firemen and provided them with a uniform and badge.

1668. The Government passes an Act which required municipal authorities to provide buckets, ladders, pickaxes and other equipment for fighting fire. The Act only applied to London, it made no provision for the training of the men to use the equipment.

1676. 600 houses in Southwark were burned down.

1680. First fire 'insurance office' opened behind the Royal Exchange. This was followed by the opening of other fire insurance companies.

1682. 1,000 houses destroyed by fire in Wapping.

1686. First manual fire engine developed that gave a continuous jet of water with every stroke of the pump. The height of the jet was claimed to exceed 100 feet. Leather hose, sewn at the seam, allowed the flow of water (with its jet attached) to be taken into a building.

1696. The Hand in Hand Fire Office resolved on the formation of a fire brigade, 'to consist of eight watermen'. Half should reside on the Middlesex side of the Thames and half on the Surrey side.

1707. Act of Parliament passed *'for the better preventing of mischiefs that may happen by fire'.* It dealt with the *'salvation of property'* rather than saving lives, it also covered that insurance offices employ watermen for extinguishing fire.

1708.

1. The Government passes the Parish Pump Act, a law that ordered every parish to keep a water (fire) pump for use in extinguishing fire.

2. The City of London, and immediate suburbs were allowed by a subsequent Act to 'unite' and if so they need only provide one engine for the united parishes.

1710. Sun Fire Office founded together with the introduction of the fire-marks placed on the outside of protected properties.

1720. Twelve London insurance companies established. The Insurance firemen are best described as 'retained'. They were paid to attend drills and calls only. Insurance companies also employed 'porters', the first Salvage Corps; the porters not only saved the goods from damage but protected it from looting and pilfering.

1725. Richard Newsham patented 'a new water engine for quenching and extinguishing fires'. (He had previously patented his water (fire) engine in the USA in 1721.)

1748. Cornhill, in the City of London, was destroyed in a fire that involved over 200 houses.

1755. A ship in dock in Shadwell, a warehouse and over 100 houses were burned out. In Rotherhithe 260 houses and many warehouses were destroyed by fire.

1765. The Sun Insurance Company acquires the first of two fire-floats: a barge that carried a manual fire pump for fighting riverside fires on the Thames.

1774. Parliament decreed that *'every parish should provide three or more proper ladders of one, two and three storeys high, for assisting persons in a house on fire to escape there from'.*

1790. An unknown Insurance fireman was killed at a fire at Aldersgate Street, London in a dispute with 'The Bridewell Boys' (A team of firemen Based at Bridewell Hospital). *Note – Often disputes arose between rival Insurance Company firemen over who had the claim to extinguish a fire.*

1794. 630 houses, and contents, valued at one million pounds destroyed by fire in Wapping.

1799. Ratcliffe, near the Tower of London, 630 houses, many warehouses were burned down and 1,400 people were made homeless.

Early 1800's. Volunteer fire brigades, without any official prompting or legal inducement, come into existence.

1812. The very first sprinkler system was patented by Sir William Congreve and installed in the Drury Lane Theatre. It was not automatic, controllable by taps that connected the sprinkler pipe work to a reservoir of water.

1815. London experiences a rapid growth, the villages of Chelsea, Paddington, Islington, Bethnal Green, Bermondsey and Kennington are linked with, and become absorbed in, the built up area of expanding London.

1816. The portable extinguisher was invented, comprising a container charged with a 'special' fluid and actuated by compressed air.

1819. Leather hose was put into use which had copper rivets, instead of stitching, to fasten the seams.

1828. The Fire Escape Society was formed due to the public concern at the extent of the loss of life that had occurred in fires in domestic property. The Society was dependent on public donations. Six wheeled fire escapes were provided and placed in streets at night. Each were manned by a competent 'escape conductor', who on hearing the alarm being raised would wheel the escape by hand to the scene and carry out the rescues of any occupants.

1824. Edinburgh brings into being a Fire Brigade Establishment, which was the first organised municipal fire brigade in Great Britain. This was in spite of London being the country's leading city, and probably the largest in the world.

1829.
1. Creation of the Metropolitan Police Force under the Metropolitan Police Act.
2. First steam fire engine. A horse-drawn vehicle on which a ten horsepower steam pump was mounted was designed and manufactured by Braithwaite and Ericsson. It was not introduced into London for another 30 years.

1830.
1. First use of a steam fire engine. A horse drawn vehicle on which a ten horse power steam pump was mounted. (Manufactured by Braithwaite and Ericsson.)
2. The Lighting and Watch Act was passed by Parliament. This enabled any local authority, large or small, that adopted its provisions to establish a fire brigade. This included the organisation of night-patrols to watch out for fires. Supply and maintenance of fire engines and the payment of proper

persons to look after the equipment. The parishes of Hackney and St Marylebone were among the first to have their own brigades of part-time firemen under a permanent 'engineer'. By the standards of the day, these brigades were well equipped and efficient.

1832. The Insurance Companies start action to form one London combined brigade.

1833 (1st January). The London Fire Engine Establishment came into being. James Braidwood, formally in charge of Edinburgh's fire brigade, takes up the post of Superintendent on a salary of £400 p.a. Eighty whole-time firemen, in grey uniforms, black leather helmets and black top boots, comprise London's new fire brigade.

1834. The 'old' Houses of Parliament, centuries old, were totally destroyed by fire. Twelve engines and sixty-four firemen were brought into action. Superintendent Braidwood is credited with saving Westminster Hall by his leadership at the scene.

1835. Plans for a floating steam fire engine submitted by Braithwaite and Ericsson to Braidwood (LFEE), which were rejected.

1836. The Royal Society for the Protection of Life from Fire was formed and the Fire Escape Society was amalgamated with it.

1837. The number of escape stations had increased to sixteen and had Queen Victoria as the RSPL's patron.

1838. The Royal Exchange in the City of London and the court office of the Lord Mayor entirely destroyed by fire. Both fire-plugs (hydrants) and the manual fire pumps froze up making them ineffective.

1841. The Tower of London Armoury is destroyed by fire.

1855.

1. The Metropolis Management Act was passed into law. It saw the creation of the Metropolitan Board of Works in London, with powers relating to streets, sewage and the control of building construction.
2. A powerful steam floating fire engine is constructed.

1858. Mr. Shand, of Shand Masons, Upper Ground, Southwark, patented a steam fire engine. Weighing over four tons it required three horses to pull it along.

1861

1. **(21st June)** A massive fire occurred at Cottons Wharf, a riverside warehouse in Tooley Street, Southwark. Nearly the whole of the LFEE brigade were deployed in trying to fight a rapidly developing riverside conflagration, including the newly acquired steam Shand fire engine and the steam-driven fire float. Braidwood was killed at this incident following a warehouse wall collapsing and burying him under tons of hot brickwork. It took two days just to bring the blaze under control. Braidwood was given a public funeral and the procession was a mile and a half in length.

2. **(August)** Captain Eyre Massey Shaw, Chief Constable and Chief Fire Officer of Belfast, is appointed as the replacement to Braidwood by the insurance companies that control the LFEE.

1862. The insurance companies inform the Home Secretary that they can no longer accept responsibility for providing a free fire service with no financial support from any public authority. A Select Committee report was presented to the House of Commons, its major recommendation was that a fire brigade be formed as part of the Metropolitan Police Force. Captain Shaw was charged with bringing forward proposals to cover the area of the Metropolitan Board of Works. His estimated costs of £70,000 p.a. were capped to a maximum of £50,000 p.a.. (This figure of £50K was arrived at with no assessment of Shaw's costings.) The City of London, which had its own police force, rejected the Metropolitan Police/fire brigade option on the basis that they would need to have a separate fire service.

1865.

1. The Metropolitan Fire Brigade Act was passed into law. It placed responsibility for London's fire service, throughout the Metropolis upon the Board of Works.

2. The London Salvage Corps was formed and maintained by the fire offices of London. It began operations in March 1866 and was inspired by the Liverpool Salvage Corps which had been formed in 1842, to reduce the loss and damage caused by fires, to help mitigate the effects of fire and of fire-fighting and to salvage both premises and goods affected by fire.

1866.

1. **(1st January).** The Metropolitan Fire Brigade formally came into existence. It covered an area about fifteen and a half miles long and ten miles wide. It ran from Plumstead in the east to Putney in the west, and Hampstead in the north to Crystal Palace in the south. The Act of 1865 authorised the MBW to purchase stations and engines belonging to the former parishes such as Lewisham, Norwood, Tooting, Hammersmith, Hampstead and Stoke Newington.

2. Captain Shaw introduces the brass firemen's helmet (silver for officers), replacing the Braidwood leather helmets.

3. The MBW oversees the construction, and opening, of nineteen new MFB fire stations (including temporary stations whilst a permanent station is being built). The stations were Bethnal Green, Bow, Camberwell, Fulham, Greenwich, Hackney, Hammersmith, Islington, Kennington, Mile End, Notting Hill, Paddington, Poplar, Rotherhithe, St Johns Wood, Shoreditch, Stoke Newington, Waterloo and Whitechapel. In the first decade of the MFB's existence, Captain Shaw secured the building of fifty-seven new land and river fire stations. A record that has never been surpassed. (*Excluded the opening of temporary AFS/NFS fire stations in an enlarged London Fire Force area during the Second World War.*)

1867.

1. The Metropolitan Fire Brigade take over eighty-five escape stations from the Royal Society for the Protection of Life from Fire.

2. All horses used to pull fire engines were hired from the firm of Thomas Tilling, who provided most of London's horse buses. (This firm supplied the Brigade's horses for over fifty years.) The 'coachmen', who in later years would be replaced by motor drivers as horse drawn fire engines were superseded by motorised counterparts.

1870.

1. The number of MFB fire stations had increased from nineteen to fifty-one. A total of twenty-five horse drawn steam fire engines, eighty-five manual engines and three floating engines comprised the brigade's appliance fleet. The number of whole-time firemen had increased to 378 from its previous 129 LFEE establishment. Whilst the original eighty-five escape stations had grown to ninety-one.

2. The creation of the London Salvage Corps by the Insurance Companies and funded by them.

3. In the Franco-German War, when Paris was under bombardment, Captain Shaw travels to Paris to act as an ordinary firemen and wins personal acclaim from the French public. (The MBW had received a formal request from the French government for fire-fighting assistance. But before the necessary arrangements could be put in place the Paris fires were under control. However, in the meantime Shaw had already left for France, heading to Paris.)

1871. Water Companies obtain the power to fit hydrants at the expense of the MBW. However, not always where the hydrants were required, rather where the Water Company thought convenient.

1873. The MFB devises methods of getting hose ashore from fire-floats.

1875. Formation of the London Auxiliary Fire Brigade. It was actually a kind of club, with entrance fees and annual subscriptions. Members provided their own uniforms, their brass helmets were painted black. They attended both drills and fires but under the direction of the MFB.

1876. Review of the workings of the MFB by a Parliamentary Select Committee. Its terms of reference later extended to fire prevention arrangements in theatres and other places of entertainment.

1877.

1. **(July)** Select Committee report published. Whilst accepting the MFB was inadequate in size and overworked, it also proposed control of the Brigade be passed to the Metropolitan Police. The report produced little positive results.
2. The Metropolitan Board of Works commissions a gallantry medal for acts of valour by MFB firemen, and to have it struck in silver.

1878. The Metropolitan Fire Brigade transfers its headquarters from Watling Street, in the City of London, to Southwark Bridge Road, Southwark. Part new build and part conversion of existing three-storey buildings it is the largest fire brigade headquarters and combined fire station in the country. Captain Shaw, and his family, take up residence in Winchester House, now incorporated in to the MFB's HQ complex.

1880. Introduction of (electric) street fire alarms and the telephone. Street fire alarms would remain a feature of London's streets for more than seventy years.

1881.

1. The first fire gallantry awards were made to nineteen MFB firemen for acts of conspicuous bravery. They were presented by Captain Shaw at a special parade. The Annual Reviews were created and would continue for over one hundred years.
2. The post of Deputy Chief Fire Officer was created.

1882. Brigade strength enlarged to 536 men.

1883.

1. A bronze medal was produced for members of the Brigade who had served with 'zeal and fidelity' without offence, for fifteen years.
2. The Royal Standard flys over Winchester House with a visit by the Prince and Princess of Wales.

1884.

1. Captain Shaw, and 73 recipients, received the first bronze medals at the Annual Review.

2. Firemen's leave was increased. Station Officers could grant 24 hours leave, District Officers could grant 48 hours leave, off duty.

1889.

1. **(21st March).** The London County Council (LCC) is created, replacing the Metropolitan Board of Works, by virtue of the Local Government Act of 1888.

2. The LCC dispenses with the requirement that recruitment into the Metropolitan Fire Brigade should be from ex-sailors only.

3. The first Royal Review of the Metropolitan Fire Brigade takes place on 27 May at Horse Guards Parade, Whitehall. It did not all go well, with the mounted police going to the aid of the Prince and Princess of Wales when uninvited crowds overran the parade ground reserved for the firemen's prize-giving and presentations.

1890.

1. The invention and adoption of horsed escapes by some provincial brigades encourages Captain Shaw to introduce them into the MFB.

2. Leather hose started to be replaced by the lighter, more flexible, canvas hose.

1891.

1. (31st October) Last day in office for Captain Shaw. He had fallen out with the newly created LCC due to a clash of personalities and policy direction.

2. (1st November) Mr. James Sexton Simonds becomes the MFB's Chief Officer.

3. Queen Victoria bestows a Knighthood on Captain Shaw, now Sir Eyre Massey Shaw.

1896.

1. Chief Sexton Simonds dismissed from the MFB with no pension and only one year's salary. Captain Lionel de Lautour Wells, a naval officer, appointed Chief Officer.

2. Captain Wells inherits the MFB appliance fleets that now stood at sixty-three manual fire engines and fifty-nine steam engines, all of which are horse drawn.

Opposite: The new Metropolitan Fire Brigade Headquarters located in Southwark Bridge Road.

1897.

1. The 'Great Cripplegate fire' started in Well Street in the City of London, and it soon spread to surrounding streets. Over fifty warehouses, some six storeys high, were destroyed. 228 firemen and fifty-one steam engines were required to quell the conflagration. The subsequent inquest recommended more fire alarms, better hydrants and more conspicuous hydrant notices. They also proposed that firemen have opportunities to familiarise themselves with the layout and construction of warehouses.

2. Captain Wells's naval background was brought to bear on the MFB's fire float fleet. Prior to his arrival the Brigade's fire floats were deep-draughted (9 feet) and unable to get close to the banks of the Thames. These floats were crewed by licensed watermen who lived some distance away from the float stations. Using designs that Wells drew up himself, firefighting on the water was revolutionised with sleeker, shallow drafted craft, with much improved boilers, built by the ship builders Messrs. Yarrow and Company. The five river stations were also modernised and re-organised. Under the new scheme there were four stations-Battersea, Blackfriars, Rotherhithe and Deptford. The staff of the Blackfriars lodged at the new Whitefriars fire station that opened on the 21st July.

1898. As a result of experiences at large fires the Brigade introduced the provision to supply hot tea and coffee at large fires. The 'canteen-van' had arrived.

1899. Last manual fire engine used at a fire.

1900.

1. First improved automatic sprinklers brought into use (from the United States) and the operation of an alarm gong, outside the building, gave an audible alarm.

2. Finchley Council purchases the first petrol engined pump to be used anywhere in the world for its local fire brigade.

3. Introduction of electric bells fitted to fire stations to alert crews when an emergency call is received, the bells were also installed in the firemen's family accommodation above the station to summon them at night.

1902.

1. Following a serious fire in Queen Victoria Street involving a five storey office building, the first crews to arrive were unable to rescue screaming girls trapped on the fifth floor because their ladders did not reach over fifty feet. A special seventy foot ladder from the Southwark headquarters fire station helped to save two of the girls. The Press published bitter and blistering articles blaming the LCC and the Brigade for its alleged failings. In contrast, the jury at the subsequent inquest gave unqualified praise to the

MFB for its actions at the incident. However, after this fire horses were no longer kept in their stables at the rear of the stations; but kept harnessed, for two hours at a time, to the escape cart. In addition hook ladders were introduced into the Brigade. A French invention, and used in major French cities, these ladders were about 13 feet in length and weighed around 28 pounds. With its long serrated hook at the top end, firemen could hook the ladder to a window sill, climb the ladder and whilst sitting astride the sill they had climbed into, raise the ladder and hook it to another window sill above them. This way they could climb to the highest floor of a building. With the use of a rescue line, which they carried with them, firemen could lower a person to the ground.

2. Formation of the Metropolitan Water Board.

The 75 foot 'long ladder' in use at the LCC-MFB HQ at Southwark.
(Permission of the London Fire Brigade.)

1903.

1. Fire engines are fitted with bells to warn other traffic to make way. Prior to that the shanty call of seamen 'Hi-hi-hi' (that they shouted when rope hauling) was used by firemen as they clung to the engines as they raced through London's streets.

2. Introduction of the first, small, motorised tender. Fitted with a tank of water, the water was expelled through hose-reel that was under pressure of carbon dioxide gas.

3. Tottenham fire brigade (outside the LCC county boundary) builds a new fire station with no stables or provision for horses.

4. There were rapid changes in the methods of fire engines propulsion.

1904.

1. The Metropolitan Fire Brigade Act 1885 stated that the Brigade be known as the Metropolitan Fire Brigade. Despite being known as the London Fire Brigade, the name could not be changed without the LCC obtaining the requisite enactment. This the LCC secured and the official title of the Brigade was changed to the London Fire Brigade.

2. A German self-contained breathing apparatus set, consisting of an oxygen cylinder, worn in the small of the back, passed the oxygen to the gas-proof re-breather bag carried on the fireman's chest. Special training became necessary for the use of this apparatus.

3. Introduction of the sliding pole into London fire stations after Captain Shaw saw the poles in use in American fire houses.

4. The first steam driven, self-propelled fire engines (The Fire King) were introduced into the Brigade. Extremely limited in number, Whitefriars fire station was allocated a Fire King. With a top speed of 25 mph, it weighed five and half tons.

5. The last street wheeled escape stations disappear from London streets.

1905.

1. Turntable ladders were introduced into the Brigade. Horse drawn, when towed along the streets in the un-extended (housed) position they were no longer than the ordinary 50 foot wheeled escape. However, when extended they reached 82 feet and were self-supporting. Operated either by hand or compressed air the ladder could rotate 360 degrees on its turntable.

2. Annual turn-out competitions were introduced and a cup awarded to the station with the fastest turn-out.

3. The LCC enters into negotiations with the MWB for the improvement of water supplies for fire-fighting.

1906.

1. London firemen formed a group called the Municipal Employees Association, which was a trade union. The LCC disapproved and the group had little success in seeking redress to its demands.

2. The birth of the annual Whaler Race when firemen from the Blackfriars river station challenge the Royal Naval ratings onboard HMS President to a whaler race on the River Thames. (No record as to who won the race.)

1907. The Public Health Act confers powers on firemen to break into premises reasonably supposed to be on fire. It also provided powers allowing local authorities to enter into mutual aid agreements and place the Captain or Superintendent of the local brigade to be in sole charge of fire-fighting.

1908.

1. **(25th August).** Sir Eyre Massey Shaw dies at Folkestone, Kent aged 78. He was buried at Highgate Cemetery on the 29th August.

2. The LCC obtains the first two petrol-driven fire engines.

1909.

1. Review of the London Fire Brigade by King Edward VII in Hyde Park. As the Prince of Wales, King Edward, was a keen 'volunteer' fireman under Captain Shaw.

2. King Edward creates the King's Police and Fire Service Medal, to be awarded to, 'those of our faithful subjects who, being members of a recognised police force or a properly organised fire brigade within our dominions, have performed acts of exceptional courage and skill or have exhibited conspicuous devotion to duty.

3. Self-contained smoke helmets (BA sets) were introduced for use 'in an atmosphere dense with smoke and dangerous fumes.' A special motor appliance fitted for smoke helmet work was based at Southwark's HQ fire station. The appliance was also fitted with a dynamo and portable searchlights, oxygen-reviving apparatus, and electric fans. (The first emergency tender.)

1911. A major extension to the Brigade Headquarters is completed and opened (Southwark fire station) and more motorised fire engines replaced their horse drawn counter-parts.

1913.

1. London now has 85 Stations and 3 River Stations.

2. Following the death of two firemen, overcome in a gas-filled sewer, the efficiency of the self-contained smoke-helmets was reviewed. The smoke-helmets were removed from the thirteen stations that had been issued with them. A supply of the helmets was retained at Brigade Headquarters pending the arrival of two special breathing apparatus carrying appliances.

1915.

1. (First World War) London firemen are exempt from conscription.

2. London fireman John Samuel Green died on the 17th September 1915.
   He was fatally injured in a Zeppelin bombing raid on London on the 8th September while saving 22 lives from a fire caused by the raid at Lambs Conduit Passage. He became trapped by the fire and threw himself from an upstairs window to escape. He died of burns and other injuries.
   Fireman Green was the one of the first LFB fatalities of World War One. He was subsequently awarded the Silver Medal.

3. The exemption from conscription was later rescinded following serious raids on London in 1917 all members of the LFB serving aboard were recalled to the Brigade.

1918.

1. Between September 1915 and 5 March 1918, 24 separate enemy air raids took place in London. Actions by hostile aircraft resulted in the Brigade being summoned to 224 fires and it rescued 138 people from danger. His Majesty King George conferred the British Empire Medal for Gallantry on 40 officers and men.

2. Seven London firemen were killed in January at a building fire on the Albert Embankment, SE1. It remains the worst London fatality of firemen/firefighters as a result of a non-enemy action fire.

1920. The two watch system was introduced (Red and Blue watches). For the first time firemen were not on duty all the time and now worked a 72-hour week.

1926. Fire-float Beta III was brought into service and was the forerunner of the later Massey Shaw fire-float.

1928. The latest design in motor-driven fire-floats is supplied to the Brigade. It had a length of 70 feet; breadth of 13 feet 6 inches; and draught of 3 feet 9 inches. It was fitted with two Merryweather turbine fire pumps, each capable of discharging over 1,300 gallons per minute.

1933. Major C B Morris was appointed London's Chief Officer and was responsible for the introduction of dual purpose appliances (fire engines capable of carrying an escape ladder or an extension ladder and both carrying their own pump). He was also responsible for the introduction of the hose-laying lorry, capable of laying out hose at speed.

1935. The London Fire Brigade's latest fire-float, The Massey Shaw, is commissioned and placed into service. It is stationed at Blackfriars river station.

1936.

1. The Crystal Palace Fire occurred at Sydenham, South London. The giant glass palace built after the great exhibition, and relocated to South London from Hyde Park, burns to the ground. The fire could be seen from most of the Capital.

2. (1936/7) The Merryweather brass helmet for firemen, and silver plated for officers (modelled after the helmets worn by cuirassiers of the French Army) were to be withdrawn from operational use. These metal helmets were conductive and a serious safety hazard as the use of electricity became widespread and the risk of live wires falling from overhead increased. They were replaced with a, lighter, compressed cork version made by Cromwell Helmets.

King George VI and Queen Elizabeth formally opening the London Fire Brigade Headquarters at Lambeth. (Permission of the London Fire Brigade.)

1937. The London Fire Brigade opens its new, purpose built Brigade Headquarters and fire station complex on the Albert Embankment, SE1, facing the River Thames. Comprising both land and river fire stations'; senior and principal officers residential accommodation; the Brigade's vehicle and maintenance workshops; drill yard and double fronted drill tower; mobilising control room and band stand, it was formally opened by HRH King George VI, accompanied by the Queen Elizabeth on 21 July.

1938.

1. The creation of the Auxiliary Fire Service (AFS) that would see some 25,000 men and women join the London AFS and augment the regular London fireman in preparation for the Second World War, and the anticipated aerial attacks upon London.

2. Fire Brigades Act 1938. This Act (which is no longer in force) provided for centralised co-ordination of fire brigades in Great Britain and made it mandatory for local authorities to arrange an effective fire service, although it did not apply to the London County Council's London Fire Brigade.

1939 to 1945. (World War II) The ranks of London's Firemen are swollen by the introduction of Auxiliary Firemen and Women. Women did not carry out any front line firefighting but were used as control officers, drivers and dispatch riders; although many laid down their lives alongside their male counterparts. As well as the London fire stations, some 300 Auxiliary fire stations (sub-stations) were set up in schools and garages etc. Trailer Pumps were provided and hundreds of London Taxis were commandeered to tow them to fires.

After a year (1939) of the so-called 'phony' war, the Blitz began on 7th September 1940 and lasted for 57 consecutive nights. On 29th December 1940 an incendiary attack on central London caused a fire storm and what was described as the second Great Fire of London. Much of the City of London burned and was destroyed with the exception of St Paul's Cathedral, which stood miraculously untouched in the middle of this firestorm.

On the night of 10th/11th May 1941 there was the last massive Blitz attack on London, 17 Firemen were killed in a direct hit at St George's Circus in South London. Less than a week later on 17th May, saw the beginning of the end of the London Blitz.

In August 1941 the National Fire Service was created. All equipment, ranks, organization and procedures were standardized across the UK. The name of 'fire-float' is changed to 'fireboat'. June 1944 saw the start of the enemy rocket attacks, V1s, launched on London. The more powerful, and destructive V2 rockets fell on London in September of the same year.

In May 1945 World War Two ended. Hundreds of thousands of Londoners had been killed by the enemy air attacks including 327 London firemen and firewomen. Additionally 3,086 were seriously injured. Many London firemen and women displayed exemplary and conspicuous bravery. One fireman received the **George Cross**, one fire woman and thirty-seven men received the George Medal, there were three OBEs, thirteen MBEs, one hundred and eighteen BEMs, eleven King's Police and Fire Service Gallantry Medals and numerous King's Commendations awarded.

1946. 'The KING has been graciously pleased to award the **GEORGE CROSS** to Frederick DAVIES (deceased). **Fireman. No. 34 (London) National Fire Service.**' In respect of his actions at the fire, in Harlesden north London in August 1945, where he went to the rescue of two children in a burning house. He knew the extreme danger he was facing, but with complete disregard of his own safety he made a most heroic attempt to retrieve the two children. In so doing he lost his life.

1947. Fire Services Act 1947 was passed into law. This Act transferred the functions of the National Fire Service back to local authorities.

1948. The Fire Services Act was enacted on the 1st April. Regulations, later issued under the act laid down a standard system of rank, uniforms and badges of rank. The London Region of the National Fire Service ceased to exist and reverted to the London Fire Brigade, under the command of its Chief Fire Officer Frederick Delve.

1949.
1. The London County Council decide to abolish London's street fire alarms.
2. The Auxiliary Fire Service is re-established.

1951. In November the first, ever, refusal of labour by London's firemen: members of the Fire Brigades Union work an emergency calls only dispute in seeking parity with police pay. Hundreds of disciplinary charges are issued but are dropped after the December, Broad Street fire, in which 3 firemen are killed and the Deputy Chief Officer is seriously injured and loses a leg.

1954. The Fire Services Long Service and Good Conduct Medal (LSGCM) was created. Those eligible for the Fire Service's LSGCM are full-time and part-time members of all ranks in Local Authority British Fire Brigades (including London). Individuals may be awarded the medal for 20 years of continuous or aggregate service in an eligible fire brigade or service, so long as they are deemed to have been very good in conduct and character.

1956. On the 21st May a fire in the Goodge Street Deep Shelter, off Tottenham Court Road, was described as 'one of the worst fires since the Blitz'.

1957. The Lewisham train disaster. St Johns, south London. Two trains collided and brought down part of a railway bridge. 90 people were killed and 138 were injured. The London Fire Brigade was highly praised for its rescue and recovery efforts.

1958.

1. Smithfield Meat Market Fire. The massive fire in the basement of the market killed 2 Firefighters who ran out of oxygen in their BA sets. In October, the government issued ``Fire Service Circular No. 37/1958" detailing the findings of the Committee of Inquiry and recommending, among other things, that all British fire brigades establish control procedures for recording and supervising breathing apparatus wearers as well as standard procedures for firefighters wearing breathing apparatus. This saw the introduction of one of the most advanced and strict breathing apparatus control systems in the world.

2. The London Fire Brigade introduce an automatic signalling device attached to their breathing apparatus sets to provide an audible warning (whistle) 15 minutes before the oxygen in the wearers cylinder is exhausted. This was widely adopted by other British fire brigades and played no small part in why the UK had one of the lowest firefighter 'in line of duty death' rates in the World.

3. The last street alarm box was also removed in this year following the introduction of the '999' Telephone system.

1959.

1. Fire Services Act 1959 This Act amended the 1947 Act; it dealt with pensions, staffing arrangements and provision of services by other authorities.

2. The Factories Act was passed into law. The London Fire Brigade had greater powers of inspection and enforcement than existed previously. It was further amended and improved in 1961 Factories Act.

1963.

1. The London County Council authorises the adoption of a new General Post Office (GPO) mobilising system to all London fire stations. This involved the transmission of calls to stations by teleprinter, a brigade wide automatic telephone system that removed the need for stations to have their own individual switchboards.

2. Chief Officer Frederick Delve is knighted. Sir Frederick Delve is the first Chief Officer since Sir Eyre Massey Shaw so to be honoured.

3. The Offices, Shops and Railways Premises Act is passed into law. At the time of its passage, the Act was intended to extend the protection of workplace health, safety and welfare under the Factories Act 1961 to other employees (some 8 million) in Great Britain. (Though as of 2008 some of it remains in force, it has largely been superseded by the Health and Safety at Work etc. Act 1974 and regulations made under it.)

1964. The London Fire Brigade introduces the Junior Firemen scheme for boys between 16 and 17 years old, who subject to passing the required test become firemen at their 18th birthday.

1965. April. The Greater London Council (GLC) was created and was the top-tier of Greater London's local government. It replaced the earlier London County Council (LCC) that had previously been London's fire authority. With the formation of the GLC the now enlarged London Fire Brigade came into being. This Brigade, which still covers the same greater London area, saw the amalgamation into the GLC-LFB the fire brigades of West Ham, East Ham, Croydon, Middlesex, and parts of Kent, Surrey, Essex and Herts fire brigades that had bordered the former LCC area.

1966.

1. The first issue of the London Fire Brigade magazine, London Firemen, was published in May.

2. The London Fire Brigade celebrates its Centenary with a special Royal review at the Lambeth headquarters attended by Her Majesty the Queen accompanied by HRH Prince Philip, the Duke of Edinburgh.

3. The Queen formally opens the new Lambeth mobilising control, (whose radio call sign was M2FH).

1967. The Hither Green rail crash occurred on the 5th November. It left 49 dead and 78 injured.

1968. The Government disbands the Auxiliary Fire Service (AFS) and London bade farewell to its auxiliary firemen and firewomen.

1969.

1. In June the London Fire Brigade successfully fought one of the most major fires in London's history. Over 50 people, many of them foreign tourists were rescued from a massive fire in the Leinster Gardens Hotel in Bayswater. Crews from most of London's 'A' Division stations were involved in ladder rescues (including hook ladders) in the early stages of the fire. Not a single life was lost at this fire as every single trapped person was rescued.

2. July: explosion at Dudgeons Wharf kills five firemen – the greatest loss of London firemen in a single incident since WW II.

3. The first operational use of High Expansion (Hi Ex) foam at a major south London fire in Peckham.

1971. 9th -11th August. A 50 pump fire, involving a riverside warehouse, occurred in Battlebridge Lane, Tooley Street adjacent to London Bridge. This was the largest fire in London in over two decades and at one point the Chief Office, Joe Milner, considered making 'pumps eighty'.

1972.

1. The Hazchem scheme is implemented across the UK following ground breaking work by the LFB, in particular DACO Charles 'Charlie' Clisby. Initially restricted to the carriage of chemicals on road tankers it would later be expanded to cover the storage of hazardous materials and provide a first strike code to emergency services attending incidents involving hazardous substances.

2. The London Fire Brigade launch a TV advertising campaign warning of the dangers of portable paraffin heaters (that had been responsible for multiple fatalities and serious fires). It was the first UK brigade to use TV advertising in this way.

1973.

1. The Irish Republican Army bomb campaign hit London from 1973 onwards. It sought to create a climate of fear over a longer period of time, trying to explode two or more devices at a time to maximise the havoc. There were 36 bombs in London in 1973.

2. The Ealing train crash on the 19th December left 10 dead and 94 injured.

1974.

1. The LFB launch an unprecedented recruitment campaign to attract prospective firemen into the Brigade.

2. Lambeth control room (M2FH) closes down and its staff are dispersed to the other three LFB control rooms.

3. Compressed air breathing apparatus sets are introduced onto Pump Escapes.

4. Introduction of a Chemical Incident Unit into the operational fleet. Attended chemical and radiation suspected incidents.

5. Some of the most indiscriminate bombing attacks and killings of the IRA's bombing campaign were carried out by eight IRA members from Dublin, who had come to London in early 1974 and aimed to carry out one attack a week. That year's bombings included the Palace of Westminster at the Houses of Parliament (June) and the bombing of a pub in Woolwich which killed two people and injured 28 in October.

1975. The Moorgate tube crash occurred on Friday 28th February 1975 at 08:46 on the Northern City Line, then operated by London Underground as the Northern Line (Highbury Branch). A southbound train failed to stop at the Moorgate terminus and crashed into the wall at the end of the tunnel. 43people died as a result of the crash, the greatest loss of life during peacetime in the London Underground and a further 74 were injured. The Brigade's Chief Officer, Joe Milner, used the phrase; 'My thousand selfless heroes' when describing the 1,000 London firemen who battled, over 5 days, to free the dying and injured from this crushed and compacted tube train. Station Officer Christopher Woods and Fireman Richard Furlong both received the British Empire Medal for their actions at this incident.

London firemen removing casualties from crushed carriages at Moorgate Underground Station. (Permission of the London Fire Brigade.)

1976.

1. The long hot summer of 1976 saw the London Fire Brigade's busiest year in post war London. In addition the numerous derelict properties were being burned by unscrupulous demolition contractors in the 1970s. Almost every patch of open green space and railway embankment appeared to burn as temperatures hit the high 90s and no rain fell for months.

2. Firemen's black helmets are painted yellow. Later new issues to firemen to Sub Officer rank came only in yellow. Black leggings are withdrawn and yellow over trousers are issued.

3. The phased withdrawal of scaling ladders and first floor ladders in lieu of triple short extension ladders commences.

1977. First national firemen's strike started on 14 November over pay and conditions. After a bitter few weeks the settlement included a system whereby pay was index linked to the pay movement among other similar groups. This meant that there was no need for national pay strikes until 2002, when the system broke down. The insurance companies picked up the final bill for the dispute with pay-outs totalling £117.5m compared with £52.3m for the same three months the previous year. The strike lasted nine weeks.

1979. A fourth watch, the 'Green Watch' is created, thus lowering the working week from 48 to 42 hours.

1980.

1. The phased withdrawal of both the hook ladders and 50ft wheeled escape ladders started. There was no replacement ladder for the hook ladder and the Fire Brigades Union had long advocated its removal from fire stations. The 13.5 (45ft) alloy ladder would replace the escape ladder across the Brigade. Pump escapes would be called Pump ladders.

2. Soho nightclub fire. In the early hours of 15th August, a man who was earlier ejected from an illegal drinking and gambling club in Soho returned with gasoline and started a fire that killed 37 people and injured 23 others.

3. Brixton fire station, in south west London, is the busiest station in the London Fire Brigade by a wide margin.

1981.

1. On the 18th January a New Cross house fire claimed the lives of 13 people, all aged between 14 and 22, attending a birthday party. The exact and true cause has never been established.

2. Over an April weekend the Brixton riots erupt in south London. It was an unprecedented civil disturbance within the UK and involved the LFB in previously untried operational tactics.

1982.

1. The first (peacetime) woman firefighter joins the London Fire Brigade.

2. On the 20th July, the IRA carried out two bombings in central London parks. The first attack came in Hyde Park around 10.40am just as members of the Royal Household Cavalry, Blues and Royals, walked past as part of the Changing of the Guard procession. This resulted in the deaths of 3 soldiers and 7 horses. The second came two hours later while people sat to listen to the band of the Royal Green Jackets in Regents Park. This killed a further seven bandsmen. Over fifty people were injured, many seriously. Pictures of the horses' corpses lying among the debris became one of the enduring images of the 'Troubles'.

1983. Last recorded rescue by a hook ladder was made at an 8 pump, persons reported fire in Fenchurch St, EC3 when a woman was rescued by 'hook ladder and lowering line' from second floor window at the rear of the building.

1984.

1. The Oxford Circus underground fire occurred on Friday 23 November at 9:50 p.m. The station is served by three deep-level tube lines: the Bakerloo Line, Central Line and Victoria Line. The three lines are linked by a complex network of tunnels and cross-passages and come to a common booking hall situated beneath the junction of Oxford Street and Regent Street. The fire started in a materials store at the south end of the northbound Victoria Line platform, used by contractors working on the modernisation of the station. This major underground fire became a thirty pump fire, although there were no fatalities. The fire gutted the northbound Victoria Line platform tunnel and the passages leading off it. Although smoking had been banned on all London Underground trains since July 1984, in response to the Oxford Circus fire, a complete smoking ban in all sub-surface stations was introduced in February 1985. Nonetheless a similar, but fatal, incident occurred in November 1987 at King's Cross tube station when it was concluded as probable that a passenger had dropped a lit match onto an escalator.

2. The London Salvage Corps was disbanded by the Insurance Companies and the London Fire Brigade took over its full responsibility for salvage work at fires.

3. The Brigade takes delivery of its new fireboat and rescue craft, the London Phoenix. It replaces the Fire Swift and Fire Hawk boats and covers the whole of the River Thames for the Greater London area.

4. The last hook ladders are removed from appliances and are to be consigned to the history books.

1985. Station Commanders take up post. One Assistant Divisional Officer (Station Commander) per station, who manages and co-ordinates the activities of four station watches in addition to performing their duties as a senior officer.

1986.

1. Abolition of the Greater London Council and the creation of the London Fire and Civil Defence Authority, a 'quango' that oversaw the London Fire Brigade and elements of Emergency Planning for the Capital.

2. Disestablishing the existing eleven divisions and creating a five area structure.

1987. On Friday 27th November a fire occurred at Kings Cross underground station. It claimed 31 lives, including that of Station Officer Colin Townsley (Soho fire station) who was subsequently awarded, posthumously, the George Medal for his actions at this fire. The public inquiry that followed (headed by Desmond Fennell QC) determined that the fire had started due to a lit match being dropped onto the escalator and suddenly increased in intensity due to a previously unknown 'trench effect'. London Underground were strongly criticised for their attitude toward fires. Complacent because there had never been a fatal fire on the Underground, the staff had been given little or no training to deal with fires or evacuation. The publication of the Inquiry report led to resignations of senior management in both London Underground and London Regional Transport and to the introduction of new fire safety regulations and procedures in the LFB.

(A model of King's Cross station was built at the Atomic Energy Research Establishment using computer simulation software; this showed the flames first spreading along the floor of the escalator, rather than burning vertically and suddenly producing a jet of flame into the ticket hall, matching the tube fire. A fire behaved as in the computer model during experiments with a third scale replica of the escalator. The metal sides of the escalator contained the flames and directed hot air ahead of the fire. The tests proved that temperatures quickly reached between 500 and 600 degrees Centigrade. When the wooden treads of the escalator flashed over, the size of the fire increased exponentially and a sustained jet of flame was discharged from the escalator tunnel into the ticket hall. The conclusion was that this newly discovered trench effect had caused the fire to flashover at 19:45.)

1988. In December the Clapham Train disaster occurred at Spencer park, in south west London. It left 35 dead and 113 people injured.

1989. Replacement of the 'old style' fire tunic (with chrome buttons), and worn for the past forty years, with a new style Bristol style fire tunic. Some 20,000 tunics were ordered at a cost of £1.9 million. This followed on from the Kings Cross fire and was targeted to improve firefighter safety. New style over trousers and gloves followed.

1990.

1. Introduction of an automatic distress signal unit on breathing apparatus sets which operate when the wearer is immobile for more than 20 seconds.

2. New Pacific style fire helmets (with visors) replace the cork firefighter's helmet.

3. The Massey Shaw fireboat (now owned by a heritage group) returns to Dunkirk with a LFB and veteran crew as part of the 50th anniversary commemorative celebrations.

4. 50th commemorative service of the Blitz held at St Paul's cathedral attended by HRH Princess of Wales and HRH's The Princes Harry and William.

5. The Brigade's new mobilising control at Lambeth (CMC) opens, albeit 6 years late. This was due to system development delays, using a Marconi system. It was the Brigade's first fully computer aided control. The CMC control was closed in 2006.

The London Fire Brigade's new Command and Mobilising Control finally opens at Lambeth HQ. (Permission of the London Fire Brigade.)

1991.

1. There are now forty three female firefighters in the London Fire Brigade. A ratio of 150:1.

2. In May, Her Majesty The Queen Mother Queen Elizabeth unveils the 'Blitz' statue opposite St Paul's Cathedral following a commemorative service to which representatives of all the UK's fire services were represented.

3. The original Emergency Tenders (ETs) and later rebranded ERTs (the word 'rescue' was added) are replaced by a new fleet of Fire Rescue Tenders with enhanced rescue capability and extended duration breathing apparatus sets.

4. Following the fatal fire at Gillender Street, east London, which took the lives of two firefighters the London Fire Brigade is served with two statutory Improvement Notices by the Health and Safety Executive.

Her Majesty the Queen Mother unveils the Blitz statue at St Pauls.

5. Leather fireboots are reintroduced. These new style boots were part of the outcome of the review of the Clapham rail crash when a request for a 'decent pair of fireboots' was made.

1992.

1. 10 April. The Baltic Exchange at St Mary Axe was partially demolished, and the rest of the building was extensively damaged in a Provisional Irish Republican Army bomb attack. The one-ton bomb killed three people, with another 91 people injured. The bomb also caused major damage to all the surrounding buildings at a cost of £800 million, £200 million more than the total damage caused by the 10,000 explosions that had occurred during the Northern Ireland's Troubles. In August 1994 the Provisional IRA announced a 'complete cessation of military operations'.

2. Southwark Training Centre gets funding for a multi-million pound refurbishment, the first complete major overall of the site since its creation under Captain Massey Shaw in 1878.

The IRA bombing at St Mary Axe – the Baltic Exchange, that left three dead and many injured. (Permission of the London Fire Brigade.)

1993. The Brigades starts it radical move from 'ranks' to roles. The work that would take a number of years heralded far reaching changes in the Brigades organisation and the creation of 'Competence Standards'.

1994.

1. Operationally the busiest year in the London Fire Brigades history with 259,000 calls being handled by the fire brigade control room staff.
2. Her Royal Highness, The Duchess of Kent formally reopens the refurbished Southwark Training School.

1995. A reorganised Brigade structure implemented. It reverts back to the three Commands from the five Areas and the phasing out of two senior ranks.

1999.

1. Greater London Authority Act 1999. This act was necessary to allow for the formation of the Greater London Authority and in turn the London Fire and Emergency Planning Authority.
2. Introduction of the 'Inferno' firefighter's uniform. LFB the first UK brigade to use this.
3. The Ladbroke Grove rail crash (also known as the Paddington train crash) was a rail accident which occurred on 5 October at Ladbroke Grove, north London. With 31 people killed and more than 520 injured, this remains the worst rail accident on the Great Western Main Line.

2000. 'Odin' becomes the first fire investigation dog in the Brigade.

2002.

1. Brigade Museum, at Winchester House, Southwark achieves registered status.
2. The term Chief Fire Officer is discontinued in favour of the Designation of 'Commissioner'.

2002/3. The Fire and Rescues Act was drafted in response to the Independent Review of the Fire Service, often referred to as the Bain Report, after its author Professor Sir George Bain. It recommended radical changes to many working procedures and it led to a national firefighter strike in 2002–2003.

2003. 12 years in research and development and at a final cost of £22 million the Brigade's bespoke Firehouse, located at the refurbished and modernised Southwark Training Centre goes 'live'.

2004.

1. The Fire and Rescue Services Act 2004 passed into law. It changed many working practices and was brought in to replace the Fire Services Act 1947

and repealed several existing acts, many going back fifty years. The 2004 Act saw the formal introduction of the Integrated Personal Development System (IPDS) that supported Fire & Rescue Services to train and develop their staff in order to meet the changing demands that face the service. It also enabled individuals to assess their development needs against a set of National Occupational Standards (NOS) and seek appropriate training and development opportunities. Ranks were therefore replaced by roles, i.e. 'managers'. The changes also removed the single level entry system for operational staff and facilitated multi-level entry, allowing for suitable staff to be recruited directly into roles other than firefighter and enabled in-service staff with potential to progress more quickly.

2. Fire and Rescue Services (FRS), in England and Wales, including the London Fire Brigade, are given a statutory duty to respond to incidents involving collapsed structures and heavy transport incidents. The Brigade, along with the FRS are provided with government supplied resilience equipment. They included; Incident response units, urban search and rescue (USAR) units and high volume pumps.

3. The Brigade's mobilising control is transferred to a new control facility in London's Docklands, only to be relocated yet again in 2011 to Merton.

4. London has the first woman in the UK to be awarded the Queen's Fire Service Medal. (*2007: she became the highest-ranking woman in the British Fire Service with the post of Area Commander.*)

2005.

1. On 5 January 2005 a second fire occurred in the ceiling void above the 'office fire room' on the second floor of the Firehouse. The first fire had occurred a year earlier. The fire itself caused minimal damage and was quickly brought under control. The major concern related to the fire risk which had been manifested in the building. The fire was caused by the auto-ignition of the mineral fibre ductwork insulation that had become contaminated by oil leaking from the ductwork. It was necessary to stop all 'real fire training' at Southwark. The facility being used only for 'cold fire training'. Real fire training had to be carried out through facilities provided by the Lancashire and Essex Fire Services.

2. The 7th July London bombings (often referred to as 7/7) were a series of coordinated suicide attacks in London, which targeted civilians using the public transport system during the morning rush hour. All but one of the 52 victims had been residents in London during the attacks and were from a diverse range of backgrounds. Edgware Road Underground Station bombing required 12 pumps; Kings Cross Underground also 12 pumps; and Aldgate Underground, 10 pumps. At 9.47am, almost an hour after the events underground, another bomb exploded on a number 30 bus in Upper Woburn Place/Tavistock Square. Euston. 13 people were killed with many more injured.

3. A new generation of Fire Rescue Units, (FRUs), are placed into operational service, which as well as their traditional roles, now includes 'line rescue and a water rescue role.'

4. Last issue of the **London Firefighter** magazine published due to changes in the Brigade's internal communications policy.

2007. Closure of Lambeth as the Brigade's Headquarters. Transfer of the London Fire Brigade Headquarters to the former Post Office Sorting Offices at Union Street, Southwark.

The Grade II listed former London Fire Brigade Headquarters' frontage on Albert Embankment, SE1. It was subsequently put up for sale for redevelopment. It remains unsold and its future uncertain. (Permission of the London Fire Brigade.)

2009. The Fire Authority appoints the Brigade's first female and non-operational Deputy Commissioner (formerly termed a Deputy Chief Officer). The new incumbent had no previous operational fire service experience.

2011.

1. The Brigade mobilising and control facility moves to Merton, South West London. Provided with a computer system by Motorola the building was originally built as the planned, but abandoned, regional fire brigade control centre.

2. November. London's Fire Planning Authority agreed proposals that saw all training for fire brigade staff in London outsourced to a private training provider for the first time in its history, Babcock Training Limited. The decision was based on a report that stated it 'would radically improve training facilities, increase the amount of time available for firefighter training and save the Brigade an estimated £66m over the next 25 years.' The decision to 'outsource' came after a previous report in 2008 reported the existing in-house firefighter training facilities were no longer suitable. This is despite a multi-million pound modernisation and refurbishment programme of the Brigade's Southwark Training Centre less than a decade earlier and which its then Chief Officer considered fit for the 21st century. A sad time for the London fire Brigade who had been training London's firefighters at Southwark since 1878.

2014. January. The London Mayor, Boris Johnson, ordered London's fire authority to go ahead with a controversial plan to close 10 London fire stations and axe 14 front line fire engines. The cuts were included in a new London Safety Plan drawn up by Fire Commissioner Ron Dobson in the wake of reductions in central Government and City Hall funding for the London Fire Brigade. It was the largest cull in London's fire cover since the 1920s.

Westminster fire station, one of the ten fire stations closed.

Last ever parade at Clerkenwell fire station; another of the ten London fire
stations forced to close. January 2014.